Advance praise for *Pearls, Politics,* ...

"A natural storyteller, Kunin combines her personal journey in politics with the stories of dozens of female politicians. Writing with wisdom, intelligence, and warmth, she provides a guide for women at all levels who might seek to enter public life. The timing of this excellent book could not be better."
—DORIS KEARNS GOODWIN, Pulitzer Prize-winning historian and biographer

"Madeleine Kunin had to imagine herself as a woman leader when those two words rarely came together. Now she teaches us from her experience, and helps us imagine the next leap into the future."
—GLORIA STEINEM, feminist and founder of *Ms.* magazine

"*Pearls, Politics, and Power: How Women Can Win and Lead* incisively analyzes the challenges women face in their bids for elected office. Drawing on her extensive political experience as one of our nation's finest Governors, Madeleine Kunin offers clear and practical advice on how women can pursue careers in politics. This book is a must for any woman interested in becoming one of tomorrow's leaders."
—PRESIDENT BILL CLINTON

"It's one matter to tell people about the challenges facing women in politics. It's another to write the story so that people will want to read it. With her vast personal experience as a political leader and her considerable gifts as a writer, Madeleine Kunin offers a new generation both pearls of wisdom and practical lessons in the real-life, nuts and bolts of politics."
—RUTH B. MANDEL, Director, Eagleton Institute of Politics, Rutgers University

"In *Pearls, Politics, and Power*, Governor Kunin lays out the what, why, and wisdom of women's political involvement not only in the U.S. but throughout the world. It is especially relevant today in light of Senator Clinton's presidential campaign and the forces impacting it because she is a woman. Interesting and informative, it is a must read for every woman who cares about having government make a difference for her children and grandchildren and is looking for a way to make that happen."
—GERALDINE A. FERRARO, former Member of Congress and 1984 Democratic Nominee for Vice President

"Here's the book we've been waiting for—an insider's view of the role of women in politics by one of America's most distinguished public servants. Governor, federal executive, ambassador, Madeleine Kunin has seen it all. And her keen eye and deep understanding of the challenge of gender in wielding power has produced a wonderfully insightful book that should be read by every woman—and man—who wants to lead."
—ROBERT B. REICH, former U.S. Secretary of Labor and Professor of Public Policy, University of California at Berkeley

"Women have always provided leadership in their families, their community, and their country. *Pearls, Politics, and Power* takes this influence to a different leadership level. A great read for an understanding of the need for continued involvement."

—NANCY KASSEBAUM, former U.S. Senator

"Every page is indelibly stamped with one word: impact. Governor Kunin clearly and compellingly captures the deep and lasting impact women have had and can have on American politics."

—ILANA GOLDMAN, President, Women's Campaign Forum

"Madeleine Kunin's story is instructive and inspiring—a must read for those who dare to seek elective office. It is a powerful book, based on real experience."

—VERNON E. JORDAN, JR., Senior Managing Director, Lazard Freres

"Kunin gives us thoughtful advice on how women can lead change. A wonderful, insightful book."

—DONNA E. SHALALA, former U.S. Secretary of Health and Human Services

"This book provides a rare insight of what it is like to run for office and win. Kunin listens to the voices of women who have been there—at the local, state, and national levels. She is inspirational, informative, and timely, calling for women to jump into the fray and make a difference for our country."

—ELLEN MALCOLM, president, EMILY's List

"Once again, Madeleine Kunin gives us a thoughtful examination of women's roles in American politics. In an effort to engage more women in the political process, Kunin uses not just her story, but the stories of elected women from both parties and all levels of office. She skillfully weaves these together to illustrate the challenges women face in running for and holding office as well as the tremendous rewards that come from public service. These stories illustrate the concerns women have about running for office in the first place, the realities they face as officeholders, and the difference they make by being there. What a useful tool this book will be in the classroom to teach about the experiences of women in politics and to educate the next generation of women for public leadership."

—DEBBIE WALSH, Director, Center for American Women and Politics, Rutgers University

"We women who have devoted our time and resources to taking on political leadership roles must also motivate, inspire, and mentor other women to surge into the ranks of politics. Governor Kunin's book is an excellent resource—and a must read. It lays out the chutzpah for tackling politics. She says, 'The worried mother syndrome is an effective catalyst for social change.' We worried mothers must act."

—SWANEE HUNT, former Ambassador to Austria and Director of the Women and Public Policy Program at Harvard University's Kennedy School of Government

"Madeleine Kunin has written a fabulous 'how to' book for women who want to make a difference in their communities, states, or the nation. Drawing on her own experience and a rich trove of interviews with women in political positions at all levels, she gives practical advice on how to get started, survive the stresses of public life, and make change happen. This slim, lively book is a must read whether you want to be more effective in your community or aspire to change the world."

—ALICE RIVLIN, former Director of the Office of Management
and Budget and Vice-chair of the Federal Reserve

"Part memoir, part manual, leavened with poignant interviews, testimonies, practical truths and (best of all) the passion of a wise and temperate activist, Kunin's work manifests two rarities in the modern world: scholarly politicians and readable scholarship. This book should become part of the women's studies curriculum in every college and university in America and is perfectly appropriate for senior level courses in public affairs in high schools throughout the land. Fair, honest, and civil— a magnificent achievement by a remarkable woman."

—FRANK BRYAN, John G. McCullough Professor of
Political Science, University of Vermont

"Madeleine Kunin makes an impassioned and informed plea for women, especially younger women, to enter politics. There is no doubt in my mind that our country and the world would be a far better place if the 'feminine values' of compassion and nurturing were to achieve their rightful place in our nation's governance. As she says, it's a wonderful thing to donate $10 to fight breast cancer, but it's a far more powerful thing to shift millions of dollars of government money to finding a cure."

—BEN COHEN, co-founder, Ben & Jerry's

PEARLS
POLITICS
&
POWER

PEARLS
POLITICS
&
POWER

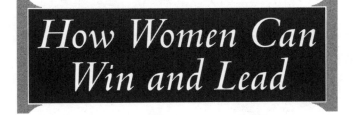

How Women Can Win and Lead

MADELEINE M. KUNIN

CHELSEA GREEN PUBLISHING COMPANY
White River Junction, Vermont

Developmental Editor: Shay Totten
Project Manager: Emily Foote
Copy Editor: Margaret Pinette
Proofreader: Ellen Brownstein
Book Designer: Peter Holm, Sterling Hill Productions

Printed in the United States of America on recycled paper.
First printing, March 2008

5 4 3 2 1   08 09 10 11

Library of Congress Cataloging-in-Publication Data
Kunin, Madeleine.
    Pearls, politics, and power : how women can win and lead / Madeleine M. Kunin.
        p. cm.
    Includes bibliographical references and index.
    ISBN 978-1-60358-010-6 -- ISBN 978-1-933392-92-9
    1. Women in politics--United States. 2. Women political activists. I. Title.

HQ1236.5.U6K86 2008
324.7082'0973--dc22

                            2007052886

Our Commitment to Green Publishing
Chelsea Green sees publishing as a tool for cultural change and ecological stewardship. We strive to
align our book manufacturing practices with our editorial mission and to reduce the impact of our
business enterprise on the environment. We print our books and catalogs on chlorine-free recycled
paper, using soy-based inks whenever possible. This book may cost slightly more because we use recycled paper, and we hope you'll agree that it's worth it. Chelsea Green is a member of the Green
Press Initiative (www.greenpressinitiative.org), a nonprofit coalition of publishers, manufacturers,
and authors working to protect the world's endangered forests and conserve natural resources. *Pearls,
Politics, and Power* was printed on 50# Natures Natural, a 50-percent postconsumer-waste old-growth-
forest-free recycled paper supplied by Maple-Vail.

Chelsea Green Publishing Company
Post Office Box 428
White River Junction, VT 05001
(802) 295-6300
www.chelseagreen.com

For our grandchildren:
Jacob, Samuel, Sara, David, Will, Lizzy, Tucker, and KJ

Contents

Introduction

It is time for a call to action, for new political leadership to emerge from the women of America. The stories of the women in this book and thousands of others like them who hold elective and appointive offices all over America are making a difference. Others work for change in their communities as volunteers, as activists. The problem is that they are too few.

We need their voices as grandmothers and mothers, wives and widows, daughters and sisters to be heard in the political debate about the future of our country. The debate may be raucous, the process complex, and the rewards not assured, but we cannot stay out of it. Each woman's experience changes the nature and content of the conversation. Politics, as Hillary Clinton said, is not for the faint of heart. But politics is where the decisions are made that determine whether our children will go to war, whether our parents will live in security, and whether Earth itself will continue as we know it.

We have been bystanders to history for too long. We have no more excuses; we are educated, we care, and we are ready to enter the arena. Times have changed since I was first elected governor of Vermont in 1985. When I walked into the Executive Office the morning after the election, I scanned the row of somber male governors' portraits with names like Ebenezer and Erastus. They stared down at me, as if to say, "What are *you* doing here?" When nine-year-old Melissa Campbell visited the Vermont State House in 2006 and came upon my portrait, she exclaimed, "Finally, a woman, it's about time!"

It *is* about time. We have seen two women serve as secretary of state, Madeleine Albright and Condoleezza Rice; one woman as U.S. attorney general, Janet Reno; and two female justices in the Supreme Court, Sandra Day O'Connor and Ruth Bader Ginsberg. For the first time in our history, we have a serious, qualified woman candidate for president—Senator

Hillary Rodham Clinton. On January 23, 2007, we saw the portrait of political leadership change in the Congress with the election of House Speaker Nancy Pelosi. During the State of the Union Speech, when the camera focused on the triumvirate of the president, the vice president and the speaker, it was as if someone had torn down the scrawled sign nailed to the tree fort that read "Girls Keep Out," and replaced it with "Women Are Welcome."

We see more strands of pearls, flower-printed scarves, and red jackets in the Congress and in corporate boardrooms, but the lineups remain predominantly muted in black and gray. We can no longer wait for incremental change; it has been too slow. Parity will not be achieved by patience. To arrive at equal representation, we must mobilize both our anger and our optimism: anger at what is wrong in America and optimism that it can be changed for the better.

And we have to take risks—risks that we don't have all the answers and risks that we may be rejected. The risk that we can no longer afford to take is the risk of continuing to accept things as they are—a country divided, governed by people who do not reflect the face of America. Bella Abzug made the case for women's participation in public life in 1977: "We can no longer accept a condition in which men rule the Nation and the world, excluding half the human race from effective economic and political power. Not when the world is in such bad shape."[1]

It is time for women to change both the content and style of leadership. Children, families, education, health care, the environment, and diplomacy must be brought to the top of the agenda, not relegated to an asterisk. Women do not vote in unison any more than men do, but there are differences, and these differences will change the outcome on many issues that now divide us.

The long debate about whether women lead differently is not over, but we know that many women are more inclusive, collaborative, consensus builders, and are more likely to work across party lines. Therese Murray, the senate president in Massachusetts, contrasted her leadership style with the man who had the job before and ruled with an iron hand, "We have a different style. They're not afraid of me. I communicate and am more inclined to share power."

Women bring something else. "In male dominated Michigan politics, we bring a level of truth that would be missing if we weren't there," said State Representative Shanelle Jackson, a Democrat. "Representing the bottom 99 percent of us," was the heart of the campaign that elected Congresswoman Carol Shea-Porter (D-NH).

Women are active in their communities: They volunteer, they contribute, and they support social causes. That is where the seeds of political activism lie. More women need to make the transition from helping people one-on-one in the nonprofit sector—vital as that is—to creating change on a grand scale in the public sector. Making a donation for breast cancer research is good, but obtaining funding of millions of dollars for research in the federal budget is so much better. "It's just a different venue with a greater impact," said New Hampshire House Speaker Terie Norelli, who had worked to reduce sexual violence in her community.

It is time to say that politics does not have to be a lifetime occupation. Just as there are different life stages, there are different political stages from volunteering to getting elected. Public office is not for everyone; but being an informed citizen, ready to speak out for what she believes, is for everyone.

Those of us who have achieved a rank in the political realm have a challenge before us—to convince young people not only that the tools of social change are available but that they have to be utilized by more women if we are to change the policies that frustrate them.

I openly wonder why we aren't reaching young women and getting them more involved in elective politics. What is wrong with the political system that participation does not seem worth the effort? And what is wrong with contemporary feminism? If younger women knew more about women's suffrage—a movement in which women labored for 100 years to exercise the right to vote—would they cherish it, rather than dismiss it?

The younger generation's concern about social justice shows that they want to create change just as much as my generation did. We have to do a better job of telling them how and why they can keep their idealism alive and create change in their time, in their way. One way is for women to tell them why it is worthwhile to enter the fray; to be the one wielding power, rather than reacting to it. "The fact that you can wake up every morning and think that you can change the world. There is no better job," said Congresswoman Loretta Sanchez.

"If you are young and you are thinking about it and you have a track record and you are passionate about the community, do it now. I believe if change is going to happen, a woman needs to do it. We are in a critical time in states and around the country. I can think of no better time for women in office than now. So don't wait," urged 28-year-old State Representative Alicia Thomas Morgan (D-GA). Making a difference is easier than most people think. "If you have a complaint, or something does not make sense, or something frustrates you, the solution is out there. The truth is out there. You as an individual probably can figure it out by believing you can, by making phone calls, by asking questions. The tools of social change are pretty tedious but they are actually available to all of us," said Amy Richards, a thirty-seven-year-old writer and social activist. What we need is a healthy dose of political optimism. "Some people get the dream sucked out of them," said Michigan Representative Shanelle Jackson. "I'm not going to let them take it from me."

We also need to change politics. It is time to take strong steps, as women, as a country, to reverse the trends at work today. Imagine a Congress, a Supreme Court, and state legislatures composed of women and people of color—not as exceptions but as commonplace as they are in the American population.

To achieve that, we must do the following:

- Make public office a civic virtue.
- Inaugurate a bipartisan national campaign to elect and appoint more women.
- Ask women to run for office.
- Embrace community involvement.
- Educate girls to exercise power.
- Teach citizenship.
- Link community service to politics.
- Implement campaign finance reform.
- Establish a mentoring bank.

- Teach negotiating skills.
- Change the political culture.

There is one recurring number: 16 percent. Women make up 16 percent of the Congress, 16 percent of top corporate positions, and 16 percent of the lower houses of Parliaments worldwide. These are record numbers for the United States, but they are low compared to many other countries. The United States ranks sixty-ninth in a list of 187 countries in the percentage of women in lower houses of Parliament. Every female head of state knows she is gaining membership in a club whose rules were designed by and for men. Some were given membership through family names, others by their own determination. Many who succeeded were able to play by the rules while continuing to maintain their female personae and introduce a gender-influenced agenda. Whether they acknowledged or denied gender differences, their very presence at the helm showed that women could be in command in countries that had never before elected women leaders.

The question that follows is: If these countries, historically and culturally far more patriarchal than the United States, elected women heads of state, why do so many Americans still question whether a woman can be elected president of this country?

What are the barriers that make it harder for women and girls to think of themselves as future politicians? Or future presidents? Raising money, facing critics, losing privacy, balancing family responsibilities are all barriers, but these elected women have dealt with them courageously.

It's time to change our picture of what political leadership looks like. This book is addressed to seventeen-year-old Jessica Riegel (and her mother) who wrote, "I could not picture myself at a mahogany desk with stars and stripes behind gleaming white teeth and stiff bobbed hair. I could not picture myself knocking on strangers' doors, or making fund-raising calls, or forming a quick, coherent answer to reporters' jabs." She asked, "Why can't politicians look and act like normal people?" At the end of a political training session, she concluded, "Well, they can." We have to change the face of political leadership so that "the woman who looks like their next-door neighbor, who jogs in the morning, who loves horror movies, spills coffee, organizes clothing drives, schleps her kids to soccer practice and orders takeout, is responsible and driven enough to represent them [the voters]," she said.[2]

It is time for the women of America to claim their full citizenship. In 1920, we won the right to vote. Now we must use that right to change what is wrong in our country.

If we need courage, we need look no farther than the political women of Rwanda who survived genocide. Women comprise almost half of their Parliament. "We had to do this," Senator Odette Nyiramilimo said, "for the survival of our children."

A Life in Politics

The question was not why, but when. "When did you decide you would run for governor?" the young woman asked, as if she wanted to know the exact moment. I thought for a second. "It was when I had a fight with the governor."

I was chair of the House Appropriations Committee, the most powerful legislative committee because it controls the budget. We had made changes in the governor's budget; some items were added, others subtracted. That was the power of the purse. Governor Richard Snelling, a Republican, was not pleased. He called a press conference and blasted me and the committee. Reporters came straight from his office to my committee room. I answered his charges point by point. It was then that I realized that I knew as much as he did, perhaps even more. Standing up to the governor allowed me to see my narrow feet stepping into his rather wide shoes.

As committee chair, I had received a working PhD in state government. Every bill that required new spending was sent to our committee. Every agency and department testified before our committee, either asking for increases in their budgets or opposing cuts. I had learned how to find out whether a program worked. I had become a power broker. I had moved from observing the power huddles of lawmakers and lobbyists to being at their center. Legislators intercepted me on my way to the ladies' room to ask for my help on their bills. In my four years on the Appropriations Committee (the last two as chair), I had become comfortable with power and confident in my ability to understand state government. I could become governor because of my *expertise*, the first prerequisite for leadership, particularly for women.

I told this story to Cheryl Hanna, a Vermont law school professor, who responded by asking, "But what made you want to do it? A lot of women believe they are qualified to be leaders, but they still don't want to go there." This is the question asked by many women who distrust the political system and doubt that the sacrifices are worth the effort or worse—that they could effect change. I knew I had to say something more than, "I wanted to make the world a better place."

That cliché—like most clichés—is partly true, but it was not enough of an answer. I told her I believed I could make a difference. The real reason was more complicated. I wanted to prove something to myself and others. I was defeated in my first race in 1982, so in 1984 I ran to prove I could win; that I could erase the word *defeat*. I didn't want to go down in history as the first woman candidate for governor of Vermont who ran and lost. I wanted my children to know that defeat need not be the last chapter, that I could try again and win. In my first race for governor (Vermont has two-year terms), I thought I could win because I was running for an open seat. Soon after I announced, the governor decided to seek another term. Overnight, I found myself in a different race; instead of a likely winner, I had become a likely loser, running against a three-term incumbent. I stayed in the race because I wanted to show that I had the guts to continue or, the other way around, that I wasn't a coward.

There were other reasons, too. I felt a connection between myself and the women in the audience; it was the nodding heads, hopeful smiles, and handshakes that lasted longer than usual. We were in this together. If I won, they won. I wanted to do it for them.

Was I ambitious? Yes, I wanted to get to the next rung on the ladder. Did I want power? Power is an explosive word, particularly when applied to women. It is one of the arrows shot at Senator Hillary Clinton by David Geffen, a Los Angeles fundraiser for Barack Obama who used to be close to the Clintons. On February 21, 2007, Maureen Dowd quoted Geffen in *The New York Times:* "I don't think that another incredibly polarizing figure, no matter how smart she is and no matter how ambitious she is—and God knows, is there anybody more ambitious than Hillary Clinton?—can bring the country together."[1]

Women are not supposed to want power, somewhat like sex. It's OK if they just receive it. So acculturated am I that it is not easy even now to say, "Yes, I wanted power." This is somewhat of a cop-out—I wanted the power to empower others. True. Women tend to look at power differently than men. Rather than having *power over* others, they are more comfortable to *share power with* others.

The challenge in exercising power is to achieve equilibrium between opposing forces and to have an ear for the people in the room and those waiting outside.

The attraction of becoming governor was that I believed my voice would be heard. I could not act without the legislature, the courts, and a majority of the voters. Even when others disagreed with me, which I had learned to expect, I could lay down the first marker. It was up to them to react. That is one definition of power in a democracy.

I confess I also found it hard not to like the sound of applause. Politicians get more than most people but not quite as much as rock stars. They also get booed, but less often.

Before I ran for governor, I had a dress rehearsal. For four years as lieutenant governor, I was an understudy to the governor. I saw that he was only human.

When we look at leaders from afar they take on huge proportions, like gazing up at Abraham Lincoln from the steps of the Lincoln Memorial. But the closer we get, the more accurately we observe them; we find they are not so tall after all. Some, like Lincoln, will always be gargantuan because he was no ordinary man. Others become surprisingly ordinary.

Part of a governor's job is solving problems. I enjoyed that process; I found it creative. As a legislator, I had learned that problems are most easily solved by asking the right questions. I gained the confidence to ask questions of experts who appeared to have all the answers. I learned "to speak truth to power," before the phrase became popular. It may not always be possible to speak *truth* to power, but it is possible to *challenge* power, to analyze its sources and question its conclusions. I soon learned that no question was a dumb question, something I had not been taught in school.

One of the few facts of political life is that it is impossible to please everyone. Politicians hate to accept that. I kept thinking if I could only say the right words, phrase them elegantly, or develop a different strategy, I could appease the dissenters. I tended to blame myself until I learned that no matter what I did, some people would continue to disagree with

Vindication
MARY WOLLSTONECRAFT (1759–1797)

A Vindication of the Rights of Woman, written in 1792 in England, was a feminist treatise in its time and still sounds bold to our ears. Like Abigail Adams, Wollstonecraft was self-educated. Unlike Adams, she led an untraditional, independent life; she had two open love affairs and a child out of wedlock and did not believe in marriage. She and William Godwin married secretly and kept separate apartments twenty doors apart.

She gained access to books at the home of a clergyman and his wife. She supported herself in the only ways available to women of her generation: first as a companion, then as a governess. Later, she opened a school with her close friend Fanny Blood. At the age of twenty-nine, she had a new "'plan of life': to live entirely by her pen . . ."[2] She did so, for the rest of her life.

Wollstonecraft was inspired to write the *Vindication* in response to a pamphlet by French diplomat and writer Talleyrand, "A Report on Public Instruction," who wrote that girls should be educated with boys up to the age of eight and then stay home where they belonged.[3] Her work immediately gained notoriety. Horace Walpole, (novelist, historian, and member of Parliament) described her as a "hyena in petticoats."[4] Years later, historians analyzed her in a way that may sound familiar to modern-day feminists: "Mary Wollstonecraft hated men. She had every personal possible reason known to

psychiatry for hating them. Hers was the hatred of creatures she greatly admired and feared, creatures that seemed to her capable of doing everything while women to her seemed capable of doing nothing whatever, in their own nature being pitifully weak in comparison with strong lordly male . . ."[5]

Her story had a tragic ending. She died giving birth to her second daughter, Mary, who later ran off to Paris with the poet Percy Shelley while he was still married to his first wife. Mary Shelley (they were later married) became famous as the author of *Frankenstein*. For years, early feminist writers ignored Wollstonecraft, fearing that her unconventional life would hurt their cause.[6]

Excerpts from *A Vindication of the Rights of Woman:*

> My own sex, I hope, will excuse
> me, if I treat them like rational
> creatures, instead of flattering their
> *fascinating* graces, and viewing them
> as if they were in a state of perpetual
> childhood, unable to stand alone. I
> earnestly wish to point out in what
> true dignity and human happiness
> consists—I wish to persuade women
> to endeavour to acquire strength,
> both of mind and body. . . . It is
> time to effect a revolution in female
> manners—time to restore to them
> their lost dignity—and make them,
> as a part of the human species, labor
> by reforming themselves to reform
> the world.[7]

me. It took me some time to acknowledge that there are no fabric softeners for the rough edges of politics. I feared—as all elected officials do—that if I couldn't please everyone, I had failed. I would be punished by losing the next election. The pressure to please can be both good and bad for the democratic process. It is bad to be accused of the sin of "doing anything to get elected." It is good to be "accountable, to listen and be responsive." Vice President Dick Cheney has expressed no interest in running for reelection or for president, which should enable him to be a statesman, rather than a politician. He does not have to listen to the voters; he knows he is right. He forces me to reexamine the virtue of a politician without political ambition.

Why don't politicians keep it simple and just listen to the voters? The answer is easy: because voters—except for rare situations—don't speak in unison. They may be closely, and sometimes evenly, divided. We say we want elected officials to "vote their conscience" but sometimes, when they do, we want to throw them out. What's a politician to do? Follow your conscience, yes, but people do not have a conscience to follow on every issue. Decisions on issues like abortion, the death penalty, and immigration often are based on a personal definition of conscience rather than on facts. Most issues do not present themselves that way. I've withheld an opinion on many questions until I felt fully informed. It was the factual case and personal testimonies that moved me in one direction or another. I've modified my positions after negotiating with the other side. Some call that caving in. Others call it diplomacy. I also have changed my mind. Sometimes that is praiseworthy—she had the courage to listen. Or she had the guts to admit a mistake. Other times it is called indecisiveness, or worse—a flip-flop, an accusation that hits women harder because of the gender stereotype that women can't make up their minds.

After three terms as governor, I decided not to run for reelection. From the time of my first election to the legislature, I had told myself that I had to keep a life outside of politics. I knew, as all elected officials know, that I might be defeated at any time. Now, after nine campaigns, I wanted to explore life after politics—to read, to think, to be with family and friends, and to write the next chapter.

I had seen too many politicians define themselves exclusively by their titles: the senator, the congressman, and the governor. When they lost that prefix, they no longer knew who they were. I had other titles, "mother" and "wife," "writer" and "professor," that had defined me before, and I could reclaim them now. Besides, I would always have, whenever I needed it, the lifelong title of "governor." Unlike when I had lost my first election, I would not be in mourning if I did not run again.

The transition to civilian life was both harder and easier than I expected. My children teased me about having to learn to drive again after having been chauffeured everywhere. Driving was not hard; finding a parking space was. The phone quieted down, and so did the mail, which was good because I had no staff to answer it. I was saved by academia, a safe haven for retired politicians who do not have a perch in a law firm, lobbying firm, or corporation. Dartmouth College gave me a new title— a Montgomery Fellow—and an office, an assistant, and a beautiful house in Hanover, NH equivalent to the governor's mansion. Vermont is one of those states without a governor's mansion.

Certain habits were more difficult to change: I had to learn how to stand in one place at a cocktail party and suppress the urge to work the room. I had to learn not to wave at cars in New Hampshire with Vermont license plates. (Vermont and New Hampshire share a common border.)

There were pluses. Time, the scarcest of all resources, was now mine to distribute. I set my own schedule. I could go to the movies, plays, concerts, lectures, and art exhibits and linger over coffee. Being in public life had meant I spent less time with family and friends. Many times I felt conflicted, particularly when my children were young.

Now I could live at a more normal pace, teaching, writing a memoir, and remaining involved in politics in a different way. I founded a nongovernmental organization (NGO), the Institute for Sustainable Communities. Holding public office was one way to create change; NGOs were another. During an election-monitoring assignment in Bulgaria in 1990, I discovered that these former Soviet-controlled emerging democracies needed assistance in managing environmental problems and making democracy work through civic participation. That is how ISC was born.

Another way to change the world is to teach, something that teachers know when they inspire their students. I met with students when I was a fellow at the Bunting Institute at Radcliffe (now the Radcliffe Institute for Advanced Study, Harvard University). When I finished my tour as ambassador to Switzerland (more on that in a moment), I became the bicentennial scholar at Middlebury College and then distinguished visiting professor at St. Michael's College and the University of Vermont. A magnanimous definition of politician is "teacher." Instead of speaking to thousands of constituents, there were twenty students in my seminar on "Women, Politics, and Leadership" at the University of Vermont.

I am as proud as I would be of any piece of legislation that one of my former students, Rachel Weston, was elected in 2006 to the Vermont legislature. At twenty-five, she is the youngest. Half a dozen others work on House and Senate congressional staffs.

"Are you still involved in politics?" I am asked. The answer is "no," but "yes."

In 1991, while at the Bunting Institute, I testified before the Senate Judiciary Committee against the confirmation of Clarence Thomas. I was on a panel of pro-choice witnesses who feared that Thomas would overturn *Roe* v. *Wade*. Anita Hill had testified earlier that when she had worked for Thomas, he had sexually harassed her. Senators were skeptical, even accusatory. "Are you a scorned woman?" asked Senator Howell Heflin. David Brock, a conservative columnist, called her "a little bit nutty and a little bit slutty." It was a charged moment for women. Thousands watched the televised hearings and saw the makeup of the U.S. Senate for the first time—a male club. (There were two women in the Senate, Nancy Landon Kassebaum, R-KS, and Barbara Mikulski, D-MD; neither served on the Judiciary Committee.) "They just didn't get it," became the catch phrase. The following year, 1992, a record number of women ran for Congress, and four new women were elected to the Senate, and those in the House more than doubled.

In early 1991, a new chapter opened. I received a call from Governor Bill Clinton, asking for my support for the Democratic nomination for president. I had known both him and Hillary from our time together at governors' conferences. I had first heard him speak at a small gathering outside the Democratic convention hall in the early 1980s. I don't remember what he talked about; I do remember that it was a visionary speech. He picked up a little baby, proudly showed her to the crowd, and said, "This is Chelsea." "Who is this guy?" I asked the person next to me. "The new governor of Arkansas," she said. This is someone to watch, I said to myself.

As I held the phone, I paused for a minute and asked him to call me back. I wanted to see if New York Governor Mario Cuomo would run. Three days later, Cuomo bowed out, and Clinton was again on the phone. "Yes," I said, wondering if he really had a chance. I campaigned for him in New Hampshire, the day after the Jennifer Flowers story broke. She had dropped the bombshell that she and Clinton had had a long-standing affair. That was the first of a series of damaging revelations. At a breakfast gathering of influential supporters in Boston, my task was to rally the discouraged crowd and convince them that Clinton could win. They almost came around.

After the primaries, I was asked to join a three-person vice presidential search committee with Warren Christopher and Vernon Jordan, Jr. The process of recommending a candidate to be Clinton's running mate was undertaken carefully. We reached consensus on Senator Al Gore, disregarding conventional wisdom that said the vice president should balance the ticket and carry a basketful of electoral votes. Gore was another Southerner from the neighboring small state of Tennessee with eleven electoral votes, he was young, and he was progressive, much like Clinton. On balance, he provided foreign policy experience and senatorial gravitas. I had long known him as a dedicated environmentalist.

After the election, we three formed the core of the transition team that soon expanded into a larger, more diverse group. My job, I believed, was to advocate for the appointment of women. At one meeting in Little Rock at the governor's mansion, we presented our recommendations for cabinet positions and the structure of the president's office. We were assured we would all be given serious consideration for the cabinet.

I did not get my first choice, administrator of the Environmental Protection Agency. Instead I was offered the position of ambassador to Canada, an attractive post of some significance, but I regretted that I would not be in Washington. I was about to go out to buy new ice skates for winters in Ontario when I received a phone call from Richard Riley, former governor of South Carolina and designated Secretary of

Education. Riley was a thoughtful, modest man with progressive views, the antithesis of what most people think of as a politician.

"Madeleine, how would you like to be my deputy? I need someone I can work with," he said.

I had to stop and think. What about those ice skates? The advantage of working with Dick Riley was that I would be in Washington, DC, part of the excitement of the new Clinton administration. The title Madam Ambassador had cachet, but I was eager to have an impact on federal education policy because of my reform efforts in Vermont. But I would be number two, not easy for a former governor. Could I carry it off?

I decided I could. The experience in Washington was sometimes hard on my ego, a city that judges people's worth exclusively by rank—secretaries at the top, followed by deputy secretaries, under secretaries, assistant secretaries, and so on down the line to special assistants. Nobody outside Washington knows the difference, but everyone in Washington does. When asked, "And what do you do?" at receptions and I replied "I'm Deputy Secretary of Education," I could see eyes search the room for someone more important. Sometimes, desperate to explain who I really was, I added, "And I'm the former governor of Vermont." I always felt defensive and somewhat disloyal when I used my backup title. It was not only that I was number two, which made me a small morsel among the power hungry; it was that I was in the Department of Education, low on the Washington power scale. I occasionally would get a "good for you," like a pat on the head (something every schoolteacher has experienced).

Secretary Riley and I worked closely together; I created a new office for education technology, developed and helped enact legislation for direct student loans, was chief operating officer of the department, and led the charge to "reinvent government." Soon after my arrival in Washington, National Public Radio did a series on "big fish in small ponds and small fish in big ponds," as it related to life in Washington. I was the perfect interview, a little fish. The upside was that I had a huge pond to swim in: schools all over America. I learned firsthand about the difference between suburban schools and urban schools, predominantly minority population schools, and predominantly white schools. Segregation by race and class existed almost everywhere. I became an education evangelist. I talked about how education transforms lives; I spoke from experience—it had transformed mine. There were days when my idealism was tested. One morning I called the principal of a school in Washington, DC, after I had read a story in *The Washington Post* about a gunman who had run through the corridor of an elementary school in Anacostia to escape the police. He was shot dead before a group of first graders. I arranged to visit the school, believing the staff should know that a U.S. Department of Education official cared and wanted to help. (I later created a DC School Office within the department.) I used the same thinking I had as governor: When something bad happened, I showed up. Here, the principal was surprised when I arrived. Anacostia is a neighborhood a few miles from the Capitol that taxi drivers refuse to take people to. In one classroom, buckets were scattered around the floor to catch the rainwater from the leaky roof. The teachers looked exhausted. The incident—although horrendous—did not seem that unusual to them. The nearby child-care center, which I visited next, was surrounded by a wall. The center was a patch of hope in a barren trash-strewn lot.

An important part of my job as Deputy Secretary of Education was to be a cheerleader for the teachers and principals who educated children against the odds of deprivation. Governing consists of praise as well as criticism. The goal is to find programs that work, figure out why, and then try to replicate them. When President Bill Clinton hosted a luncheon for present and past governors in the Library of Congress the day before his first inauguration, he told us, "For every problem in America there is a solution somewhere. Our challenge is to replicate it and make it work everywhere." I went in search of those solutions and found them: a school providing health and dental programs to students and families; schools open twelve hours a day, seven days a week, in Harlem because of Geoffrey Canada, who put his vision to work. I will not forget the words of Howard Lappin, principal of a Los Angeles school barricaded by a twelve-foot high fence to keep the drug pushers out: "Don't tell me these kids can't learn," he told me.

When I began my political life in the Vermont legislature, I did not know that my career in public service would take me from the state to the national to the international level. The most important decision I made was to close one door so that another could be opened. Timing was also on my side. If a Democratic president had not been elected in 1992, I would not have received these federal appointments. It was a good sequence—moving from governor to deputy secretary to ambassador—because I used what I learned in each position and applied it to the next. I could be an effective Deputy Secretary of Education because of my experience as governor. The big differences between politics in Vermont and Washington were the aggressive power of lobbyists and the fierce partisanship of lawmakers. I developed a new definition of power. It had little to do with gender, unlike when I was governor. Education is a female enclave, but even here, as with principals and superintendents, most of the leaders of lobbying organizations and unions were male. Gender was not a factor in 1996 when I became ambassador to Switzerland; another woman ambassador had served earlier, and Swiss—mostly male—government officials took me seriously. They had no choice. I was the U.S. ambassador. Not until I arrived in Bern and presented my credentials to the president did I realize that the American ambassador had special access. This would not be the only time I would meet with the president; I could see him whenever I needed.

Each person's political life follows a different trajectory, making it hard to say what works best. The only advice I have is—don't be afraid to move on.

Knowledge of the federal bureaucracy in the Education Department helped me cope with the bureaucracy of the State Department as ambassador. I would not have had the patience (which I sometimes lost) with State Department procedures if I hadn't been schooled earlier. I had, on occasion, attended cabinet meetings and high-level policy discussions. It helped to know the major players in the Clinton administration when I needed their help. From the Swiss perspective, my greatest asset was my access to the president and first lady. They were thrilled to have an ambassador who had government experience. Almost all prior American ambassadors to Switzerland were political appointees who had never served in government and had a limited knowledge of the country and no language skills. This has been equally true in Republican and Democratic administrations. Born in Switzerland, I retained enough of my Swiss-

German dialect to carry on a conversation. I also spoke German and French. Americans have such a poor reputation for language skills that mine were thought extraordinary. When I got off the flight from New York on August 16, 1996, I held a press conference at 7 A.M. at the Zurich airport. I opened with a few phrases in *Schwiezerdeutsch*. Months later, I continued to meet people who remembered.

Many positions are carried out most effectively through management by "walking around." This holds true in the public sector. I knew that to become a good ambassador I had to meet the public, just like when I was governor. The job description for all ambassadors is the same: to foster good relations between two countries. Most of that happens outside government offices. Ambassadors who have not held public office have difficulty understanding that. Whenever and wherever I appeared, officially or socially, I was there not only as an individual; I represented my country. My first clue that I did not represent myself, but my constituents, had been given to me as a new legislator. When the speaker recognized me, I was not Mrs. Kunin. I was "the member from Burlington."

Early in the Clinton administration, because of my Swiss background, Larry Lawrence, Clinton's choice for the American ambassador to Switzerland, had asked me to brief him for his Senate confirmation hearings. I had been offered that position earlier, but at the time I thought it would be too easy an assignment. Switzerland was a quiet country where nothing was happening. Now something was happening. The issue was the Swiss banks. After World War II, the banks failed to return money deposited in secret numbered accounts by Jewish families (taking money out of Nazi Germany was punishable by death) before the war for safekeeping. Holocaust survivors or victims' heirs had attempted to retrieve these funds after the war. For more than fifty years, few accounts were found, despite repeated requests. Time was running out because the survivors were aging, and many were destitute. New pressure was put on the Swiss government and the banks by survivors and their lawyers, aided by the State Department, members of Congress, and the Jewish World Congress, chaired by Edgar Bronfman, former chair of Seagram Company Ltd. They had become a powerful coalition by the time I arrived. Before my departure, I had been briefed on the banking issue by a low-level

Foreign Service officer. Neither he nor I knew that this question—the role of Switzerland during World War II—would soon be in the headlines in both Switzerland and the United States. It would occupy me almost daily for the next three years.

My Senate confirmation hearing, compared to that of my predecessor, Ambassador Lawrence, was boringly uncontroversial. Lawrence became the poster child for an appointee who had made large political contributions but had no knowledge of the country or government experience. He barely squeaked by. Jesse Helms, chairman of the Senate Foreign Relations committee, was the man I was worried about. He was most helpful to me by not showing up. He let the fair-minded, polite vice chairman, Senator Richard Lugar, conduct the hearing.

Ambassadors continue to live in style. I did not know if I could afford to do so. Almost all the ambassadors who preceded me were independently wealthy and could augment their State Department allotment with their personal funds. I had been recently divorced and was living on my income. How would I manage? My answer was Theresa Murray, a recent New England Culinary School graduate from Montpelier, Vermont. She was an excellent chef. More importantly, she knew how to budget. My butler, James (his real name), purchased American wines. I knew we were doing well when, during a reception, the French ambassador, sipped his California Chardonnay, and said to me, *"Ce n'est pas mal."* ("Not bad.")

There was a more serious side. One of the first people who came to my office was a former Swiss ambassador to the United States who was on a committee newly created to search for dormant bank accounts. That marked the beginning of daily staff briefings, meetings with government officials, private groups, Jewish groups, historians. Information, as I had already learned, is essential to power. Meanwhile, in Washington, Senator Alphonse D'Amato, chairman of the Senate Banking Committee, kept the issue in the media. Waving newly released World War II–era documents in the air, he regularly lambasted the Swiss. A few governors and legislators threw out the idea of a boycott of Swiss banks and Swiss goods, sending a frisson of fear down Swiss spines.

Such attacks found the Swiss unprepared. American–Swiss relations had been harmonious as far back as anyone could remember. The Swiss were proud of their links with America. An exhibit displayed in the halls of the U.S. Congress was entitled, "The Two Sister Republics." Perplexed, they asked, why are they ganging up on us now? Perhaps Americans are jealous of our banks, some speculated.

I faced a diplomatic challenge: to maintain a good relationship with the Swiss while simultaneously prodding the banks and the government to resolve the "Jewish accounts" question—a clear case of "good cop, bad cop." All the mediation skills I had learned as governor were put to use.

New issues surfaced daily: Nazi-looted gold purchased by Swiss banks from the German national bank throughout the war may have enabled Germany to buy arms; Jewish refugees had been turned back at the border into the hands of the Nazis; Swiss businesses had done business with the Germans; Nazi-looted art was sold in Swiss auction houses—the list continued to grow.

The Swiss responded by defending their most sacred principle, neutrality. They had no choice, they said. To survive, surrounded by Nazi-occupied countries, they had to maintain relationships with both sides.

I met with a small group of Parliamentarians led by the speaker of the lower House of Parliament and the chairperson of the Judiciary Committee; both were women. Swiss women did not gain the right to vote until 1991, but the percentage of women in their Parliament was greater than in the United States. Switzerland now has its second female president.

The Parliament voted to conduct a study of Switzerland's role during World War II by international historians. There were two ambassadors sitting in the gallery during the debate, the Israeli ambassador and myself. The next day, both our photos were on the front page. I had made my statement by showing up, an important decision that I had learned early in my career.

The banks decided to take a first step to find the holders of accounts that no one had claimed—they would publish their names. The Swiss habit of meticulousness was useful; the banks had kept excellent records. One morning, I read the list in *The Financial Times*. I paused. There was my mother's name, Renée May. (Several years later, I received a check in Swiss francs, about $100, which I shared with my brother. The sum may have originally been higher; the bank had subtracted annual fees.) Suddenly I became part of the story. Political how-to pamphlets rarely discuss the emotional side of politics. How does one remain objective? Is it helpful to connect personally with an issue, or is it dangerous? I would soon find the answer. The next day I was asked by the State Department if, under the circumstances, I could keep my objectivity. I assured them that I could. I always had been proud of my Swiss heritage; now a shadow had fallen on the Alps. I was tested on the day I met with the head of the Swiss Bankers Association, Herr Georg Krayer, around a shiny oblong table in a conference room on the top floor of Bank Sarasin & Cie SA in Basel. Originally, I had been invited for lunch. I tried not to put too much meaning in the last-minute cancellation. The conversation began politely and then turned contentious. Herr Krayer denied there was a problem. Most Jews would not have deposited money in Swiss banks during the war. They would have sent money to America. I disagreed. I tried to explain why there was a problem. When a claimant came to the bank to look for a family account, the bank asked for documents, including a death certificate. These were not issued by concentration camps, I explained. As I spoke, I saw that the Jews had no power—they were paperless, pleading with the stolid Swiss banks. Their requests had been easily ignored all these years. They had no standing. It was as if they had not existed. I could not let that happen again. The banks' arrogant attitudes and unrealistic procedures were equivalent to a denial of the Holocaust itself. I controlled myself, shook hands, and said a polite adieu.

I took the elevator down to the bank lobby where I met Germaine Molina, a cousin who had written me a letter of congratulations. We had never met, although I had known her sister, Mimi, who lived in Paris. We embraced like the long-lost cousins that we were and walked down the street to Chez Mario, her favorite Italian restaurant. As I started to tell her about my conversation with Herr Krayer, tears spilled down my cheeks. Why couldn't I have been a better advocate for those Holocaust victims? Why couldn't I make him understand that this debate over bank accounts was not only about money, it was about a form of atonement— the only form of atonement now available? It was not atonement for the sin of commission—the Swiss did not kill Jews. The former Swiss president had angrily exclaimed after one particularly vicious D'Amato attack, "But Auschwitz was not in Switzerland!" The need for atonement was for the sin of omission—they did nothing, they were bystanders. Worse, they did not acknowledge the reality of the Holocaust, in part because their neutrality shielded them from it. Harsher critics would say that they profited from it. I may have felt something akin to survivor's guilt because I was Jewish; I felt personally responsible for getting their money back.

My religion had not been an issue in my political life. Vermonters, if they knew I was Jewish, didn't seem to care. When I arrived in Switzerland, I was identified in some news articles as the Jewish American ambassador. I was asked whether Clinton had appointed me at this time because I was Jewish. My denials, I sensed, were not always accepted.

Keeping personal feelings separate from public policy is considered a necessity in diplomacy and most areas of public life. It doesn't always work that way. Some melding of the two is inevitable. We are all products of our life experiences that recall our emotions. They have their place; they can be positive instigators for action, but they also can be negative if they overwhelm objectivity or obscure solutions that make good sense. As a diplomat, I had to be trusted as a fair arbiter by both the Swiss and my government. I could not express the sadness and frustration I now felt to anyone but Germaine. Over lunch she told me stories about the French side of my family; cousins who, after they made it over the border to safety from France, had been placed in Swiss internment camps, others who had been turned back, a cousin who had been imprisoned in Paris and never returned, those who had died at the hands of the Nazis. I wished that she had been at my side at the oblong table, on the top floor of the bank when I talked to Herr Krayer.

Three years later, a settlement was reached between the three major banks and Jewish plaintiffs. They were awarded $1.3 billion in restitution. It was not a perfect solution. Many account holders still have not been found, and the banks have not always been cooperative. Despite my repeated requests, the Swiss government had refused to participate in the negotiations; it was the banks' problem, and Swiss citizens should not have to contribute their tax dollars. The settlement created closure to the extent that it was an acknowledgment that the banks had made mistakes. Whether the banks reached that conclusion because they feared the issue was beginning to damage their trustworthiness in the global finance industry, or whether they had a change of heart, is impossible to say. Several months before I left, I heard Herr Krayer say in a speech that he regretted the banks' behavior. They had made mistakes. I wanted to believe him.

I do not take sole credit for this resolution; many were involved, including Ambassador Stuart Eizenstat who often visited Switzerland and had made restitution to European Jews a priority. I was in Switzerland, prodding the Swiss to take action at every opportunity and complimenting them when they did the right thing, as they did with their study. It was done with such Swiss thoroughness, in seven volumes, that when the thick summary came out six years later, many had lost interest. One of my favorite memories was a visit to a Bern Gymnasium (high school). A group of students had taken the initiative to establish their own fund for Holocaust survivors, including Jews, gypsies, and homosexuals. They raised enough money to send significant checks to each group. As it turned out, I was the right person at the right time. I had played a role in setting the record straight for Jews who had had no records.

When I was first named ambassador, my mother would have been thrilled. She often had told my brother and me that "anything is possible in America." But even she could not have foreseen when she left Switzerland in wartime with two young children that her daughter would return one day as the American ambassador.

The Barriers

"Slimy," "lying," and "boring" immediately came to mind when I asked a group of 100 high school juniors what they thought of "politics." This was the crème de la crème of the high school crop, attending Girls State at the Vermont State House. Boys and Girls State are American Legion–sponsored lessons in citizenship in which girls and boys are selected by their high schools to meet separately as senators and representatives in the state legislature, write laws, and elect a governor and other officers.

Two responded differently: "making laws" and "representing the public," but they were far outnumbered.

I should have waited for more discussion before I jumped to the next question.

"How many of you would think of running for office?" A few hands rose halfway.

I tried a different approach. "How many would run for the School Board?"

Yes! Fully a third raised their hands.

"For city or town council?"

Half the hands went down.

"Appointive office in state government?"

Another half went down.

"For the state legislature?"

Approximately eight or nine remained in the air. I dared not aim as high as governor for fear of losing them all.

When I talked to the newly elected governor of Girls State for 2007, Olivia Teer, she was thrilled with her recent victory, but she too demurred. "No, I wouldn't run for office. Maybe school board, some day," she told me.

Why so much hesitancy? Women make up 16 percent of the Congress and 23 percent of state legislatures. These are record numbers for the United States, but they are low compared to women in other countries. What are the barriers that make it harder for girls to think of themselves as future politicians? Two analysts have said women lack political ambition because of "traditional gender socialization."[1] The future looks no better; "the prospects for gender parity in our political institutions are bleak."[2]

Dirty Politics

Placing total emphasis on gender socialization is a mistake because it blames women for being themselves and assumes that neither they nor the political system can change. The biggest deterrent for women is the nature of politics itself. Too many women cannot envision themselves in an arena where their portraits are rarely seen.

The words *dirty* and *politics* fit together so well that few people separate them. Clean words like *public policy* get more respect. Many women wish they could do policy without becoming sullied by politics. The two are interlocked—for better or worse—in a long-term relationship. Policy doesn't happen without politics, that messy negotiating process by which laws are made. I often heard repeated a quotation from Otto von Bismarck, who wrote that "Laws are like sausages; it is better not to see them being made." The public is not only suspicious of politicians' motives, it has become used to the idea that politicians lie about themselves and their opponents, that they accept campaign contributions from special interests, and that they will do or say almost anything to get elected and reelected. The worst accusation one politician can hurl at a rival is "playing politics."

When politicians were ranked for respectability in a national poll a few years ago, they landed just below car dealers. In September 2007, the U.S. Congress received a favorability rating of 19 percent. Individual congressmen and congresswomen do better, or they would not get reelected term after term. Governors do considerably better, with an average approval rate of 53 percent.[3] School board members and local officials are looked

The Legacy of the Mystique
BETTY FRIEDAN (1921–2006)

The headline in Betty Friedan's obituary in *The New York Times* was "Betty Friedan, Who Ignited Cause in 'Feminine Mystique,' dies at 85." The obituary stated that the book "is widely regarded as one of the most influential nonfiction books of the 20th century."[4]

When *The Feminine Mystique* was published in 1963, I belonged to a book club in Cambridge, Massachusetts. The discussion was a turning point in my life. Half of us felt that, at last, someone was saying what we had been feeling and could not express, the frustration of the housewife who has given up her education and dreams to find fulfillment in domestic life. The other half of the book group vehemently disagreed with Friedan, defending their wife/mother roles. Little did we know that these divisions would continue until today.

Friedan was born in Peoria, Illinois, and graduated from Smith College, where she edited the campus newspaper. She married and had three children and later was divorced. At her fifteenth college reunion, Friedan conducted a survey of her Smith classmates about their education and present lives; this material became *The Feminine Mystique*. She cofounded the National Organization for Women (NOW) and helped found the National Abortion Rights Action League (NARAL). Friedan angered some feminists when she feared that if lesbians were included in the movement, feminism might be equated with lesbianism. She changed her mind at the Women's Conference in Houston in 1977 when she seconded the motion for a resolution in support of lesbian rights. Her star is not as high for the present generation as it was for mine, in part because she wrote only

on benignly because they fly under the political radar until a controversial issue puts them on the screen.

The perception that all politics is dirty and that it has little to do with public policy is a major deterrent for women. Not only can't they see themselves there, they are not sure they want to see themselves there. How do we convince women that the rewards are worth the price of admission? The women who have been elected have to tell our stories. We have to be honest about how hard it is to get elected and to serve in public life. "Politics is not for the faint of heart," Senator Hillary Clinton correctly observed. Women need to know what they will encoun-

about the lives of white college-educated women.

When I went on a trip with her in 1995, one woman after another approached her at every airport; they all used almost the same words: "You changed my (or my mother's) life." She continued to speak, write, and stir controversy until her death.

In *The Feminine Mystique* Friedan identified "the problem that has no name" as one that

> . . . lay buried, unspoken, for many years in the minds of American women. It was a strange stirring, a sense of dissatisfaction, a yearning that women suffered in the middle of the twentieth century in the United States. Each suburban wife struggled with it alone. As she made the beds, shopped for groceries, matched slipcover material, ate peanut butter sandwiches with her children, chauffeured them to Cub Scouts and Brownies, lay beside her husband at night—she was afraid to ask even of herself the silent question—"Is this all?"[5]

She concluded,

> Who knows what women can be when they are finally free to become themselves? Who knows what women's intelligence will contribute when it can be nourished without denying love? Who knows of the possibilities of love when men and women share not only children, home, and garden, not only the fulfillment of their biological roles, but the responsibilities and passions of the work that creates the human future and the full human knowledge of who they are? It has barely begun, the search of women for themselves. But the time is at hand when the voices of the feminine mystique can no longer drown out the inner voice that is driving women on to become complete.[6]

ter in the arena, so that they will be prepared. But they also must be told about the rewards, "the fact that you can wake up every morning and think that you can change the world," noted Congresswoman Loretta Sanchez (D-CA).

Dealing with Conflict and Criticism

Politics is inevitably about conflict; it is the chamber in which opposing opinions and values meet and clash. Unlike a discussion at a dinner party, where conversation is usually civil and no one else has to know who said what to whom, public life is sometimes nasty and always public.

Attack mode discourse is not a new phenomenon. The British invented yellow journalism in the eighteenth century. Scurrilous attacks were written (sometimes under pseudonyms) by Thomas Jefferson against Alexander Hamilton and by Hamilton against his enemies. Lincoln was attacked throughout his presidency, depicted as monkey in cartoons. Nineteenth- and twentieth-century suffragists were ridiculed for their beliefs. The British feminist Mary Wollstonecraft was called a "hyena in petticoats."

Throughout history, women and men who dared to express their contrary beliefs were attacked by more than words, by clubs and guard dogs, sometimes followed by imprisonment and death. These forms of attack remain prevalent in parts of the world today.

What distinguishes the twenty-first century is the ease with which verbal attacks are disseminated—through blogs, the Internet, and talk radio. We will never know the names of the many women who would have been superb presidents, senators, congresswomen, and state legislators but were deterred by the fear of public attack. We do know the names of the women who have stepped into "the muddy pool of politics" and emerged relatively unscathed in both their personal and public lives.[7] We can learn from these women what it is like to be in the line of fire and survive. It means developing a thick skin, but not so thick that it provides insulation against necessary criticism.

I did not become totally accustomed to public criticism, but I learned not to agonize over it. As a legislator and lieutenant governor, my campaigns were mild compared to what I experienced when I ran for governor; the burner suddenly was turned on high. I reassured myself that no one reads or hears each word as carefully as the candidate and her family. There is the old adage, "Don't worry about what they say about you as long as they spell your name right." It is meant as a joke, and it is a joke. They don't always spell your name right. All politicians worry about "what they say about you" because this is who others think you are, even if you are not.

Experience helps. Compartmentalizing helps. Laughter helps. Good media relations help, but the media are fickle. Having a good shoulder to cry on certainly helps. Still, public life in a democracy requires public scrutiny, sometimes fair, sometimes unfair.

There are three thresholds that women have to step over before they can see themselves as candidates for public office: raising money; giving up time; and losing privacy.[8] There are three more, according to Jo Ann Davidson, former Republican speaker of the Ohio House of Representatives, now co-chair of the Republican National Committee, who conducts training sessions for Republican women. They are: fear of risk taking; a lack of confidence; and it's not the right time in their lives.

Raising Money

Money is the commonly used gauge to determine a campaign's viability. For some women, that taints the whole process. How can a person stand for issues, for social change, for integrity, and be beholden to other people's checks? True, the way campaigns are financed in the United States needs to be reformed. The U.S. Supreme Court decision declaring part of the McCain-Feingold Act unconstitutional changes the conversation about federal campaign finance reform. A few cities and states have stepped in with public financing. (For further discussion, see p. 207.) In the meantime, there is no alternative: Women candidates have to raise as much money as anyone else if they want to be competitive. Emily's List, an organization that raises money for candidates who win their endorsement, trains fund-raisers because that is how they can help women run professional campaigns. Raising money is not always a chore. Some people like to give to candidates, and a surprising number expect no quid pro quo. (There is more on this on p. 208.)

Raising money is not the only deterrent. Not having money is another. "I don't think it's feasible for a person without the financial means to run," said Amy, a student at the University of Vermont.

A large number of men and women in Congress are wealthy, but some are not. It is not necessary to draw on personal funds to run for office. I never did. Congresswoman Carol Shea-Porter (D-NH) opened her campaign account with a personal check of $100 and never had to add more of her own funds. The hardest financial strain is the need to have another wage earner or savings to support a family while carrying on the full-time job of campaigning. Congresswoman Laura Richardson (D-CA) had to take out a second mortgage "to feed the campaign." Atlanta Mayor Shirley Franklin (D) lived on her savings while she campaigned. I was fortunate to have my spouse support us, but that is not possible for many women and men.

Time

Campaigning is all consuming. Clare Giesen, head of the Women's Political Caucus, compared it to having a six-month-old baby; it needs constant attention.

Life after winning is almost equally demanding, but there are more opportunities to control the schedule. I worked my way up gradually, lessening the shock. My first elective office was the legislature in 1972. Vermont has a part-time citizen legislature that meets from January to June, four days a week. My children were young—two-and-a-half, six, eight, and eleven—and I usually could make the thirty-seven-mile commute between my home and Montpelier in time to be home for dinner. I found a great nursery school for my youngest child, and there was Mabel Fisher and later Shirley LaBelle—two women who enabled me to become a legislator. I prepared some meals at 11 P.M. the night before. My husband learned to make "stay-a-bed stew." (Recipe: Keep stew in the oven all day at a low temperature.) Neighbors and friends helped with carpooling.

The next step, lieutenant governor, required more hours but was still considered a part-time job. The children were getting older. I presided over the Senate and attended events year round but could still be home for dinner most nights. When I was elected governor twelve years later, my three oldest children were in college, and my youngest was in high school. I had prepared myself and my family for the life ahead.

Congresswoman Tammy Baldwin (D-WI) calls this career process "the stepladder approach. I think somebody who has never run for office and all of a sudden runs for Congress is in for a shock."

The gradual approach makes it easier to manage time, fund-raise, and handle the loss of privacy; you get used to the rise in temperature like slowly stepping into a hot tub, lowering your body one inch at a time.

My four gubernatorial campaigns and the job were extraordinarily demanding because governors never punch a time clock. The job is 24/7. Even so, I set boundaries for family and personal time.

When I first ran for governor in 1982, female candidates were advised not to include pictures of their families in promotional material. They were afraid of being asked, "Who's taking care of the children?" I ignored that advice. The hardest part was taking the family picture, getting my husband and four children to smile as if they meant it and including the family dog and cat. For some women, serving in the legislature is easier than having a full-time job. Governor Kathleen Sebelius (D-KS) said her job had required much travel. Running for the legislature was a pro-family choice because she could spend more time with her children, ages two and three-and-a-half months.

Thirty-two-year-old Democratic New York City Councilwoman Jessica Lappin had her four-month-old baby cooing in the background during her interview. She had recently returned from maternity leave from the council—an unusual request from an elected official, but one that her constituents understood.

"You make sacrifices in the time that you would spend with family and friends. The way I deal with that is to set boundaries. The time that I do set aside to spend with friends and family is special time and is nonnegotiable time. I turn off my cell phone. I turn off my BlackBerry. I really enjoy that time, and I don't let myself feel guilty about it. I see a lot of my colleagues thinking that you have to be at every single event. You don't. For it's more about choosing what is more important in your personal life and what is most important in your political life than you would in any profession."

Other women also make time within the high demands of constituent politics.

When Sylvia Larsen (D), president of the New Hampshire state senate, first ran for city council, her husband, a trial lawyer, was concerned because their youngest child was still in nursery school and she wouldn't be home on Monday nights when the council met. "My husband committed to staying home with the kids, and in return for his support I promised him a hot dinner every Monday night, and he still gets that—but now I have hired someone."

Hiring someone to do the everyday chores is what many women do, at least those who have the income. They give up carpooling, doing the laundry, going to the dry cleaners, and even cooking. How much to delegate is a personal decision. Often it depends on the husband or other caregiver, on how much spouses or partners are willing and able to share family responsibilities. The answer also depends on how strongly they support their spouse's goals.

U.S Senator Debbie Stabenow (D-MI) was twenty-eight when she became the youngest person ever elected to the Ingham County Board of Commissioners. Later, when she was a divorced working mother, her four-year-old son Tom wore a T-shirt emblazoned with "Vote for My Mom."[9] It worked. She now says that T-shirt should be commonplace.

Privacy

The loss of privacy is a frequent deterrent for both women and men. Mothers are particularly concerned because they feel an added responsibility to protect their families, who should not have to suffer because of them.

Kansas Governor Sebelius said the loss of privacy "is tough, and to be honest, there is no other occupation you can choose which has this kind of personal intrusion unless you are in some kind of scandal in your other life. I do think there is an opportunity to find some balance. My experience has been that the press has been pretty good at staying a step away from my kids. My children were two and five when I entered public office, so they grew up in the town where I was either a legislator or insurance commissioner, and then they went off to college."

I managed to keep my children out of the news, but I did keep my fingers crossed that they would stay out of trouble. Bill and Hillary Clinton have set a good example for other politicians by making stories about their daughter Chelsea off limits, a policy that succeeded in main-

taining much of her privacy. After the first flurry of press attention
to the Bush twins' drinking habits, they have managed to shed most
paparazzi.

It's harder for younger children. Washington Senator Patty Murray's
twelve-year-old daughter was pleased to move to Washington, DC, after
her mother was elected to get away from her school because she had
found it hard to face her classmates during the campaign when they had
criticized her mother. She was embarrassed to see her mother's picture
everywhere—in the newspapers, on television, and on posters. Today
Murray says her daughter is a stronger feminist than she is and enjoys
disagreeing with her mother on some issues.[10]

After she was elected to her first term in the U.S. Senate, Murray
discovered that managing her family life and her political career remained
a challenge. The family moved to Washington, and her husband took on
more child-care responsibilities:

> Over the years, many people criticized me because I wasn't home
> with the kids. And they criticized me because my husband "had
> to" move to Washington when I got elected. What kind of a
> mother was I? What kind of wife was I? But I got into poli-
> tics because I'm a wife and mother. Who knows better about
> the issues that affect children and families than someone who is
> experiencing them?[11]

The loss of privacy is often most pronounced when campaigns turn
"ugly."

Republican Congresswoman Deborah Pryce faced a tough reelection
campaign in Ohio in 2006, and she had to face this question head on,
day after day:

> I think it's easier if you walk into it with your eyes open; that the
> candidate herself is prepared. When you see what it does to your
> family and people who didn't make a conscious decision to display
> themselves open to the world. . . . That I think affects women more
> than it does men. To see siblings groan under the weight of nega-
> tive ads and that type of thing. Personally I deal with it by ignoring

it. The last election was the worst I have ever been through. I just have a policy of not listening to the radio station so I don't have to hear the ads.

Congresswoman Pryce announced in August that she would not seek reelection so she could be with her five-year-old adopted daughter. She had lost a child earlier.

Congresswoman Loretta Sanchez tries to ignore the ugly side of politics. She said, "So what. Whatever. Just get past it. I don't care what people say about me. If it's true, it's true. If it's not, it's not. Women are sensitive. So are men. Men are the biggest crybabies, I've found. We are all sensitive."

Her younger sister Linda Sanchez (D), also a California congresswoman, explained that she developed a thick skin because "I grew up in a family of seven where my brothers teased me unmercifully, and that sort of prepared me for politics."

She was in a six-way Democratic primary in her first campaign:

> I was the front-runner, and they were all attacking me. I learned to take that and respond when it was appropriate and not respond when it wasn't appropriate. During one of the last debates, one of the other candidates was accusing me of not being Latina, of changing my name to pander to that vote. [She had resumed her birth name after her divorce.] My mom was in the audience, and I could see her getting agitated. She was getting angrier and angrier. She stood up and said, "You don't even know what you are talking about. Both me and my husband are immigrants from Mexico." I felt really bad. I knew she was trying to (a) set the record straight but (b) protect me. It's sort of embarrassing to have your mom fighting your battles.

During my first gubernatorial campaign, one of my children went up to my opponent and asked, "Why don't you like my mother?" Fortunately, he was nice about it.

Each family reacts differently to a parent's political career. Judging by the number of sons and daughters who follow in their parents' footsteps and run for office, the experience is not necessarily damaging. Some children thrive by living in a political household, others do not, and many are proud of their mothers' political involvement. The higher the office, the more demanding the schedule, and the greater the scrutiny. That is equally true in the private sector. But the spotlight in the public sector is harsher because politicians' children are supposed to be perfect. When Geraldine A. Ferraro's son was arrested for selling drugs at Middlebury College, both she and her son suffered greater notoriety than had she simply been Gerry Ferraro, not Gerry Ferraro first woman candidate for vice president.

Single women feel equally threatened by loss of privacy. "If you had an abortion that would be brought up. It ties into reproductive rights. Nothing seems to sell like the privacy of women politicians," noted a young woman I talked to while researching this topic.

Women with children get asked questions about the kids; unmarried, childless women also get questions. I asked never-married Arizona Governor Janet Napolitano (D) whether her marital status was an issue. "There is always a whisper campaign if you are single. I was asked up front, 'Are you gay?' and I said, 'No, I'm just single.' The whisper campaign is always there, but as you can see, it hasn't stopped me."

How untraditional can a woman's personal life be before she has to rule out running for public office? Divorce is no problem today for either women or men unless a spouse seeks public revenge. When Governor Adlai Stevenson of Illinois ran for president in 1952 and in 1956, voters asked if a divorced man could be elected president. The question died down with the election of Ronald Reagan and seems to have disappeared with the candidacy of Rudy Giuliani, the thrice-married candidate for the Republican presidential nomination.

Today, the question is sexual orientation. Congressman Barney Frank (D-MA) is openly gay and survived a scandal with a male prostitute. He has been reelected fourteen times. Congresswoman Tammy Baldwin (D) from Madison, Wisconsin, is the only openly lesbian woman member of Congress.

Was her being a lesbian ever an issue? I asked. She responded:

Always, yet not an issue that prevented me from being successful in terms of my election and in terms of my time in office.
We certainly live in a country and a world where homophobia
still exists, but frankly, sexism still exists, racism still exists.
Being a woman, being a lesbian, all those issues you have to deal
with. There are clearly some people who would never dream of
voting for me because I'm a woman and because I'm a lesbian.
Fortunately, that's a small number. But I think my biggest challenge is simply assuring all of my constituents that I will represent all of them. I'm not running for office just to work on
women's issues or just to work on gay issues.

I find especially in the heat of the campaign that every major
newspaper in my district had to write the "Can a Lesbian Win?"
article. But I also think that is a fair article to write, although
I think they can only write it once. This has never happened
before, so it's history making, and it would be silly to pretend
this is not something they should write about.

For Christine Quinn (D), New York City council speaker, being
openly lesbian has not been an issue. "Other people might think that I
wouldn't get leadership support in a speaker's race, but I never thought
it would be an issue."

So, is it just because she's in New York?

"I would like to think it could be true in a lot of places . . . that people
don't really care anymore, but you have to be willing to take that risk and
go find the answer for yourself."

Arizona State Representative Kyrsten Sinema (D) took the risk in a
so-called red state; she is openly bisexual. Asked what obstacles she faced
she replied: "Oh God! I'm a Democrat in a very conservative legislature.
And I'm a progressive Democrat. So that has been difficult. Also, when
I was elected I was the youngest elected person in the State of Arizona.
I was only twenty-eight, being a young woman who is single and openly
bisexual—all those things made it pretty difficult for me. I hadn't been
embraced by the Democratic Party when I first got there. In fact, the
Democratic Party had financed hit pieces against me. Of course that's all

gone now. We're great friends, and they love me. But at the time, many people saw me as threat to the establishment."

What has changed since the days of Stevenson's divorce is that much of the country has broadened its acceptance of nontraditional families, including homosexuals. They are among our neighbors, friends, colleagues, and our children. What is not tolerated is a politician who is hypocritical, who proclaims one set of values and lives by another. This was what forced Congressman Mark Foley (R-FL) and Senator Larry Craig (R-ID) to abandon politics because of their homosexual behavior after having been adamantly opposed to gay rights.

It is ironic but true that to protect privacy it is advisable to give up privacy by revealing as much personal information as possible, before anyone else does. A recent example was former Congressman Newt Gingrich's (R-GA) announcement on Fox News that he had been having an affair while he was attacking Bill Clinton for his affair with Monica Lewinsky.

An elected official is no longer a private citizen, in big ways and small. I could never make a quick stop at the supermarket just before dinner; people who had questions, opinions, and problems would stop me at the produce section, the meat counter, and the checkout line. I couldn't brush them off, because I didn't want to offend them. These conversations were often valuable—they were my ear to the ground. Former President George H. W. Bush asked what a bar code was while at the supermarket. No politician since has wanted to appear that ignorant about groceries—to appear disconnected from the voters who put them in office.

Risk

Men hate losing as much as women do, but women seem more hesitant to take the risk. If they fail, they take it personally. My generation believed men were much better at risk taking because they had the advantage of growing up playing sports—you win some, you lose some. This generation of young women is different; they are the Title IX babies. They know how to win, how to lose, how to brush themselves off and try again. Still, many are loath to jump in. When I asked a group of young women if they had thought about going into politics, one said, "What if no one votes for me?"

The British call running for election "standing for election." A candidate does stand there, in broad daylight for strangers to say, "I like you" or "I don't like you." Public failure is different from having a cake fall in the privacy of an oven, losing an argument with a friend, or even being dumped by a boyfriend. Not everybody has to know about those. It is easier to say, "Don't take it personally," than it is to do. When I lost my first race for governor in 1981, I was devastated, even though I had known all along that I was in a tough race. When I had first announced, there was an open seat. Several months later, the incumbent governor changed his mind and decided to seek a fourth term. Overnight, my prospects for winning turned upside down: A race I could win became a race I could lose. The final days' frenzy of campaigning convinced me that I could pull it off; the polls were wrong. On election night after the returns came in and I had to give my concession speech—one of the hardest things a candidate has to do—I looked at my staff and saw some of them crying. I wanted to say, "I'm sorry, I'm sorry." During the next days, I was in mourning; I wanted to hide.

How did I get the courage to run again one-and-a-half years later? Not all losses are alike. A respectable loss is different from a devastating loss. That is how I succumbed to political amnesia, forgetting the last race and moving on to the next. I experienced something similar to the pangs of childbirth; I forgot the pain as soon as I was given the baby to hold.

Standing at the precipice is frightening. Amy Sheldon, a 40-year-old natural resources planner who is thinking of running for office, told me that she had contemplated running for office but hesitated: "I don't want politics to be my whole life—King of the Mountain one day, Humpty Dumpty the next."

Politics does not have to be your whole life. Neither does your job. Either can be lost without notice. The challenge is to try to make losing less personal.

Senator Susan Collins (R-ME) found out that after she lost her first race, another opportunity appeared. She is certain that had she not run and lost her race for governor, she would not have won her subsequent race for the U.S. Senate. "When I ran for governor in 1994, I won an eight-way Republican primary, but I lost the general election badly. I got clobbered. And then Bill Cohen [U.S. Senator William Cohen, R-ME], about 14 months later, made his decision to not run for reelection." That is where risk taking came in. After her campaign for governor, she "was totally broke. I couldn't afford health insurance." Then, she asked, "Should I give up a good job and be uninsured again? And there were no guarantees. I thought about it, and I thought about it, and I concluded that I didn't want to get to age 85 and wish that I had done it and be regretful that I had been too afraid to take the risk of losing again."

The same sequence held true for Senator Dianne Feinstein (D- CA); after serving as mayor of San Francisco, she ran for governor in 1990, lost a close race, and then was easily elected to the Senate two years later because she had become known and respected statewide.

Confidence

"I'm always doubting myself, and even when I'm proven wrong, I don't digest it," one of my students admitted. Such remarks surprise me. These are the women who were raised by parents who encouraged their daughters to believe they could do anything. They should be confident. Some are. Kesha Ram is the president of the student government association at the University of Vermont (UVM). "I feel like we are stereotyping women by saying that we are passive. I think that is a social thing we create for ourselves. I think that women are just as assertive as men in certain situations."

Another young woman who was part of a discussion group of UVM students and graduates put it this way: "I like the idea of being involved but not running. I think there is arrogance, a certain public persona that you have to take on to go through the whole election process; a process of being so publicly scrutinized. Once I was there I wouldn't mind it, but even in high school I remember running for office and going back and forth, and there was nothing personal about it. That is what really throws me off; you have to expose all your personal decisions."

These women have opinions; they are deterred from expressing them by seeming "arrogant." "I don't want to come off as a person who knows it all," Olivia Teer, the Girls State governor, told me.

Representative Rachel Weston, the youngest member of the Vermont Legislature, recalled that when she first contemplated running: "Running is a fairly scary thing."

What was the scariest part?

"For me, one was having to make it public that I wanted to be a representative and not being afraid to claim that. It seemed like it might come across as aggressive or might come across as pretentious. It was difficult for me to say, OK, I'm twenty-four, and I'm willing to do this. Also the fear of being laughed at because when you think of politicians you have this view of an older man, generally in a suit, and I was still walking around in my flip-flops."

These fears are not new to Carol Gilligan, a psychologist and author of *In a Different Voice.* Her studies indicate that girls between the ages of nine and eleven are confident and display strong leadership qualities. Once they reach adolescence, likeability becomes more important, and they tone their opinions down to maintain their friendships. They want to remain part of their circle and not stand out, which often means standing alone. The irony is that an elected official stands alone under a watchful public eye, but she can remain standing only if she is not alone. To continue to get elected, she has to surround herself with supporters who will vote for her and some who will work for her. The energy flow between a politician and the public can appear to be similar to that in a relationship, and like a relationship it can also be broken.

Weston said she was learning how to deal with the emotional side of politics. "I think anyone who runs for office has to be very strong emotionally—not getting down on yourself because people don't agree with what you are thinking or not becoming an egomaniac because people really like what you are thinking," she said.

A politician can feel like a yo-yo on a string, up and down, up and down. Sometimes it's hard to get the right spin to make it snap up again. To be effective, a public person has to be engaged, involved, and often passionate; but to survive, she has to maintain a separate space she can call her own and to which she can return when the day is done. Politics is a serious game; decisions are made that directly affect people's lives— sometimes life-or-death decisions—but it is still a game that requires keeping some distance from the board.

"It's Not the Right Time in My Life."

Women, more often than men, fear that if they take on something extra, their carefully balanced lives will fall apart. Sometimes they are right. *Juggle* is the verb most frequently used by women who have multiple responsibilities. But they are not always right. Falling back on "it's not the right time in my life" is an acceptable answer and still leaves the door open. The problem with that answer is that it may be the right time to run because in politics timing is almost everything. When a seat opens up because the incumbent is not running again, it's time to jump in. My first race for the legislature was for an open seat. I knew the occasion might not soon present itself again. Opportunity is not patient; it does not wait for the candidate. The challenge for women is to prepare them-selves so when the clock strikes, they are ready.

Congresswoman Debbie Wasserman-Schultz had not planned to run right away for the Florida House when

> . . . in 1992 [Representative Peter Deutsch, for whom she had worked for four years] called me at home in the middle of the night during the reapportionment session and said, "Debbie that last map I saw"—and I had just gotten married the year before that—"your house is in my district. [He was going to run for Congress]. So you should take advantage and run now." I had to resign from my job by law. I was 25. I spent about a month talking to my husband about the financial implications. Could I afford to give up my job and have no income during the campaign? My husband was really supportive because he knew this was my dream. He said "You should do it."
>
> All the power brokers told me I shouldn't run. I went and

paid my homage to all the condo chairmen and leaders, and they patted me on the head, mostly the men, and said "That's very nice honey, but it's not your turn. There are lots of people in front of you, you've only lived here three years. You would be a good candidate down the road."

I said, "I really have a lot of good ideas, and I think I have something to add, so I'm going to run, and I just hope you support me after the primary. Please do that."

They all said, of course we'll support you if you win the primary. I had $21,000 in a 107,000-person district—I was outspent by two of my opponents. I won a six-way Democratic primary with 53 percent of the vote and won against the Republican with 54 percent of the vote. I was the youngest woman ever to be elected to the state legislature in Florida history.

What Makes Women Run?

Given the obstacles—and I have not exhausted the list—what makes women gain the confidence, take the risk, give up their privacy, raise the money, endure public criticism, and run for office? What enabled Hillary Clinton to run for president and the sixteen women in the Senate, the eighty-seven women in the House, the 1,793 women in state legislatures, and the thousands of women serving in local elective office lift one foot and then the other and step over the line between private and public life?

The women I spoke with fall into two general categories. Some were introduced to politics at the family dinner table. Their parents were involved, either holding office, working for campaigns, or keenly interested in current events. That was our house when my children were growing up. My son Adam was invited to his girlfriend's house for dinner, and he came home and said, "Mom, guess what? They don't talk about politics."

The other group of women crossed the line because of a personal experience, often related to their children's safety or education. I started out by asking my neighbors to sign a petition to get a red flashing light at the railroad crossing. I was worried my children might be injured on

their way to school. The "worried-mother syndrome" is an effective catalyst for social change. It is also a comfortable way to step into the public
arena because when women act on behalf of their families, they do not
see themselves, nor do others see them, as politicians acting in their
self-interest. Education, safety, health, and environmental issues are the
"caring" issues, traditionally associated with women.

Concern about children catapults many women over the line between
private and public life. "A mom in tennis shoes" became the slogan for
Patty Murray (D) when she ran for the U.S. Senate in 1992; her son was
fifteen and her daughter was twelve. "Politics was the furthest thing from
my mind. I had never been to our state capitol. I was working as a parent
volunteer for the Shoreline Community Cooperative School, which was a
wonderful parent–child education program sponsored by the community
college. My kids attended the preschool."

One day the teacher announced the school would have to close because
"the state legislature was taking the funds away":

> I decided to go to the state capitol in Olympia to talk to
> some legislators and convince them of their mistake. Finally,
> one legislator I'd pigeonholed . . . let me know what he really
> thought . . . "Lady, that's a really nice story, but you can't get
> that funding restored," he said. "You can't make a difference.
> You're just a mom in tennis shoes."[12]

Murray was so incensed that she set out to prove him wrong. She put
together a list of 15,000 parents. "We showed up at every hearing. We
were a presence. We were heard. It took almost a year, but we got the
program reinstated." Being a "mom in tennis shoes" turned out to be an
asset rather than a liability.

Before Texas Representative Leticia Van de Putte (D) decided to run,
"We sat down with my children and discussed what it would mean if
mommy actually went to the legislature, an hour away. My four-year-old,
the epicenter of the family—asked, 'Why?'"

"Because there are not enough mommies there," her 10-year-old
replied. "That's when it hit, out of the mouth of babes," she said.

There is another reason some women take the plunge. "For me it boils down to not being satisfied with the choices of candidates. I wanted somebody who was going to be a passionate advocate and somebody who had the energy and the desire to roll up their shirtsleeves and fight for us every day," said Congresswoman Linda Sanchez (D-CA). "I felt I had the drive, the desire and the determination to really be an advocate in Washington." She ran despite what Democratic Party leaders told her. "'Oh, you're too young. Wait your turn. Why don't you try running for the school board first, if you care about education?' It was patronizing."

The childhood experience of receiving a spoonful of politics with porridge at the breakfast table has inspired many women to run. But it is not the only recipe. No one in my family had been elected to office. My grandfather, whom I did not know because he died a few months after I was born, ran for the Zurich city council and lost. My mother told me he gave great speeches. When I was governor, I discovered a great-aunt who had been postmistress in Texas, but I did not know her. What I knew was that my mother read *The New York Times* and listened to radio station WQXR (the equivalent of public radio). Our family knew and cared about what was going on—still the most important perquisite for public life.

Vermont Secretary of State Deb Markowitz, 45, grew up in an observant Jewish family who believed in *Tikun Olum* ("repair the world"). "Every night at the dinner table we had to tell what good deed we had done that day. I often just wanted to get it over with, but it stayed with me."

At Senator Susan Collins's (R-ME) dinner table, politics was always discussed because both her parents served at different times as mayor of Caribou, Maine. "I was always empowered and taught to give back."

Speaker of the Vermont House Gaye Symington's (D) great-uncle was Stuart Symington, senator from Missouri. Her community did not know that when they elected her. What they knew was that she had created a community center out of an abandoned 1850 building, which had been at times a gym, a library, and a high school. "The building brought people in the community together, and that's how people knew me."

Senator Amy Klobuchar (D-MN) had her first political experience as a class officer in high school, raising money by selling lollipops for the senior prom. "We went door to door, so I had to create a whole organization. We saved enough money to have the prom at the Livingston Hotel, which was really nice."

Not all daughters shared their parents' politics. "I was raised by a very conservative Mormon family, which clearly I'm not. I'm a very progressive agnostic today. I developed a skill to make my own mind up and to resist criticism and to stick with my own path and not do what others were doing," said Representative Kyrsten Sinema (D-AZ).

Congresswoman Loretta Sanchez's (D-CA) parents were "both immigrants and not educated. My parents raised very aggressive kids [her sister, Linda Sanchez is also a member of Congress], kids that thought they could do anything they wanted. They didn't have the opportunities we had, so they stressed education, they stressed being involved in the community and giving back to the community."

Vermont Senator Diane Snelling (R) had politics in her genes. She went "from being the daughter of [a former governor—the governor I first ran against and lost to] to being the candidate myself." Her mother had been lieutenant governor and a state senator. Still, she had reservations. "I am an artist, so I had thought I would stay away from politics. I ran for select board in 1985 and served six two-year terms, but that was community service." When her mother didn't run again, she told Snelling, "They want you." Her response was, "I was much too private and stayed away from large crowds, but I had to think about the opportunity." Ultimately she ran because "I grew up in a family where there was extreme dedication to public service. Apparently, I learned a lot without realizing it when I was a child."

Senator Claire McCaskill (D-MO) agreed that her 2006 victory had been tough. "It was particularly hard emotionally to get where I needed to be." Earlier, she had run against an incumbent governor in her own party. "It was inherently a very lonely journey. We succeeded in winning that primary by a wide margin and then lost the general (election) narrowly." Like Collins and Feinstein, her governor's race paved the way for her Senate victory.

Her start in politics? "From the very bottom, state representative as a very young lawyer, at twenty-eight, and slowly chinked my way up the ladder," she said.

Her political sights were set

. . . at a very early age. My parents were active but not particularly powerful. My mother was elected to city council when I was in high school, and my father had a political appointment for a brief period of time. My mom was somebody who was constantly doing what women in this country have done as the primary role, and that was she was asking people to come stuff envelopes. We went to a lot of political rallies. So I was exposed to it as a young girl and enjoyed it.

Beginning probably in junior high, no later than high school, I started visualizing me as a political candidate and holding office. I believe very much in visualization. When people can see themselves in that job, then they are comfortable in making the job their goal. More and more it will be easier for women to see themselves in political office because more and more we have women as governors and senators.

It also involves an incredible amount of risk and willingness to confront and willingness to accept personal rejection in a public way. Those are things that are difficult for all people and particularly difficult for women.

She thanks her parents for giving her encouragement:

My father, bless his heart, was kind enough to tell me that I didn't need to worry about the fact that I was a bossy woman, and that even though men would have a hard time with it, there would come a time in my life that I would find men who would relish the fact that I was smart. Dad gave me permission. Mother was the one that pushed. She is very outspoken and loves politics.

How Do You Become a Politician?

Lawyers go to law school, doctors go to medical school, accountants study accounting, beauticians go to beauty school, and realtors take a test. How do you become a politician? What is the right preparation? Are there courses a woman should take in high school or college? Is it necessary to get a law degree or a master's degree in public administration?

The problem is that there is no road map or set of Global Positioning System coordinates to tell a person what route to take to arrive at destination "public office." One reason women—and many men—do not consider running for office is that the process is more opaque than transparent, more mysterious than obvious. Any American citizen, theoretically, can run for office. The only legal requirement is age: eighteen, or thirty-five if you want to run for president. The perception is different.

"It's a lot of who you know. If women don't have these connections, how do they get them?" asked one UVM student in our discussion group. The belief persists that "who can run" is decided in the smoke-filled back room (even if smoking is no longer allowed in most gathering places) by men with paunches that hang over their belt buckles, puff on cigars, and let the ashes fall on their trousers. A glass of whiskey or a sweaty beer bottle is seldom out of reach. How accurate is that picture today?

Yes, there are still back rooms where deals are made by the "good old boys." But we soon may be able to put them on the endangered species list. Their population varies from region to region, state to state, and city to city. Increasingly, somebody in the room has said, "Open the windows, and let in some fresh air." Still, many women are convinced that they are not welcome in these rooms, smoke filled or not. The assumption is that the process is controlled by an elite who know the rules, and those rules are not written down. They can't be found on Google, or MySpace, or on a special blog.

"We have to de-mystify the political process," said Donna Brazile, campaign manager for Al Gore's 2000 presidential race. The "mystery" of politics works like a tightly meshed screen placed over a window—it's hard to see inside. The assumed importance of "who you know" rather than "what you know" tilts the playing field against the average civic-minded citizen who is not well connected and does not have access to a circle of rich donors. Connections and a hefty bank account do help; both can be acquired.

How do you get in the door? In a rural state like Vermont, politics is more accessible than in New York or California. The first step to enter any political organization—rural or urban—is the same; it's called showing up.

When I went to my first neighborhood Democratic caucus in 1971, I was surprised to hear myself nominated by a neighbor to be a candidate for the city council. He mistakenly thought I wanted to run. That had not been my intention, but I didn't dissuade him. I didn't win, but I gained instant recognition by having shown up with four friends. The old guard was certain we were trying to "take over" the caucus.

Volunteering in a political campaign, as well as attending a party caucus, a political fund-raiser, a neighborhood meeting, are the first classes in Politics 101. There you find out who the players are and how the system works. Most political groups eagerly welcome fresh faces, particularly young people. A newcomer is an extra hand and a potential convert, something needed by all parties and causes.

Senator Mary Landrieu (D-LA) came from a political family; her father, Moon Landrieu, was a popular mayor of New Orleans for many years. She did not think of herself as a potential candidate until she went door to door for the campaign of a friend of the family. "Some of my friends and fellow campaign workers came up to me and said, 'You're very good at this. Have you ever thought of running yourself?' Of course, I didn't. But suddenly I found myself thinking, 'They're right, why not?'"[1]

Getting Started

A campaign volunteer usually will be assigned menial tasks such as making phone calls, doing data entry, stuffing envelopes, and doing literature drops. Women used to be relegated to the drudgery section of campaigns, but increasingly they are running major campaigns for both female and male candidates, including Susan Estrich for Michael Dukakis, Donna Brazile for Al Gore, and Mary Beth Cahill for John Kerry.

No matter the assignment, working on a campaign provides a reality check on whether politics is for you. "If someone is interested in public policy or in a job as a public official, then get close to the campaign and learn, watch from the inside, see what the process is like. If you do that, it will be much less intimidating to you. You'll realize this [winning an election] is not rocket science. It's called trying to make sure people find out who you are and why you could do a good job. There are so many women who could do this and just don't realize it," said Senator Claire McCaskill (D-MD).

Another assumption made about women and men who run for office is that they have to have the right personality. They rule themselves out because "I like to say what I think" or "I'm not an extrovert." The ability to say what "you think" is a core political attribute—without it, why run? Moderation is learned all too soon. Shyness, too, can be overcome. When I was elected governor, my 1952 classmates at Pittsfield (MA) High School were astonished. I had been the shy, quiet one, never a cheerleader.

Many in politics are shy. Atlanta Mayor Shirley Franklin admitted that when she first ran, "I had to overcome some shyness. I had never spoken in public before." She advised, "It's equally important for a woman to be liked as well as to be smart. You can't just be the smartest person in the room." Perhaps some run for office to overcome shyness. Then they discover it's fun to connect with people, shake their hands, get them to smile, and say something nice.

Many candidates discover a new side to their personalities when they campaign. So did I. Two earlier jobs helped me become more outgoing, waitressing and teaching. Every summer while in college and graduate

Not Equal, Superior
BELLA ABZUG (1920–1998)

Bella Abzug was impossible to miss in a crowd; she always wore a wide-brimmed hat. "I began wearing hats as a young lawyer because it helped me to establish my professional identity. Before that, whenever I was at a meeting someone would ask me to get coffee."[2]

She was elected to Congress on an anti-Vietnam War platform and became an outspoken advocate for civil liberties and women's equality.

The daughter of Russian immigrants, Abzug grew up in poverty in the Bronx and went to Hunter College, where tuition was free. She received her law degree from Columbia University and was married and devoted to her husband Martin. They had two daughters.

After serving three terms in Congress, she ran for the all-male Senate in 1976 and lost the primary by less than one percent. Her subsequent efforts to run for mayor of New York and Congress were unsuccessful. She continued to have a powerful public voice. In 1990 she founded WEDO, the Women's Environment and Development Organization, an international activist and advocacy network.

I first met Bella at a conference of newly elected women legislators at Mount Holyoke College in 1973. Her voice bellowed out to the audience as if she were performing in a Wagnerian opera. Each time I saw her, standing on the podium or sitting in a wheelchair, she showed an undaunted fighting spirit that inspired everyone around her.

In " Five Cents on the Subway," she wrote:

> When I was young, it wasn't easy to challenge the traditions of Harvard Law School. When I was ten, I had decided that I wanted to be a lawyer, and at the all-women Walton High School and at Hunter College, I had been elected student body president, good training for the law. Everyone told me that if I wanted to be accepted as a lawyer I should go to the best law school, but when I applied to Harvard, I received a letter stating that it did not admit women.
>
> In 1942 only 3 percent of the nation's lawyers were women. I was outraged (I've always had a decent sense of outrage), so I turned to my mother. In those days there was no women's movement, so you turned to your mother for help. "Why do you want to go to Harvard anyway?" she asked. "It's far away and you can't afford the carfare. Go to Columbia University. They'll probably give you a scholarship, and

it's only five cents to get there on the subway."

Columbia did give me a scholarship, the subway did cost only five cents in those days, and that's how I became an advocate for low-cost public transportation.[3]

In 1977, she delivered a speech at the First Plenary Session of the first National Women's Conference in Houston, and here is a sample of her wisdom:

Some among us may prefer a future that simply continues the past. Our purpose is not to tell women how to live or what to do. It is simply to say that women must be free to choose what they do.

Housewives, or homemakers, if you prefer, earn nothing at all, though this nation could not function for a day if the millions of women who work exclusively in the home were to stop doing what they do so lovingly for their families.

We can no longer accept a condition in which men rule the Nation and the world, excluding half the human race from effective economic and political power. Not when the world is in such bad shape.

We can argue about whether women, if we arrive at the stage where we do share power with men, will create a better world. I believe we will. I believe that if we had the

opportunity we could figure out ways to spend some of the $300 billion spent on armaments each year for more rational and humane purposes—like feeding the hungry, housing the homeless, creating jobs, preventing disease, ignorance and illiteracy.

Personally, I am not interested in seeing women get an equal chance to push the nuclear button. I do want to see women and men work equally together for a peaceful world in which my daughters and your sons and daughters can live without fear.

The women's movement has become an indestructible part of American life. It is the homemaker deciding that raising children, cleaning, cooking and all the other things she does for her family is work that could be accorded respect and value. It is the young woman student asserting she wants to play baseball, major in physics, or become a brain surgeon. It is the working woman demanding that she get the same pay and promotion opportunities as a man. It is the divorcee fighting for social security benefits in her own right, the widow embarking on a new career, the battered wife seeking help, the woman running for public office.

school I waitressed. Working for tips is not unlike working for votes. The customer has to be pleased. In those days we didn't say, "I'm Madeleine, and I'm your server tonight." It wasn't that personal, but I learned how to make small talk with my "tables." I also learned the meaning of manual labor when I befriended the other waitresses and the people sweating in the kitchen—these were their full-time jobs. I have been a good tipper ever since.

Teaching taught me how to think on my feet. Before I stepped into a classroom for the first time to face fifty freshman English students at Trinity College in Burlington, Vermont, I ducked into the ladies' room and stayed there as long as I could. What scared me? That I would not think of anything to say, nobody would ask a question, and I would fall into a terrifying chasm of silence.

The most comfortable position from which to launch a political career for some women is to serve on the school board. It allows them to be home for dinner, not have to raise much money, and, in some cities, be nonpartisan. That's where Republican State Representative Vida Miller from South Carolina began. "I had a record of accomplishment on the school board and felt I knew the community."

Former Governor Jeanne Shaheen (D) of New Hampshire was involved in student government, and then, "I had been a teacher for several years. You can't usually be too shy standing up in front of a group of high school students and succeed."

Terie Norelli, (D) New Hampshire Speaker of the House, was a high school math teacher, good preparation for serving on the committee on energy, science, and technology, she explained. "We were dealing with very complex issues; not everybody was interested in the nitty-gritty of electric restructure." She was and developed her area of expertise.

Several women were social workers before they became candidates, including Congresswoman Carol Shea-Porter (D-NH) and Senator Barbara Mikulski (D-MD). They made the transition to politics because they discovered, like Representative Sinema (D-AZ), that as a social worker, "I was able to help deal with emergency issues. I was able to help these families meet their basic needs, but I wasn't able to change the basic laws of the system."

All candidates agree that there is no single set of credentials for running for office. "I think you need to learn to speak and to write. You don't need a special degree," said Congresswoman Deborah Pryce (R-OH).

"I tell young women all the time, there is no certain degree you need. You have got to really like people, you have got to embrace public speaking, you've got to be willing to take risks, and you've got to ask people for money. If you can do those four things, you can run for office," said Senator McCaskill (D-MO).

Vermont State Senator Jeannette White (D) served on the select board (equivalent to city council in Vermont) for nine years before she "decided I wanted to give the legislature a try."

"I've been a corn de-tassler, camp counselor, waitress, UPS truck loader—3:30 A.M.–8 A.M.—factory worker [in a book press], University of Vermont Council on Aging—that's what won me the election, because I knew everyone in Windham County [where she lives] from all walks of life."

Congresswoman Loretta Sanchez (D-CA) tells women "to get some experience somewhere. Be a good teacher, a good doctor, a good lawyer, a good manager at McDonald's. Do something and be the best you can be at it. And once you have got that under your belt, maybe in two to five years or however long, and you want to be a politician. Do it. In your spare time, work on a campaign. See if you are even going to like it. You have to be able to ask people for money, you have to be able to put up with insults. You have to be able to work hard. You have to like people. If you don't like people, then don't get into the business."

What did she do before she ran? "I was an investment banker for 14 years." Her sister, Congresswoman Linda Sanchez (D-CA), had practiced law and worked in the labor movement, which "helped me understand a lot of the issues that working families faced."

Senator Dianne Feinstein (D-CA) tells young women to "start on the school board, go for a spot on the town council. Earn your spurs. That's the key. Don't flit around like a moth—light and leave, light and leave. Develop a portfolio of expertise—something you're really good at, so that people will turn to you. Develop your credibility, your integrity, show people they can trust you. Make a contribution. Be effective, because once you show you are effective, you're a force to be reckoned with."[4]

Conflicting advice: Take lots of different jobs, even corn de-tassler—so everyone can get to know you—or develop one area of expertise. One size clearly does not fit all women. They tend to have more diverse backgrounds than men because women often do not plan a political career, and they run for office later after their children are grown or as a second career.

But there are some trends. Some women started out in high school as class president, others discovered their political passion in college, many have worked on campaigns, and a significant number have served as legislative interns or staff.

Senator Collins (R-ME) was president of the student council at Caribou High School. She worked for Maine Senator Bill Cohen, also a Republican, for twelve years in Washington, which "gave me a familiarity with the way the Senate worked and with some issues that I would not have had. But it doesn't have to be in the public sector; you can volunteer, serve on your planning board. Reading a lot, that is helpful."

Congresswoman Baldwin's (D-WI) interest in politics was sparked in middle school "when I was involved in student council and student government." A guidance counselor told her to get involved in a program "that contributed to my giving public service very serious thought."

I was not involved in student government until I went to college, when to my surprise, when I was editorial page editor of the college newspaper, I was named Woman of the Year by the University of Massachusetts, a title that embarrassed me because I was certain I could not live up to it. Many women become politically involved in their communities when a local or national issue prompts them to attend a meeting, write a letter to their congressional representative, sign a petition, or organize a meeting themselves.

Senator Barbara Mikulski (D-MD) was about to get her doctorate in public health when

> . . . fate intervened. . . . I got a call from a social-worker friend. She said, "You've got to come to a meeting tonight at the church." She told me about a plan for a 16-lane highway that would run

through the neighborhood. . . . I was outraged by the plan. . . . They were going to destroy Baltimore so there would be a highway for people living in the suburbs.

At the meeting, people shared their fears and talked about their lack of power. The Democratic establishment, the mayor— everyone was behind the highway.[5]

"What can we do?" they asked. Mikulski built coalitions and saved the community. "The highway forces didn't know what hit them." Her successful campaign led to the next step: winning a seat on the Baltimore City Council in 1971. In 1976 she was elected to Congress, and then years later she became the first woman Democratic senator elected in her own right.

In Vermont, Gretchen Morse was awakened early one morning by the road crew, ready to pave the scenic dirt road in front of her house that went through a covered bridge. "I jumped out of bed and ran outside in my nightgown and stepped in front of the bulldozer." It worked. Soon after she was elected to the legislature.

"Involvement is the best way to prepare yourself, whether it is just your local party apparatus or a campaign," according to Congresswoman Pryce (R-OH).

Involvement means community involvement for Donna Brazile, a political commentator. She observed that most women start out as community activists.

That was true for New Hampshire Speaker Norelli (D), who didn't know she was preparing herself for a political life when she worked on issues and advocacy for women. She

. . spent a number of years working for organizations that work for survivors of sexual assault and worked to support pro-choice candidates. What made me change my mind about running for the legislature was the person who recruited me; she framed it differently. You've worked on all of these issues, if you are in the legislature, you can continue to work on all of these issues, it's just a different venue with greater impact because it would have a statewide impact. That was the reason I changed my mind. I'm in my sixth term now; at first, I figured I would make a two-year commitment.

Those who fear they are not capable of making the leap from activism to elective politics may be surprised to learn that they have already laid the foundation. Local activists have built up a network of supporters, and they have a cause that releases their political adrenalin—two strong pluses in a political campaign.

It was a local issue that galvanized New York City Councilwoman Jessica Lappin (D), who was elected when she was thirty. She had worked in Senator Patrick Moynihan's office and for a member of the City Council, and "I thought about being the candidate at some point." She decided to run when she got involved in a fight about the location of a water main shaft and a marine transfer station in her neighborhood. "I think having done both, being a grassroots activist and having worked on the city council, I had a good sense of how to marry the two."

Working as an intern or a legislative aide is a common experience for many in public life. It provides an unobstructed view of how politics works. Senator Amy Klobuchar (D-MN) explained,

> I worked for Vice President Mondale [from her state of Minnesota] in the summer of 1980. My first job was to do an inventory, looking at all former vice presidents and their staffs' furniture. I would crawl under the desks and mark them with numbers. After that I did some speech writing and some research. I really enjoyed working for him. I'm not sure how many people started in Washington by doing furniture inventory.

Senator Klobuchar discovered that not only was Vice President Mondale a good boss, he also became her mentor. "When I got back to Minnesota I had a lot of student loans and wanted to work in the private sector. I worked in a law firm with Walter Mondale." Later, he encouraged her to run for office.

New Hampshire State Senator Sylvia Larsen (D) had worked for New

Hampshire Governor Hugh Gallen as a "backroom staff person" before she ran for City Council. She took time off "to stay with my two children" but then "started looking at my skills, and I realized I knew how to enact legislation. I had always written speeches, answered mail, done research, written laws, always done all the parts, so since I was capable to do all the work, I thought I should run."

Texas Senate Democratic caucus leader Leticia Van de Putte is the neighborhood pharmacist and grew up half a block from where she lives now. She knows everyone in her district.

A common credential for women in politics today is a law degree. When I graduated from college in 1956, I did not know a woman lawyer. Neither did I know that a law degree could be a useful credential for careers other than law. Representative Sinema (D-AZ), first elected at twenty-eight, learned that if she "really wanted to change the system" she had to do two things: "to go to law school and understand how laws are made, who makes them, and how lawyers have so much power in our country—and then to run for office."

She achieved both goals, running for office while she was in law school. "I graduated about four weeks after my election. I really wouldn't recommend that for anyone else . . . it was pretty tough. But I wasn't a typical law student; I had been working for ten years in my community."

Senator McCaskill (D-MO) used her law degree to become an assistant prosecutor:

> For a period of time I was the only female felony prosecutor in Kansas City. When I was in a job like that and I was trying to be credible with the victim, with the boss, with the judges, and all of my fellow prosecutors, and they are 99.9 percent men, I had to learn to tough it out and not be afraid to forge ahead. That training and that environment were very useful.
>
> I say to young women lawyers all the time who are interested in politics, that going the route of working in a prosecutor's office is an incredibly wise move because it not only teaches you how to think on your feet, you learn to embrace risk and confrontation and it looks great on your résumé.

Three women governors were state attorneys general: Jennifer Granholm of Michigan, Janet Napolitano of Arizona, and Christine Gregoire of Washington state.

Florida Congresswoman Debbie Wasserman-Schultz (D) did not go to law school, but she

> . . . knew I wanted to run for office when I was in college. I got bitten by the political bug and got really involved in student politics and college Democrats. Instead of going to law school, I got my master's degree in political campaigning at UF [University of Florida]. I did a lot of internships and worked on a lot of campaigns. I knew I wanted to run one day, but I thought the path I would take is the one most women take, that I would get married and that I would have kids, and later on when they were older, I would run. I went to work for a Florida House member in the middle of graduate school who recruited me to be his legislative aide.

She had planned to be an office intern, but when his legislative aide left, he offered her the job. She debated whether to leave graduate school, but he encouraged her to stay, saying, "Your degree is valuable to me." "I did get my master's while I worked for him. That has been my life ever since, constant juggling and balancing."

There is no single credential essential to running for office. But as in any career, more is better, both knowledge and experience. It is impossible to prepare for every question that comes up because politics touches on every aspect of life. The curriculum could be endless. I majored in history as an undergraduate at the University of Massachusetts and received two masters' degrees: one from the School of Journalism, Columbia University, in 1957 and the other in English literature from the University of Vermont in 1967. I used it all, as well as whatever I have learned since. As governor I had to decide on issues ranging from determining the safety of a nuclear power plant to preventing the spread of the HIV/AIDS virus. Information gathering is different in politics than it is in school.

Most of the information that elected officials rely on is current and oral—it is provided by the media, lobbyists, and the public, and it is often biased. To discount bias, it is important to ask the right questions. On her deathbed Gertrude Stein asked her companion Alice B. Toklas, "What is the answer?" Not hearing a response, she asked, "Well then, what is the question?" To know what the question is requires some knowledge, a lot of skepticism, and great curiosity. It helps not to be intimidated by all expertise but to know whose expertise to trust. That distinction is not always clear.

Information gathering is one problem, assessing public opinion is another. Those who speak loudest are sometimes the minority, but they are the best financed and most capable of mounting an effective campaign. Those who speak softly also deserve to be heard. The challenge for an elected official is to try to weave different voices into a cohesive fabric called consensus—a prerequisite for action. That is an acquired skill not easily learned. It helps to be a good teacher and use different educational tools. Former Vice President Al Gore educated the public about global warming through his documentary, *An Inconvenient Truth*, and it helped to create greater consensus.

One frustration experienced by those in public life is that there is never enough information, and it doesn't arrive in time. No matter how many staff members conduct research, how many constituents speak out, how many thick reports pile up on the desk, decisions have to be based on the best information and advice available at the time. There is no waiting for the definitive volume to appear. The vote has to be cast when the bell rings.

Although some elected officials carefully prepare for their political careers, others have a "Eureka!" moment when everything becomes clear. That's what happened to U.S. Senator Barbara Boxer (D-CA) in 1992 when she watched the interrogation of Anita Hill during the Supreme Court confirmation hearing of Clarence Thomas.

It happened to Leticia Van de Putte on children's health. "I got mad. I was angry at the politics aimed at health care. Every cow in Texas had to have a full set of vaccinations and be registered, but there wasn't anything for kids, like no money for vitamins for prenatal care."

Representative Loretta Sanchez (D-CA) heard a wake-up call that same year. "In 1992, I was flipping the channels, and I came across the Republican National Convention, and Pat Buchanan was giving his speech; his 'pull up the draw bridge and keep the immigrants out' speech. I was so outraged [her parents are Mexican immigrants], and I was a registered Republican at the time—I went down to the registrar's office the next day and changed my registration to Democrat. And then I started giving money to Democrats. They were all losing. Then I decided I had to do it myself. Bob Dornan was my congressman, and I tried to meet with him on an education issue, and he refused to meet with me. So I went home and said to my husband, 'I am going to run for Congress.'"

"Had you run for anything before?" I asked.

"I had run for City Council two years before and I had lost." She hadn't raised enough money because she didn't know how important money was. "That didn't scare me off. The next time, I said, 'I'm going to run and win. I'm going to beat this guy,' and I did."

Dornan had a reputation for being the most conservative member of Congress and making offensive remarks. To a Los Angeles television reporter he said in 1992, "Every lesbian spearchucker in this country is hoping I get defeated." Dornan was so confident of his victory over Loretta Sanchez that he told the *Orange County Weekly:* "She can't beat me" because "Bob Dornan is a father of five, grandfather of ten, military man, been married forty-one years. She has no kids, no military experience, and no track record. I win." Dornan lost by 984 votes. He later accused Sanchez of voter fraud. The election was declared valid by the Congress.

Congresswoman Baldwin caught the political wave while watching the Democratic convention in 1984 in her apartment

> . . . in Madison on my tiny television, in my unfurnished efficiency, watching Geraldine Ferraro walk across the stage to accept the nomination. I am not usually emotional, but I had tears streaming down my face that night. I am sure that played some role in getting involved as quickly as I did. I immersed myself in all the facets of politics after college: an internship

in the governor's office, volunteer work outside, worked on pay equity and comparable worth. I started monitoring county board meetings. I remember watching a debate and thinking "I'm as smart as any woman in this group. I could do this job."

Role Models and Mentors

"The only time that I ever thought of getting involved in politics was when I knew a female politician. She was a politician I could touch. She was real. I would see her in town. This wasn't something she always knew she wanted to do. She just decided. It was nice to know that," said Aubrey, a student at the University of Vermont. "I think it helps to see other women in the job. I believe very much in visualization. When people can see themselves in that job, then they are comfortable in making that job their goal. More and more it will be easier for women to see themselves in political office because more and more we have women as governors and senators," Senator McCaskill (D-MO) said.

Every woman who is in a position in which women have never been before becomes a role model simply by being there—the woman we see chairing a corporate board and the woman presiding over the U.S. House of Representatives. Her presence says: This is where women belong.

The distinction between role models and mentors is blurry, they can be either women or men; the difference is that mentors take a special interest in a person, offer encouragement, experience, and advice. Role models can be distant. In college I was impressed by Benjamin Disraeli, prime minister of England from 1874–1880, because there had never been a Jewish prime minister. He was also a novelist, a combination I admired. He was not exactly a role model, but he fed my imagination.

My legislative mentor was Representative Emory Hebard, chair of the House Appropriations Committee, a conservative Republican. He gave me responsibility, trusted my judgment, and lobbied for me to succeed him as chair of the committee after he was elected state treasurer. Male mentors were crucial to many other women in politics: Senator Jim Jeffords for Representative Heidi Scheuermann (R) and Commissioner

Karen Meyer, Vice President Walter Mondale for Senator Amy Klobuchar, and Senator William Cohen for Senator Susan Collins.

When I was younger, Eleanor Roosevelt was a role model because of her courage and independence. My mother read her column, "My Day," religiously. I admired Golda Meir, prime minister of Israel. When I got married and had children, I read about Mary Bunting, the president of Radcliffe College, married to a doctor. If she could have four children and a career, perhaps I could too.

Female role models were once rare. "In my day women were supposed to copy Jackie, not Jack, Kennedy. If I aspired to anything, it was to marry a politician. I married an artist instead, so I had to become the politician," observed Vermont state senator Ann Cummings (D).

I didn't discount Jack Kennedy. He was not a role model, but he was a model of an American president who brought joy, wit, and intelligence to politics, as was Adlai Stevenson. I volunteered briefly in Stevenson's presidential campaign while a student at Columbia University School of Journalism and wept when he lost.

Role models are often composites of historical and contemporary figures. I've spotted many in the obituary pages of *The New York Times*.

Mentors and role models also can be found at home. Vermont Senator White (D) listed her parents. Representative Copeland-Hanzas said, "There are a lot of strong women in my life. My mom and grandmother are both very strong people." Senator Cummings's grandmother was her role mode:

> Her husband deserted her during the Depression, leaving her with six young sons to raise on her own. She worked for the WPA [Works Progress Administration] and eventually opened a coffee shop. She never complained, and she never depended upon a man to take care of her.

Assemblywoman Nellie Pou (D) of Patterson, New Jersey, whose parents came from Puerto Rico before she was born, said her mother "was short but strong." She is the first Latina to be elected from her 220,000-member district.

Alaska minority leader Beth Kurtula's (D) greatest role model was her father. He was the state's longest-serving legislator, thirty-four years. "So I've been around it my whole life. I always knew I would regret it if I didn't try doing it." Still she needed mentors once she was elected, "Somebody who wanted to help me learn . . . the guy who I was lucky enough to sit by in my first four years where I got real well grounded."

Senator Margaret Chase Smith (R-ME) was mentioned most often by women senators. Senator Elizabeth Dole (R-NC) and Senators Snowe (R) and Collins (R), both from Maine, all referred to her. "She was senator the entire time I was growing up. She was always present," Collins said. "When I was eighteen, I went to Washington as part of the Senate Youth Program. I met Senator Smith, and she took me into her private office and spent nearly two hours talking to me, which I can't believe when I look at my schedule. Although I didn't know it at the time, I think that was my first step on my path to running for the U.S. Senate twenty-five years later. I hold her seat. I have her creed and a picture of her on my wall," said Collins proudly.

"Her" picture was important to legislators in New Hampshire, Vermont, and other states who have had women governors. And "her" picture is important in states where women hold the gavel as speakers of the House and Senate presidents.

Hattie Caraway (D-AK), the second woman to serve in the U.S. Senate (the first to be elected), inspired Senator Blanche Lincoln (D-AK) to run for office. Caraway received unexpected support from Senator Huey Long of Louisiana who said, "We've got to pull a lot of potbellied politicians off a little woman's neck."[6]

Atlanta Mayor Shirley Franklin had worked behind the scenes, as chief administrative officer and then city manager under Mayor Andrew Young. "Two former mayors forced me to consider it, Maynard Jackson and Andrew Young. It took me a year to think about whether I could do it, both run and serve. Some people forget the "serve" part. I had to consider my family obligations and my financial ability, and moving from the background to the foreground." She now has the distinction of being the first black woman to be elected mayor of a major southern city. She's one of thirteen women mayors in America's 100 largest cities. In 2005, *Time* listed her as one of the five best big-city mayors.

Mentors don't have to be politicians. Speaker Terie Norelli (D-NH) was inspired by the executive director of the pro-choice New Hampshire chapter of NARAL. "She was 'that one person.' I admired her for her ability to make connections and work in the political arena across party lines and to develop leadership in other people. [She] was one of those people in my life who encouraged me to take on leadership roles," Norelli said.

When Barbara Mikulski (D-MD) became the only woman in the Senate, "It was tough, absolutely. I didn't have any natural mentors to show me the ropes. I had to seek my own mentors."[7] As a result, Mikulski has mentored every new female senator, presenting them with thick notebooks about how to get things done in the Senate.

When a mentor is not available, women can seek them out. Most politicians are willing to play that role, particularly those interested in helping young women get into politics. Many women who were thinking about running for office have sought me out. I have never refused them.

Kesha Ram, University of Vermont student government president, said she got excited about politics after reading about female senators. "I feel as though there is so much reason for hope. Women are dominating in college. I am really positive about women in politics. So much is changing right now. Barbara Boxer said, 'Women equal change.' It's just so exciting to see how much of a dynamic shift there is."

Women and Leadership

Leadership cookbooks that list the ingredients for effective leadership are more popular than ever. Almost every successful CEO has been impelled to divulge his secret formula. Most have bemoaned the lack of leadership "in our time," exemplified by Lee Iacocca's latest book, *Where Have All the Leaders Gone?:*

> Had enough? Am I the only guy in this country who's fed up with what's happening? Where the hell is our outrage? We should be screaming bloody murder. We've got a gang of clueless bozos steering our ship of state right over a cliff.[1]

Men throughout history have struggled to define leadership, benign and not benign, from Jesus to Hitler, from Aristotle to Machiavelli. Leadership meant male leadership. There was no other, unless we count Joan of Arc and Queen Elizabeth I.

The omission of women from leadership books was not due to oversight or prejudice. It was understood that males "are superior, more powerful, and that they represent the 'norm.' . . . In fact, sexist, patriarchal values are so deeply engrained in society's consciousness that they are largely invisible."[2]

Today, women have assumed new leadership roles in politics, business, higher education, and other venues in which they had never before appeared. "Firsts," such as the first woman president of Harvard University, Drew Gilpin Faust, continue to make headlines. The seconds and thirds take longer. Surprisingly the figure is the same—16 percent—for the number of women in the U.S. Congress and the number of women in top corporate positions. Why has progress been so slow? Do women have a different leadership style, and if so, does that help or hinder their advancement? Or are their leadership skills not sufficiently recognized by a business and political culture that remains predominantly male?

James MacGregor Burns, who has made a lifelong study of leadership, divides leadership into two types: transactional, which "depends on hierarchy . . . it requires the ability to obtain results, to control through structures and processes";[3] and transformational leadership, "which occurs when a leader engages with a follower in such a way that both parties are raised to higher levels of motivation and morality with a common purpose."[4] Transactional leadership is considered more masculine and transformational is considered more feminine. Some studies give women an advantage, others do not. Tracey Manning observes, "If transformational leadership is more androgynous, women managers may not have to cope with a perceived contradiction between being women and being effective leaders."[5] If she is correct, women political leaders would be free to be themselves without feeling pressured to lead in the more traditional male style. A challenge for women in leadership is to develop a comfortable, loosely fitting leadership style that works, regardless of the culture.

Judith Rosener was one of the first to identify a distinctive female leadership style in a 1990 *Harvard Business Review* article, "Ways Women Lead." More than 170 scientific studies of gender and leadership style followed.[6]

Sally Helgesen, in *The Female Advantage: Women's Ways of Leadership*, applauds women's leadership style as the panacea for the new, more complex economy. Peter Drucker noted that "Over time women have evolved a successful leadership style that rejects the military model in favor of supporting and empowering people."[7] Patricia Aburdene and John Naisbitt, authors of *Megatrends for Women*, write that future management styles "uncannily match those of female leadership. Consultants tried to teach male managers to relinquish command-and-control mode. For women it was different, it just came naturally."[8] If women are so good at relinquishing command and control, why aren't more of them in control?

One answer is that most institutions remain male dominated, and discrimination still exists. "Discriminatory attitudes are often veiled in inaccurate 'facts' about women's capacity for leadership. Women are presented as not aggressive enough, lacking the self-confidence required for the job, and not being serious enough about their careers to climb the corporate ladder."[9]

Are women more likely to succeed when they portray aggression, confidence, and seriousness? Not necessarily. In the 1982 court case *Hopkins v. Price Waterhouse*, Ann Hopkins "had more billable hours than any other person proposed for partner that year, she had brought in business worth $25 million, her clients praised her, and her supporters recommended her as driven, hardworking and exacting." She was denied partnership because "she had interpersonal skills problems, overcompensated for being a woman," and needed a "course at charm school." The good news was that she won her case and that this happened twenty-five years ago. The story remains illustrative today because women leaders in business, politics, and elsewhere often face a no-win situation, damned if you do, and damned if you don't; they are either too tough or too soft. Kathleen Hall Jamieson identified this as the double bind in 1995.[10]

Recently the double bind was defined as

> . . . the clash . . . between two sets of associations: communal and agentic. Women are associated with communal qualities, which convey a concern for the compassionate treatment of others. They include being especially affectionate, helpful, friendly, kind and sympathetic, as well as interpersonally sensitive, gentle and soft-spoken. In contrast, men are associated with agentic qualities that convey assertion and control. They include being especially aggressive, ambitious, dominant, self confident and forceful, as well as self-reliant and individualistic. The agentic traits are associated in most people's minds with effective leadership.
>
> As a result, women leaders find themselves in a double bind. If they are highly communal, they may be criticized for not being agentic enough. But if they are highly agentic, they may be criticized for lacking communion. Either way, they may leave the impression that they don't have "the right stuff" for powerful jobs.[11]

Catalyst, which has been tracking women in corporate leadership since 1995 when there was one woman CEO of a Fortune 500 company, found

The Fight for Equal Rights
ALICE PAUL (1885–1977)

The Nineteenth Amendment to the Constitution would have been further delayed if it were not for the militant tactics of Alice Paul, a feisty woman born into a Quaker family. She was a teacher and social worker and received five advanced degrees, including a PhD and a law degree. It is notable that many of the suffragists were Quakers.

Paul explained in a 1974 interview, "When the Quakers were founded . . . one of their principles was and is equality of the sexes. So I never had another idea . . . the principle was always there."[12]

It was when she had been a student at the London School of Economics that she experienced firsthand how radical English suffragists fought for the right to vote, led by Mrs. Pankhurst. There she was arrested, went on a hunger strike, and was force-fed, an ordeal she would experience again after she returned to the United States in 1912 and began to

work for suffrage with her friend Lucy Burns. Hundreds of women were sent to the Occoquan Workhouse, where they were treated brutally. Prison officials sent Paul to a sanitarium in hopes of having her declared insane.

It is hard to believe that women were willing to go through such hardship to obtain the right to vote, a right that many women do not exercise today.

Paul targeted Democrats, including President Wilson, for their refusal to support suffrage. In frustration, she formed her own group, the National Woman's Party. They organized the first women's march down Washington's Pennsylvania Avenue on the day before President Woodrow Wilson's inauguration. That was the day they would draw a large crowd, already gathered for Wilson. Five thousand women took part, many of them roughed up by taunting bystanders while the police stood by.

in a recent study that now there are thirteen. At this rate of change, it will take seventy-three years for women to reach parity with men on corporate boards. Ilene H. Lang, Catalyst's president, is puzzled by the numbers:

> Women have been 45–50 percent of the labor force for decades and they have over 50 percent of managerial and professional positions for well over a dozen years. Companies need and want them. But at senior leadership levels, what is holding women back? There are people who would have you believe it's because

Congress passed the Nineteenth Amendment in 1919, forty years after it was introduced. Now it had to be ratified by thirty-six states. Tennessee was the last. The vote was tied forty-eight to forty-eight when twenty-two-year-old Representative Harry T. Burn had planned to vote "Nay." Just before the roll call, he received a note from his mother: "Dear Son, Hurrah! and vote for suffrage. Don't forget to be a good boy and help Mrs. Catt [Carrie Chapman Catt] put the 'rat' in ratification." The next day he explained he had changed his mind because "a good boy always does what his mother asks him to do."

After ratification, in 1923, Paul began a new campaign for passage of the Equal Rights Amendment. She continued fighting for the amendment up until her death in 1977, without success. It has recently been reintroduced by Congresswoman Carol Maloney with more than 200 sponsors.

On the march in Washington, Paul had this to say:

There had never been a procession of women from any corner of the world or in Washington. . . . Nobody ever dreamt that women—you were always seeing these Elks and people going around in processions—but they never though of women doing such a thing.

She also believed that women often have a strong bond to work together and support each other in their struggles.

It was a feeling of loyalty to our own sex and an enthusiasm to have every degradation that was put upon our sex removed. That's what I had anyway. It was just a principle that I—if I belonged to any group and that group was regarded with contempt, given no power, and handicapped in every way possible way . . . I couldn't imagine not (helping out). . . . I couldn't dream of sitting down and seeing these women have such a hard fight, and not wanting to share in it.[13]

women don't want to, or that they are not ambitious. There is no data supporting that. But there are barriers that they have to overcome that are more difficult than the barriers men face.

What has to change? The workplace culture and the expectations, both positive and negative and the stereotyping around women's capabilities—the basic notion of what does a leader look like and what does a leader act like—stereotyping on the part of both men and women. Smart companies recognize that talent is really important, for the most part leadership jobs don't require

big bodies and a lot of brawn, they require brains and sensitivity
and ability to collaborate, to think clearly, to problem solve.

How does Catalyst change leadership stereotypes? Lang described the
process at Goldman Sachs:

> They reviewed their whole performance management process.
> They didn't change their standards, but they rewrote the script
> of how you conduct performance evaluations—how you chal-
> lenged feedback that is stereotypical in nature. So, if somebody
> says, she has sharp elbows, let's talk about how men have sharp
> elbows, sort of pushing back. They don't accept things like, she
> just doesn't fit.

The same stereotypes exist for women in political leadership, particularly at the executive level; creating awareness of how we stereotype
women in leadership is a necessary step toward recognizing genuine leadership skills.

Political leadership has been defined as "the power a leader exercises
through his or her relationships. The people with whom the political
leader interacts, and how he or she interacts with those people, become
essential in defining the strengths and weaknesses of any political
leader."[14]

Burns notes in *Leadership*: "The sharper the conflict, the larger the roles
of leaders will tend to be."[15] Burns created a distinction between leadership and power:

> Leadership, in short, is power governed by principle, directed
> toward raising people to their highest levels of personal motive
> and social morality, and tested by the achieving of results measured
> by original purpose. Power is different. Power manipulates people
> as they are; leadership as they could be. Power manages; leader-
> ship mobilizes. Power impacts; leadership engages. Power tends
> to corrupt, leadership to create.[16]

When I asked Vermont Representative White for her definition, she replied after much thought, "A leader inspires and guides people to move in a direction or toward a goal in a way that allows them to claim it as their own."

Daniel Goleman's bestseller, *Emotional Intelligence*, seems to play to women's strengths. He writes that leaders who have emotional intelligence and are

> . . . high in emotional self awareness are attuned to their inner signals, recognizing how their feelings affect them and their job performance. . . . typically know their limitations and strengths and exhibit a sense of humor about themselves. They exhibit a gracefulness in learning where they need to improve, and welcome constructive criticism and feedback. Accurate self-assessment lets a leader know when to ask for help and where to focus in cultivating new leadership strengths.[17]

The barriers between different kinds of leadership are breaking down:

> It is argued that effective leadership requires a combination of traditional masculine (transactional, highly logical or authoritarian) behaviors and traditionally feminine (nurturing, democratic and relational) behaviors, as well as sex-neutral dimensions (inspirational, motivational, charismatic).[18]

A meta-analysis of forty-five studies on whether women have a distinct leadership style concluded that that they do—somewhat. Most women, however, combine both female and male styles. Women did distinguish themselves on one count—they

> . . . adopt a more participative and collaborative style than men typically favor. The reason for this difference is unlikely to be genetic. Rather, it may be that collaboration can get results without seeming particularly masculine. As women navigate their way through the double bind, they seek ways to project authority with-

out relying on the autocratic behaviors that people find so jarring in women. A viable path is to bring others into decision making and to lead as an encouraging teacher and positive role model.[19]

This gender observation is good news for the rejuvenation of democracy. If more women participate in government, they may be more participative and collaborative than men, which could result in a more representative and effective government.

Women in the Corporate World

This gender observation is also good news for business. Jenny Ming, born in Canton, China, and the recently retired CEO of Old Navy, a division of Gap, Inc., described her journey to the top:

> I realized that I've got to try it even if I fail. I think there is a bigger regret of not doing something than a regret of failing because in failing you learn about yourself.
>
> I grew up thinking the boss or the leader had to be a white male, older, speaks well. It took me a while to realize that leadership has changed in the last ten years. I find that women today are better equipped to be leaders because today women are more attuned to not dominate. Most women tend to be better consensus builders. A good leader has to be a good listener first.

Ming supervised 40,000 people. "Communication is very important. I don't think I always know everything. It is hard today as a leader to know everything, to have all the answers. Most women are comfortable to say 'I don't have the answer, but let me go out and talk to people and come back to you on this.'"

We compared our experiences as CEO and governor. She said, "That's why the politician goes out [to meet people] because when you are in your office and listening to what people feed back to you, it's only the point of view that they want you to hear. I don't know if that's ever what you have asked yourself—is that really what's out there?" Yes, I did. I asked her how she defines leadership.

"Knowing when to be in the thick of things, and when to lead. Lead means to use your full vision and let others run with it and do it."

PepsiCo's new chairman and CEO, Indra Nooyi, fifty-one, is an example of a new kind of woman leader whose philosophy is "bringing together what is good for business with what is good for the world." *Forbes* magazine ranked her the fifth most powerful woman in the world, one of the few female Fortune 100 leaders. PepsiCo does nearly $40 billion in sales, operates in 190 countries, and employs 168,000 people, she explained, calling it a "little republic."

Her philosophy was gained at the family dinner table in Madras, India, where her mother would

> . . . challenge my sister and me to explain what we would do if we were elected prime minister or president of India. Every day it was a different job she would throw at us.
>
> She'd ask us a simple but compelling question: What will you do to change the world? After we had each responded, my mother would decide who would deserve our support. At the time, I thought it was a fun game. But in reality, my mother was teaching us a lesson: She was instructing us in how to live a good life. She wanted us to make a difference in the world. She wanted us to use whatever power we were granted to do good. So, how do we translate the principles that contribute to the good life into a company that contributes to the good society?[20]

She acknowledged that it was odd that a CEO would ask this question, but she is a different CEO.

Carly Fiorina, president and CEO of Hewlett-Packard from 1999 to 2005, had a less positive experience in the corporate world. Her abrupt firing stirred controversy. In her memoir, *Tough Choices,* she tells her side of the story. She describes a scene early in her career when her new boss introduced her as his newest sales manager. He began the meeting by saying, "'I'd like you to meet Carly. She's our token bimbo.' Then he laughed and said, 'Actually, she's our new sales manager.' I laughed, too, and did my best to dazzle the client with my knowledge of their mission." After the meeting she said to him, "'You will never do that to me again.' My anger outweighed my fear of speaking to him like that. He looked me up and down and replied, 'OK. Sorry. Tell me, were you ever a cheerleader?'"[21]

There are some challenges that *all* women in power face.

Women and the Military

The best analogy to the once all-male political world is the once all-male military world. In both cases women have stepped into a culture that had been created by and for men to protect and defend their citizens, in politics by law and in the military by might. The earliest leaders were warriors, using command and control to defend their land. The language of leadership arose from the battlefield: kill, vanquish, defeat, emerge triumphant. The modern military has made a concerted effort to include women. A study done by the Canadian military notes that women who work in a male-dominated work environment "are subjected to more negative instructions," including sexual harassment and gender harassment: "If she acts in traditionally masculine ways she may have good evaluations from her supervisors but poor evaluations from followers. If, however, she acts in traditionally feminine ways, followers may be satisfied but superiors will judge her as ineffective."[22] The military is glorified in Brian Mitchell's book *Women in the Military, Flirting with Disaster:* "The uniforms, the rank, the danger, the purposefulness, the opportunity to earn the respect of men and the admiration of women—all contribute to the military's enduring hold on the imagination of men and boys, and all are now threatened by the military's eagerness to present a female-friendly face."[23]

Mitchell goes on to explain that if you want to create solidarity in a group of men,

> . . . you kill the woman in them. . . . This can only mean that to possess feminine characteristics is directly opposed to success in

the military. How can we expect our young men and women to respect, follow and look up to female leaders, when from the very beginning of their careers, they have been trained to despise all things that are feminine?[24]

How much has the military changed? Significantly, according to the Dean of the U.S. Air Force Academy, Brigadier General Dana H. Born: "One of the things I like about the military is that today it is very much gender neutral," she told me. Twenty-one percent of the 2007 entering class are women, a statistic that is approximately the same for all the academies. In September 2005, women comprised 14.6 percent of active duty personnel in the U.S. Armed Forces and 15.4 percent of the officers. I know of no other institution that has women in leadership in proportion to their numbers in the organization.

General Born was in the first class of 1979. "Did you feel any difficulty in expressing your feminine side as well as your tough side?" I asked. She responded,

> I think that is always difficult in the military. I was always an athlete; that helped. But I do know I struggled tremendously fitting in and being professional with the guys. I was hesitant to wear makeup. Women struggle with expressing their femininity and still fitting into the dominant male culture. Women now will wear makeup. We had to wear our hair short, we now allow women to keep their hair long as long as they can put it up into an acceptable braid or bun, within two minutes.

Judy Woodruff featured women's combat roles in Iraq and Afghanistan on July 5, 2007 on public television. The program opened with the funeral of twenty-two-year-old army specialist Karen Clifton, one of eighty women killed in the wars. Officially, women are barred from combat occupations; but today the front lines have disappeared, and women drive Humvees and trucks, escort military convoys, serve as military police, and fly helicopters and planes—all the activities that place them in danger.

When asked if she had experienced any difficulties as a woman, Carolyn Schapper, a sergeant in the Virginia Army National Guard replied, "I did have difficulties at first with the commanders."

Woodruff: "Difficulties in what way?"

Schapper: "Just that I didn't really know what I was talking about, maybe because I was a female. But it all turned around one day when one of my gunners got shot and I took command of the convoy to get him back. And I got high praise from the infantry sergeant major when we got back. . . . So I had to prove myself to them that I was capable of doing the same job as a man.

Women in the Media

The most visible women in society today are women in the media. Barbara Walters broke into the club in 1976 when she cohosted the ABC evening news. Before then it was rare to hear a woman's voice presenting the news. My 1957 classmate from the Columbia School of Journalism landed his first job as a news anchor at WCAX-TV in Burlington, Vermont. I did not think to apply. I worked at the same station, writing advertising copy and a script for a children's puppet show.

How much have the media changed? Today it is rare to see a group of talking heads that does not include at least one woman. Female reporters have become commonplace. Katie Couric broke through a long-established barrier when she moved from hosting a morning talk show to anchoring the evening news at CBS. She remains closely watched.

"Now the News: Couric Still Isn't One of the Boys," was the headline in *The New York Times*, July 12, 2007:

> Katie Couric has dominated everything about the network evening news competition—except the ratings—since she joined the "CBS Evening News" in September. Being younger than the previous anchors, being far more written about in celebrity coverage on everything she does outside the office, being, of course a woman: these factors set Ms. Couric apart from the men who

did the jobs at the three networks for more than 20 years, Dan Rather, Tom Brokaw and Peter Jennings.

The perception is that Couric's news program is softer due to her morning show credentials and because she is a woman.

Female leaders in the corporate world, the military, the media, and in politics receive special scrutiny because there are so few. In each case, it is impossible to determine how much of that scrutiny is because of who they are, regardless of gender, and how much is because of their gender.

Gender, because it is the first lens through which we form our impressions of people, always will be a factor. As the public gets accustomed to seeing women in roles that had been once held by men, gender will be less likely to preclude objective judgment.

Two quiet revolutions have occurred in the last thirty to forty years that provide a stronger foundation for women in leadership, women's access to higher education and to team sports.

More women than men graduate from college today, whereas in the 1960s the reverse was true. Today, 56 percent of undergraduates are female. By 2014, it is projected that 60 percent of bachelor's and master's degrees and 50 percent of PhDs will be awarded to women.

Women in Higher Education

There are eight Ivy League college presidents, and for the first time, half of them are women: Ruth J. Simmons, a comparative literature scholar, at Brown; Shirley M. Tilghman, a molecular biologist at Princeton; Amy Gutmann, a political scientist and philosopher, at the University of Pennsylvania; and, most recently, Drew Gilpin Faust, a historian, at Harvard. The four met at a panel discussion in the spring of 2007 in Cambridge, Massachusetts, chaired by Judith Rodin, the first woman president of any Ivy League institution—the University of Pennsylvania. She is now president of the Rockefeller Foundation. The presidents agreed "that women do not have a separate and distinct management style."[25]

Rodin said, "Leadership styles are on a 'very, very broad continuum. Just as . . . for men." Yet, she said that while at Penn her "maternal instinct brought out a side of my leadership."

None of the women confessed to a grand plan to be where they are today, but Rodin said she had ambition. "In our time it was called aggression—it wasn't called ambition. . . . I was, and am proud to be fiercely ambitious."

Three noted the importance of their mentor. Gutmann, Simmons, and Tilghman were all administrators at Princeton University and shared the same mentor, Princeton President Harold Shapiro. "He would deny credit," Gutmann said, "but he should get credit."[26]

Faust's Harvard appointment followed a stormy phase in her predecessor's tenure. Larry Summers's name remained in the headlines for months after he had given a speech attributing the lack of women in tenured positions in science to a number of factors, including women's lower innate scientific ability and their unwillingness to work an eighty-hour week. The resulting storm provoked an ongoing debate about the role of women in academia. Summers's remarks may have indirectly led to the appointment of Faust to prove that Harvard, once a bastion of male privilege, had changed. Faust's mother, a Southern lady, had once told her, "Dear, it's a man's world, and the sooner you find that out the better." Faust did not heed her mother's warning. The significance of Faust's appointment is not to be underestimated. Harvard, the school that once barred women from the all-night Lamont library, had undergone the equivalent of a sex change operation.

In total, 23 percent of college presidents are women; the highest number is at two-year colleges. The Massachusetts Institute of Technology is headed by a woman, Susan Hockfield, but most other major research universities are headed by men.

How contagious is leadership from one field to another? Will Faust's portrait, when it is hung, carry a message to Harvard's female students that they may become leaders? Do Oprah Winfrey and Martha Stewart tell young women that they can grow up to be as successful as they are, in any field? Do Madeleine Albright, Janet Reno, and Condoleezza Rice give us different expectations for ourselves? And do Serena and Venus Williams have the same effect? There is a cumulative impact that successful women have on our imaginations. We may not want to be exactly like them, but we may want to be more than we are. Some leadership skills are crosscutting: ambition, courage, vision, and persistence. These can be widely emulated. The impact that successful women have on society is more than being specific role models—they convey the broader message to a large constituency that women can compete and succeed.

Women and Sports

Before Congress passed Title IX in 1972, only one in twenty-seven high school girls participated in sports. Today it is one in three, an 847 percent increase, according to the Women's Sports Foundation.[27] The law's clout stems from the requirement for equal spending on sports for female and male students, in proportion to enrollment.[28] College-level sports participation by women has increased 411 percent in the thirty-five years since Title IX was passed. Overall, the numbers changed from 300,000 girls and women to 3,000,000. Parents and grandparents know what Title IX has achieved. My nine-year-old granddaughter Sara plays girls' soccer on Saturday mornings. I experience a special thrill when I see hundreds of little girls, from kindergarten on up, playing soccer in their brightly colored team T-shirts. What are the consequences of Sara's soccer skills for women in leadership? "We're five years away from having it become evident. The Title IX babies are now in their early 40s," said Donna A. Lopiano, chief executive officer of the Women's Sports Foundation. Still, there are results. Eighty percent of senior women in corporations played sports, and research shows that "athletes are more political and civic minded than their non-athletic peers."[29]

"It's not terribly important that they stay in sports, it's important that they use the confidence and poise and chutzpah that they get from sports to succeed in all walks of life," Lopiano added.

Ironically, as women's sports participation has increased, the number of female coaches has declined. Before Title IX, 90 percent of women's teams were coached by women. Today that number has been cut in half. The law raised the profile of women's sports to such an extent that coaching women's teams has become more attractive and lucrative for men. Men coach women's teams, but only 2 percent of men's teams are coached by women.

Female Lawyers

A similar pattern is found in women and the law: More women are entering the field, but fewer women than men are in leadership positions.

Women have been graduating from law schools and entering firms "in virtually equal numbers for at least 15 years," but according to an MIT study, women make up only 17 percent of firm partners.[30] Women leave the partnership track "mainly due to the difficulty of combining law firm work and caring for children in a system that requires long hours under high pressure with little or inconsistent support for flexible work arrangements. . . . Most of the female lawyers live with spouses or partners who have an equal or greater commitment to their careers and contribute an equal or higher percentage of the household income so that both have severe time constraints."[31]

One consequence of the seepage of women lawyers from top positions is that the pool of potential women political leaders also is drained.

My stepdaughter-in-law, an obstetrician, found a similar pattern in her medical practice. She manages a group of ten physicians. She offered them partnerships, but the female obstetricians would rather be her employees than assume the added hours and responsibility of partnership.

Coaches, lawyers, CEOs, doctors, or politicians—the results are the same: The ambition to attain a leadership position is tempered, particularly for women with children, by the reality of time constraints and the discovery that it is difficult to do it all. Does that explain women's attrition on the leadership ladder as simply a matter of lifestyle choice, or are other factors at work? Some women don't want to give up having what they see as a "full life" with their families to get to the apex of their professions, which may provide insufficient rewards. The other answer is that the legal profession has remained inflexible to the work/family needs of both women and men. If talent is to be retained, corporate policies have to change to become more family friendly. A few law firms are beginning to move in that direction.

Women on the Court

Although giving a hand up and working collaboratively are two ways that women can help other women, there are still examples of lone voices, brave women making a difference. Sandra Day O'Connor and Ruth Bader Ginsburg stand out.

When Sandra Day O'Connor was named to the Supreme Court by President Ronald Reagan in 1981, she was the 102nd individual and the first woman to serve. Until the appointment of Ruth Bader Ginsburg in 1993, she remained the only woman on the nine-member court, a distinction now held by Ginsburg. O'Connor graduated near the top of her class at Stanford Law School in 1952, but no firm was willing to hire her; one firm offered her a job as a legal secretary. When she retired in 2006, she was lauded for staking out the middle ground in a sharply divided court, voting with the majority on many five-to-four vote decisions.

A Washington 2003 dateline story read:

> It now seems almost impossible in this city of unrestrained superlatives to overstate the influence of Sandra Day O'Connor in her 22 years [she served two more years] on the nation's highest court. Justice O'Connor has firmly established herself as the single most important voice on a nine-member tribunal that decided some of America's most difficult and politically contentious issues, including abortion, religion, race, and the death penalty.[32]

Jan Crawford Greenburg asked O'Connor in an interview after she had announced her retirement, "Would you like to see a woman take your place, or do you think it will be nice to see another woman?"

O'Connor replied: "I hope there will always be women, plural, on this court."

Describing her style and demeanor in the court room, Greenburg said:

Justice O'Connor you know, she's very much the "no nonsense" Arizona, you know, cowgirl and she was first out of the box, in almost every argument to ask the first question.

She looked for the practical effect of the law. Discussing a case which involved whether a police officer could order passengers out of a car during a search, she said, "Do you mean to detain a pregnant woman with a baby in the rain?" . . . getting again to the point of how would the law be applied, how would it affect people, how would it affect women, how would it affect children, obviously things that she was very sensitive to.[33]

O'Connor's wish for "women" on the Supreme Court was not granted. Once again, one woman must speak for all. Ginsburg grew up in a Brooklyn neighborhood of mostly poor, working-class immigrants. After Cornell, she attended Harvard Law School at a time when Dean Erwin Griswold could ask the women of the class what it felt like to occupy places that could have gone to deserving men. Two new court appointments, Justice Samuel A. Alito Jr. and Chief Justice John G. Roberts Jr., have moved the court to the right, placing Justice Ginsburg in the minority on many five-to-four decisions. She has begun to read some of her dissenting decisions from the bench, an unusual practice.

In response to the Court's five-to-four decision banning late-term abortions, Ginsburg said in a dissenting opinion (joined by Justice John Paul Stevens, Justice David Souter, and Justice Stephen Breyer):

Today's decision is alarming. . . . It tolerates, indeed applauds, federal intervention to ban nationwide a procedure found necessary and proper in certain cases by the American College of Obstetricians and Gynecologists. . . . And for the first time since *Roe*, the Court blesses a prohibition with no exception safeguarding a woman's health.

She then went on to quote from an earlier case (*Planned Parenthood of Southeastern Pennsylvania v. Casey*):

Women now have the talent, capacity, and right "to participate in the economic and social life of the Nation. . . . Their
ability to realize their full potential, the Court recognized, is
intimately connected to their ability to control their reproductive lives. . . . Thus, legal challenges to undue restrictions on
abortion procedures do not seek to vindicate some generalized
notion of privacy; rather, they center on a woman's autonomy
to determine her life's course, and thus enjoy equal citizenship
stature.[34]

On salary discrimination, Justice Ginsburg wrote the dissenting opinion (joined by Justices Stevens, Souter, and Breyer) in the case of a
Goodyear Tire and Rubber Company manager and a female manager,
Lilly M. Ledbetter. Ledbetter sued the company for pay discrepancy that
took place during the twenty years of her employment. The Court ruled
she could not sue because the 180-day deadline for filing a suit had
expired. In Ginsburg's dissenting opinion, she wrote:

The court's insistence on immediate contest overlooks common
characteristics of pay discrimination. Pay disparities often occur,
as they did in Ledbetter's case, in small increments; cause to
suspect that discrimination is at work develops only over time.
Comparative pay information, moreover, is often hidden from
the employee's view. . . . Small initial discrepancies may not be
seen as meet for a federal case, particularly when the employee,
trying to succeed in a nontraditional environment, is averse
to making waves. . . . It is only when the disparity becomes
apparent and sizeable, *eg.*, through future raises calculated as a
percentage of current salaries, that an employee in Ledbetter's
situation is likely to comprehend her plight and therefore, to
complain. Her initial readiness to give her employer the benefit
of the doubt should not preclude her from later challenging the
then current and continuing payment of a wage depressed on
account of her sex.

Women are making significant inroads on state courts. Their numbers have increased in the last four years. The National Association of Women Judges reports that women comprise 24 percent of the nation's judges, and seventeen states have female chief justices. Alabama recently elected Sue Bell Cobb, a sharp contrast to one of her predecessors, Justice Roy Moore, who was removed from his post because he refused to move a monument of the Ten Commandments from the courthouse, despite the orders of a federal judge. Alabama is one of a handful of states that have partisan judicial elections. Cobb's opponent, Drayton Nabers Jr., made a pro-life stance on abortion his issue. Judge Cobb, who had served twenty-five years as a trial judge, refused to state her position. She had a campaign ad that said, "I'm the only candidate who's put thousands of people behind bars, plays the piano at church, and keeps kids out of jail." Alabama's prison population is the fifth largest in the nation per capita. "We can't outbuild ourselves out of the crime problems. We must do the hard work of fixing people," she said.

Imagine a Supreme Court composed of five women and four men. Not all the women are liberal, but they all share common experiences. The votes would not be five women against four men on many issues. But it is possible they could be five-to-four in the other direction.

Gender Bias

Given the gains women have made, the perception is that the bad old days are gone; there are laws that protect women from discrimination, and there is a culture of political correctness that constrains gender bias.

Direct discrimination is more rare than it once was, but the message that women are inferior to men remains deeply imbedded in both men's and women's psyches. It ranges from the Catholic Church's prohibition against women priests, to the practice of Sharia law by some Muslims, to Orthodox Judaism, and to the controversy within the Episcopal Church over the ordination of women priests. One example of unconscious gender bias was revealed when some symphony orchestras decided to change the way they conducted auditions. To make the competition for orchestra seats gender neutral, the musician was asked to sit behind a curtain that was long enough to cover her or his shoes. The result? Many more female musicians made the cut.

Science, a field in which objectivity would seem more assured, provides another example. In a study done in 1968 and replicated in 1983 by Jennifer Freyd of the University of Oregon,

> . . . college students were asked to rate identical articles by specific criteria. The authors' names attached to the articles were clearly male or female, but were reversed for each group of raters: what one group thought had been written by a male, the second thought had been written by a female, and vice versa. Articles supposedly written by women were consistently ranked lower than when the very same articles were thought to have been written by a male.[35]

Freyd writes that gender bias and discrimination against women take many forms, from sexual harassment to the "more ubiquitous and insidious problem of subtle and unconscious sexism impacting daily life." Further, she writes:

> One error people make is assuming that gender bias and discrimination require a conscious sexist ideology or a conscious attempt to discriminate against women. In fact, however, psychological science has overwhelmingly demonstrated that sexist behaviors, gender bias, and discrimination can and do occur without these conscious beliefs or attempts to discriminate.
>
> A second error people often make is believing that discrimination is "out there" but not "here."
>
> A third error is the belief that bias, though present, is negligible in effect. The problem with this is that a large number of nearly negligible effects all working in the same direction can easily cumulate to very significant aggregate discrimination.[36]

How much do women experience gender bias in politics? Answers vary widely to this question. "I don't belong to the women's caucus, and I don't identify as a feminist. I feel 100 percent accepted everywhere I work and an equal participant. I don't feel we need to break barriers. I have never been sexually harassed. I never feel like there have been obstacles in my way because I am a woman," Vermont Representative Patti Komline (R) told me.

Vermont Representative Rachel Weston (D), the youngest member of the House, had a different experience. When she first introduced herself to one of the older representatives, "who could have been my father," he told her he would have liked to have been introduced to her with her clothes off.

Alaska minority leader Beth Kurttula (D) said women still have to work harder, and says,

> I still feel the sexism. I think it's a little tougher for women. When I don't raise my voice people perceive that as being too nice . . . they perceive you as weak when they say, "Oh, you are too nice. What they really misperceive is the strength that comes through calmness. They think that if you are not a screamer, if you aren't swearing and fighting, you are not a strong person. There is a lot of pressure on you to be someone who you aren't and to stoop down to the level that some people do.

Most women in public office agree that gender has an impact on their leadership style and on the policies they promote. They often offer a much different perspective, incorporate different leadership styles, and have different ways of resolving conflict.

That was the gender difference detected by Senator McCaskill (D-MO). "I think that women, generally, are more focused on trying to find common ground." When she and the governor had a conflict, "the women wanted the conflict between me and the governor resolved. It was uncomfortable to them. Men enjoy the fight, and I think most women enjoy solving the problem. Although I have to admit, for me, I love to win, and I hate to lose. So there is that competitiveness I have that I think is healthy."

The mothering role, in many women's experience, influences their leadership style and substance. In a working paper, "Leadership: What's Motherhood Got to Do with It?" Sumru Erkut, PhD, writes:

> . . . in contemporary U.S. society, leadership continues to be viewed as a masculine activity. Yet, in a study of 60 women leaders (Winds of Change Foundation, 2001) close to 40 percent of prominent women from a variety of fields spontaneously made reference to motherhood when describing a good leader or leadership training.[37]

One woman was quoted in this article as saying,

> One of the best training grounds for leadership is motherhood and if you can manage a group of small children, you can manage a group of bureaucrats. It's almost the same process. . . . It's partly team building. And a family is partly team building, too. Getting kids to work together and to feel the family feeling and not hitting each other, and so forth. [38]

When Speaker Terie Norelli (D-NH) was asked how she managed 400 state legislators (New Hampshire has the 2nd largest legislative body in the world), she credited her deputy who managed five day care centers, an obvious qualification. "She is very calm. She doesn't try to whip people into shape," she said.

Yes, Gender Does Make a Difference

How do gender differences affect policy? Congresswoman Loretta Sanchez (D-CA) explained,

> We think in different ways. We approach things in different ways. When Nancy Pelosi was on the appropriations committee and we had just gone through the whole Kosovo incident, that was a very debilitating conflict for women because many Muslim women had been raped as tools of war. In the Muslim situation, you are shunned or stoned because it is your fault if you were raped. She realized that if we didn't change that, if we didn't help the women to become whole, then the family would not become whole, and the society was not whole. What does that mean? It means putting $100 million into mental health for women. This never would have happened if there wasn't a woman on the committee.

The difference between female and male legislators is that women bring different life experiences into the debate. They change the conversation. Drucilla Ramey, the head of the National Association of Women Judges, told me that having just one woman on a court has an impact. She can describe sexual harassment as no man can. Many men are also advocates for so-called women's issues, but they have not experienced them personally. The difference is intensity, and in politics, intensity matters.

Intensity not only changes what gets on the agenda; it changes what gets to the top of the agenda. Politics is competitive not only about who gets elected but also about what gets done. There are limited amounts of time, money, and political capital to go around. Those who fight hardest and refuse to give up usually win.

Terie Norelli (D-NH) explained the relationship between her "mom" role and her agenda:

> If you are a woman, if you are a mom, then chances are you are the one who is interacting with the schools and monitoring your children's education. If you are a mom, you are probably the one who is taking your kids to the doctor, and maybe you've had them to the emergency room. So you are figuring out how your health insurance works, so you know something about health care. A lot of people don't. We have experiences based on either our everyday life or what we do professionally or what we do in the community.

Asked about gender differences, Assemblywoman Pou of New Jersey focused on "the lighter side. A man can go to an informal event, take off his jacket and tie," and he's appropriately dressed. "A woman has to bring a different set of clothes. For an evening event, he simply puts his jacket and tie back on." Again, the woman has to bring a different set of clothes. "Casual, business, or formal, he's always appropriately dressed," she laughed.

What differences do women make on the issues? The biggest difference that women make in elected office as they move from being outsiders to insiders is that they bring their experiences, values, and priorities into the political process.

Nowhere was that more evident than with the historic election of Speaker Nancy Pelosi.

"Today, we have broken the marble ceiling. For our daughters and granddaughters, the sky is the limit, anything is possible for them." Those were the words spoken by House Speaker Nancy Pelosi, sixty-six, before Congress during her inaugural address. In the first paragraph, she had thanked her family for "their love, support, and the confidence to go from the kitchen to the Congress."

No prior speaker had mentioned the marble ceiling or the kitchen. Neither had he asked his grandchildren to surround him on the podium.

Her presence changed the image of Congress; from black and gray to color—pearls, politics, and power. The substantive role of the speaker—knitting together a unified Democratic agenda and getting it adopted—had not. She was ready—ready to be second in the line of succession for the presidency.

Pelosi learned politics at an early age, schooled by "Big Tommy," her dad, Thomas J. D'Alesandro Jr., a congressman and Baltimore mayor.

She waited to run for Congress until 1987 when she was forty-six and her youngest child was in high school. How did she, as a liberal and a woman, get elected to the third most powerful position in a country whose leaders are predominantly male and more conservative than she is? Conventional wisdom would hold that she could rise to a leadership position only once there was a critical mass of women and liberals in Congress—about one-third. She defied expectations by leapfrogging over these barriers, an indicator that most assumptions about politics can be overturned.

CNN's Wolf Blitzer interviewed Pelosi shortly before her election as speaker, noting that she would be making history. She replied, "Well, I appreciate your saying that, and I think one of my first acts, postelection, will be to become a grandmother for the sixth time. We're anxiously awaiting the birth of our grandchild, who is due the first week in November. So a good omen. We'll get ready for our new grandbaby as we get ready for a new Congress."

Is that who she is, a sweet grandmother? Not quite. Illinois Congressman Rahm Emmanuel, chairman of the House Democratic Caucus, told me that Pelosi is as tough as he's seen in politics. "I'm from Chicago, and I know tough. I have never seen anyone tougher, stronger, and more determined than Nancy Pelosi. That's what I love about her," he told me.

Vermont freshman Congressman Peter Welch agreed,

> She is brutally tough, but in the sense that she knows what has to be done and is willing to do what is required to get it done. Her leadership style is based on knowing the issues, on respecting the work of the other members, respecting their points of view. She creates an environment where people want to cooperate

much more than if she were just using a hammer. She is one of the most gifted political people I've ever seen.

When Larry King asked her what had surprised her about the job, she answered, "Well, I'm usually not one to be surprised. I like to be prepared for everything." She has been prepared, disciplined, and focused throughout her political life. To keep everyone "in line," she does what many women politicians do best—build consensus.

Pelosi's skills enable her to work successfully in the world of "inside" politics where her constituency is the other 434 members of the U.S. House of Representatives. There is little doubt that she could not, as Hillary Clinton is doing, run for president because she is considered too far outside the mainstream. The right wing tried its best to scare voters before the 2006 election by the threat of Pelosi becoming speaker, caricaturing her as an extreme left-wing San Francisco liberal. That attack did not prevent voters from electing a sufficient number of Democrats to create a Democratic majority in Congress. If Pelosi were to run for president, the dynamics would change. It is easier to be defined by 232 Democrats in the House than a population of millions of voters.

That is one reason that Parliamentary systems are more likely to elect women. The political party will have had time to receive a more complete biography of who a woman is. They will have vetted her before the voters have a chance to appraise her. The challenge for Clinton is to go beyond the cardboard cutout picture voters are given of all candidates in a U.S. presidential campaign. Speaker Pelosi has a less daunting task because she has been introduced to the public with a strong recommendation— that of her peers.

Congresswoman Carol Shea-Porter (D-NH) moved from the outside to the inside on November 8, 2006. Nobody thought she had a New Hampshire snowball's chance in hell of winning against a strong incumbent. She was a social worker. Her campaign theme was, "New Hampshire doesn't have anybody sticking up for just regular people, what I call the bottom 99 percent of us."

She decided to run after seeing the aftermath of hurricane Katrina and was "so disturbed by what I experienced and what I saw and I knew that we had to do better." When she put $100 of her own money in a bank account to launch her campaign, "My kids said to me, 'Mom, please don't embarrass us or you.' My husband I have to say was terrific. He said, 'Listen, if you want to go out there and do it, do it.'" She asked a friend to run her campaign who said, "'I have never been a campaign manager,' and I said, 'I have never been a candidate. We are probably starting off at the right point, we'll learn together.'" She said, "I think I am going to win because I believed everybody wanted what I wanted. My ears were close to the ground; as a grassroots person I could feel the volcano rumbling underneath."

She observed other elections and concluded, "what we were missing was the heart in it, we needed to make emotional connections. I really was an optimist and I think that is the first ingredient that you have to have—optimism, especially when the numbers are down."

Her campaign was a family affair. Her daughter was her press secretary until she returned to college:

> My mother was unbelievable. She was a Republican for eighty-three years. She changed her party on her eighty-fourth birthday. She'd had enough. I call that the drip-drip theory that you just keep putting out the truth, the facts. Not too many. Just a couple of facts that show people what reality is and then tell them what you plan to do about it.

While she was filming a commercial, her mother had come to watch. She asked her mother to sit beside her. After we both say the country was going in the wrong direction, "my mother looks at the camera, leans forward, and says, 'Vote for my daughter, she's a hard worker and I know she'll do a good job.'" Experts told her to get rid of the ad, but she said, "No, it's my mother and me, and it's how we feel about one another and the whole effort." Everywhere she went, voters then asked her, "How's your Mom?" The feature attraction at a political event was, "Carol's mom is coming!"

Now that she's in Congress, I asked her if it's living up to her expectations:

> When people ask what's it like in Washington, I say, "It's like having Thanksgiving dinner with your dysfunctional family every day; you love them, but there are differences there."

She knows that she will have to raise more money next time, as she already has two opponents, and the GOP is taking shots at her. "It's like looking at ducks nibbling at your ankles. Annoying as heck, and it doesn't hurt a bit."

Shea-Porter proves that the same rules do not apply to everyone, everywhere, every time. Each election is unique, based on the concerns of the voters and the characteristics of both the candidate and her opponent. The only necessary constant in this game of chance is the candidate's commitment to change and the passion with which she conveys that to the voters—making the prospect of her election not only her victory but also theirs. That is the "heart" that Shea-Porter saw was missing and that enabled her to convince the voters that "we all really need the same things, that I would work for all of them."

The ability to connect to a diverse group of voters enabled African American Laura Richardson (D-CA), forty-five, to win a special election to Congress from California in the summer of 2007. Her district is "at least 40 percent Caucasian, maybe 35 percent Hispanic, and 16 percent African American, maybe about the same of Asian. There was a slight majority of women, I think that helps as women are running," she explained. She is part of a new trend: African Americans representing diverse districts.

Richardson moved up quickly, from six years on the City Council, to serving in the California Assembly for one year and eight months, to Congress:

> When I was running in this last race, the press constantly asked about race [African American versus Hispanic], and I would constantly try to get them back to the point that I really didn't

think the voters cared so much what race I was, because they cared about my experience, did I have the ability to do the job.

Her inspiration to run comes from her mixed-race background. "At a very early age I learned that there were injustices and that we needed people who were willing to stand up."

She said this is the job she loves because

I enjoy when I see the difficulty that someone has and I have the ability to step in and help. If the government is not giving them fair options, I have the ability to fight on their behalf and to say, "You have to do this." To me, there is nothing more enjoyable than to see a horrible situation and to be able to help fix it. That's just like the best thing to me. I really enjoy it.

What keeps her fighting for her constituents is her faith. "I'm a Christian. I believe in God. Seriously, I go to church, I pray, and I ask God to help me to take care of his people. The continual education and growing spiritually is what encourages me."

As the youngest woman of color ever to serve in the Michigan House of Representatives, twenty-seven-year-old Shanelle Jackson (D) brings the outsider perspective to politics on three counts. I asked her, as a young African American woman, "How is it different for you? Is it youth, being African American, or being female?" She responded,

It's all three. It is very challenging. It is great because I am living my dream. It is still a white man's system, they don't know, they have never seen a "me." I have never worked with so many white men. Everyday, it is a challenge, I am learning so much about their characters.

Unlike Richardson's, Jackson's Detroit district is 90 percent African American.

"What do you think you bring as an African American woman?" I asked her. Jackson replied,

Truthfully, I think we bring—in a male-dominated Michigan politics—we bring a level of truth that would be missing if we weren't there. I have observed that the black men don't say much, they kind of follow. What black women do, because of our place in society, because of the role we have been put in, we have the tendency to be more aggressive, to be more assertive. We speak up. I feel like I don't have anything to lose. I feel like, if not me, then who? I am not afraid of them.

And, she reminds herself constantly of why she chose this path to begin with. She has the faith and belief that things will get better. She talked about Dr. Martin Luther King Jr. and

... what it was like for him in his young twenties, knocking on doors of people in the rural South and saying to black people, "I want to help you get empowered, come on, we are going to this rally," and having those doors slammed in his face because people never thought it could change, and they were governed by fear. But he kept on going, and it only takes one, it only takes one to change how things go, to be a world changer.

She added, "Some people got the dream sucked out of them. And I'm not going to let them take it from me. So it's just faith and hoping and remembering that."

Linda Sanchez was thirty-three when she ran for Congress in California, following in the footsteps of her sister Loretta who had been elected in 1996. As a young Latina woman, she knows that she is representing the growing Latino community where there are few Latina women in power:

Every organization I have been a member of, it's usually the women who hold that organization together. They're the ones that recruit the members, do the newsletter; they are really the worker bees, and they are not always the ones that have the titles. Women are much more hardworking and focused on the needs of their communities. And I think that's true tenfold in the Latino community. Women are the ones who hold the families together. I would love to see more Latina women running for office, especially at the federal level. You know, there are still obstacles. Especially generational obstacles within their own community, because there is sort of an Old World mentality among many male Latinos, especially if they are older, about a woman's place being in the home. There is resentment when women are successful or women are in high visibility positions.

Her sister, Loretta, agreed, "We are very underrepresented in politics at this point. It's just a matter of time when women realize the men aren't getting it done so we have to get in there and do it ourselves." The Sanchez sisters' father may not be typical of Latino men. He had high hopes for his daughters: "It's amazing my father thought my mother should stay home and cook for him, but he was different with his daughters. He thought I was going to be Madam Curie on a spaceship."

A father's encouragement was important to Asian American Congresswoman Doris Matsui (D-CA):

He had three daughters, and he always made sure that we were women who understood the feminist side of things and also understood that we could do everything else we wanted to do. I never really tested it that much, but I always felt that he had that confidence in me. It's interesting when a father gives that to a daughter. You don't ever lose that. It's just there.

She was born in a Japanese internment camp in Poston, Arizona during World War II[1] "They [Matsui's parents] never really burdened us with it. They never talked about it at all. I think what they did was to try to make us so thoroughly American."

I asked, "That there would be no question of your patriotism?" and she responded,

Right, we didn't understand Japanese customs, we didn't speak Japanese, we spoke English. I think they felt, raising us, it would be a better way. They were born in this country, and still they had to go to the camps. My parents' grandparents came in 1890–1900, and yet this happened to them. I think it was a big hurt, because they were citizens and the government turned against them and thought they could have been traitors—yet they never lost faith in this country.

Now I think about it more, as an elected official, because you think about the fact that our country made a mistake, you certainly don't want that mistake to ever happen again. Because of what happened to my parents and grandparents, I am much more sensitive about that.

Matsui's response revealed a perspective that only she could bring.

Do women, regardless of party, vote differently from men? The latest study of women in state legislatures, done in 2001,[2] confirms the findings of a similar study done in the 1980s. A majority of female and male legislators agree that the increased presence of women made a difference "in the extent to which the economically disadvantaged have access to legislatures and the extent to which legislatures are sympathetic to the concerns of racial and ethnic minority groups."

On policy issues, "Within both parties, women are more likely than men to support more liberal or moderate positions on a variety of issues, including abortion, hate crimes, civil unions for gays and lesbians, and racial preferences in job hiring and school admissions."[3]

Three-quarters of women and men in state legislatures agree that the presence of women has changed attitudes about legislation affecting women's concerns. Many women feel a special responsibility to become advocates for these issues, but not for these issues alone.

Women lawmakers are also more likely than their male counterparts to oppose government-funded school vouchers, the death penalty, and a constitutional amendment to permit prayer in public schools.

Democratic women outnumber Republican women, 61 to 39 percent, and Democratic women are more likely than men to describe themselves as liberal: 40 to 23 percent. I asked Jo Ann Davidson, co-chair of the Republican Party, why there were fewer Republican women. She replied

that as the Republican Party moved to the right, it had been more difficult for women to get elected.

Many women political leaders exhibit a somewhat different leadership style than men and have some different legislative priorities, but
not all women behave differently from the male norm and rarely would a
woman lead differently all of the time. It would be unrealistic to expect
such uniformity. Even slight differences, however, can produce different
results.

Deborah L. Rhode concluded, in *The Difference "Difference" Makes,* that
women did not have a distinctive leadership style and that women managers, judges, and politicians had not made a significant difference, except
for issues of particular concern to women. She noted that, "Some of the
worst voting records on women's rights belong to women."[4] For women to
make a difference in the outcome of critical issues, not all women have to
agree. It would be absurd to think that they would. Men don't, why should
they—the majority—be expected to sing in unison? A simple majority of
women supporting a particular issue may change the outcome.

Most of the divisive questions of the day either pass or fail on close
votes. Let us suppose that the Congress is debating a new family leave
policy, one that would provide a paid three-week family leave for childbirth, adoption, or care of a family member. Present policy is unpaid
family leave for three weeks, but only for businesses with more than fifty
employees. Let's do the math. Assume there are thirty-five women in the
U.S. Senate. Twenty of the women support the bill, fifteen oppose it.
The sixty-five male senators are divided: Thirty-three support it, thirty-
two oppose. Add the thirty-three men to the twenty women who support
the bill, and the result is a majority of fifty-three votes for paid family
leave. Women's votes can provide the "tipping point" on such close votes.
The point deserves to be underscored. Not *all* women must agree, not
even a *strong majority* must agree, to make a difference in whether a bill
passes or fails.

Women, the study shows, are more likely than men to "report that
the attitudes of their constituents would be the most important consideration in determining how they would vote (42 percent versus 33
percent).

The difference women make in politics cannot be weighed in votes alone. The conversation changes when women are at the table; that may determine the content of a bill or whether there will *be* a bill.

On the Inside: Playing by the Rules, Power, and Working with the Jerks

When women "get beat up," they take it more personally than men, said New Hampshire Speaker of the House Terie Norelli (D).

The key to dealing with conflict, Vermont Representative Margaret Cheney (D) said, "is not to take it personally. I have learned that it is better to take it on and not avoid it. It helps diffuse it."

"Listening and being respectful at all times is key, and I demand that of my kids. You have to be respectful of opposing opinions if you are ever going to sway someone or work for a compromise," said Vermont Representative Komline (R).

Vermont Senator Jeanette K. White (D) explained:

> I have learned not to punch and kick and pull hair and bite but may do some of those things in different ways. Conflict is not bad, and I don't think we should avoid conflict. It sharpens our own vision of things and helps us think critically. If we don't deal with conflict or let it out, we have just suppressed it. Most people you have conflict with, you still have to deal with them in the future.

That's the difference between a conflict in private life and in public life. After a fight, it's possible to ignore someone who is disagreeable, even vow never to speak to that person again. Not so in politics. In a legislative body, the person you hated yesterday will still be there the next day, and it's best to smile and say "Good morning," because there is a strong possibility that yesterday's enemy will become today's friend. Coalitions are fluid, and issues change. The saying "Politics makes strange bedfellows" is more or less correct.

As governor, I could not stay mad because I had to work with legislators on both sides of the aisle and from all points of view; I would often forget the old adage, "don't get mad, get even." I also had to face different constituencies, some of whom agreed with me and others of whom did not, sometimes vehemently.

I had learned early during my legislative years that not all disagreements create enmity. The death of Cola Hudson, the Republican representative from the small town of Lyndonville, in January 2008 led me to reminisce. We had sat around the same table in our committee in 1973 when we were both freshman legislators. To the best of my recollection, we never voted the same way. That did not stop us from becoming friends. We could tease one another. It was the height of the women's movement and I tried to explain it to Cola without much success. I had objected when the chairman had referred to a 54-year-old secretary as a "girl." He just laughed and threatened to form a "Men's Liberation" committee. It became our standing joke. We couldn't have been more different. I was a liberal Democrat from the big city of Burlington, suspect on all counts. I wasn't born in Vermont or in the United States. His Vermont lineage went back for generations.

I learned many things from Cola Hudson. He worked as a custodian in the elementary school. Except for a few courses, he did not have a chance to go to college. But that did not mean he wasn't smart. Now, as I look back, I believe he had wisdom. He didn't like government, but he liked people. One summer he invited me and my family for a picnic at his farmhouse at the end of a dirt road. I invited him to my son's bar mitzvah, his first time in a synagogue.

On the last day of the session he gave me a copy of Ralph Waldo Emerson's essay, "Friendship." It was inscribed, "A true and valued friend. A <u>Vermonter</u> in the finest sense of the word." If I could have inscribed a book to him, I would have said the same thing to him.

What About Compromise?

"I tend to have a cynical view of our democratic system. As a politician, you have to compromise your beliefs. That is something I struggle with.

That's what a lot of women feel, they don't want to get involved in the so-called 'dirty politics,'" said Grace, a UVM student in our discussion group. Is it "dirty politics" to compromise? It depends. The public believes politicians will readily compromise their values if that enables them to get elected or reelected.

Representative Beth Kurttula (D-AK) said,

> There are issues where I have absolutely firm lines that I won't compromise. My constituents know those . . . being anti-death penalty, being pro-choice are absolutes in my book. Actually, it's very rare that there isn't room for compromise. It means look at the issue and all the sides of it, trying to see if there isn't middle ground.

"What do you see as the difference between compromise and selling out?" Representative Kyrsten Sinema (D-AZ) was asked.

> I call it the Political Whore check. If I wake up every morning and I can look in the mirror and I think to myself, "What am I going to do today? Is it honorable? Is it just? Is it right for my community?" If I can answer all of those questions by saying "yes" and feeling good and clean inside, then what I am doing is OK. If there is anything nagging at the back of my head—that's wrong, and I can't do it.

She explained that she could not accept proposed amendments from a lobbyist to an Arizona clean air act because it would kill the bill. The bill was not perfect, but it had her support. "I've given up on this all or nothing. I used to believe in that when I was very young, but it is not real. I believe it is better to work your way toward what is right than to say, 'I'm not going to do anything until I get what is perfect.' You're just not going to get it."

Voltaire was the first to observe, "The pursuit of the ideal is the enemy of the good."

There is an assumption that a politician can avoid conflict if she or he simply does what the constituents want. The problem is that not all constituents agree. Often there is no clear majority. Assemblywoman Nellie Pou (D-NJ) has a constituency that is both urban and suburban: "We have an incredibly diverse community, the two largest being Latinos and African Americans. But we also have a large Arab community. Speaking out on issues that become a concern to one group and trying to get everyone around the table to understand it is [the art of compromise]."

Congresswoman Pryce (R-OH) also has a mixed constituency:

> I have constituents from the university. I have a large gay and lesbian population. I also have huge farmlands, and those are very conservative. I try to explain my moderate positions. Compromise is very important. It's a hard lesson women all have [to learn] that you can't make everyone happy [more than men]. You do want to please others. You do want them to appreciate you and like you—you can't be everything to all people.

Pryce has this advice for dealing with conflict:

> I think women should always be who they are. I don't think we should try to fit in the men's way of doing things just because that's the way things have been done for centuries. We bring something very different to the political process, and part of that is very much needed—bringing peace.

Peace—for either women or men—is sometimes hard to achieve. Divisions arise not only among different constituencies; more often there is a single issue that divides all constituencies. Examples are civil unions, the death penalty, and abortion. Voters may be divided down the middle; the politician has to make the choice. These gut issues are usually decided by personal values more than by information, and when a politician changes her or his mind on them, that switch is suspect. On less volatile issues, I frequently learned that the other side had something valuable to offer, and I was influenced by a new perspective or information. Compromise, in the best sense, is a creative, exciting process. Instead of dividing the question down the middle or accepting half a loaf, a new common ground is plowed to produce a result that neither side had envisioned: a win-win. Knowing when and where to compromise, knowing how much to give and how much to hold out for are some of the most difficult and most frequent decisions that politicians have to make, sometimes several times a day. Not all votes are the same: The "Yea" or "Nay" button is pushed automatically in most instances because the issue is not controversial. Other votes are agonizing because the "right thing to do" is not obvious. If a lawaker does not have a strong opinion one way or another, votes are influenced by various constituencies, by political parties, by colleagues, and by lobbyists. There is no "undecided" column. (In the Illinois legislature and in a few others, lawmakers can vote "Present.") Often, the correct choice does not become apparent until days, months, or years later. Because politicians have to make decisions so often and so fast, they lean on their values, their experience, and the people they most trust. They also weigh the impact on the next election.

There is a line, fine as a spider's thread, between a flip-flop and listening to the voters. One is cowardly, the other is not. The public is frustrated when politicians refuse to listen to them and won't change their minds; "What's the use of writing letters or sending an e-mail when you know his mind is made up?" is a frequently heard complaint. The public is equally disdainful of politicians who do not have the courage to stick to their opinions. Navigating a safe course between Scylla and Charybdis is one of the daunting challenges of political life.

The public often gets impatient, even disgusted, with compromise because the political process is not transparent and is overly complex. Why can't a simple majority stop the war in Iraq? How hard is it to get sixty votes to override the president's veto or stop a filibuster? Politicians wish the public were more patient and more understanding of the Byzantine process of lawmaking. Inch-by-inch compromise is essential to move any major issue forward. The public will never accept this premise, and perhaps it shouldn't, because if the voters did not express their impatience and frustration, even less would get accomplished.

Are women better than men at compromising across party lines? There is some evidence that they are. Minority leader Kurttula has sixteen Democrats out of forty senators to work with in Alaska:

> I have a close friend who is a Republican, and she can normally bring at least five votes with her. With the two of us, we have managed to swing the voting on the floor on important issues. We just came out of a special session in Alaska on elder care, and that is exactly what we did there. The first rule of the legislature is to know where your votes are, go talk to people, go to work. Don't just think you can stand up on the floor and give a flowery speech and win.

Connecticut Governor Jodi Rell (R) explained, "Even in my days in the legislature [she served 10 years], we always joked that if you just left us (women) alone, we could get so much done in a lot less time. I remember doing bills on domestic violence, and we worked together, and nobody cared about Republican or Democrat."

New Hampshire Speaker Norelli (D) said she tries to work across party lines. "Perhaps I am not the person to sit down with the other side, but I know who to ask about that. . . . [it's important] to understand the other's perspective and to build compromise."

Two of the most successful governors, according to *Time* magazine, are Kathleen Sebelius in Kansas and Janet Napolitano in Arizona. Both Democrats run red states with predominantly conservative Republican legislatures. Each has had success in getting legislation through and getting reelected. Sebelius noted that,

> People will happily cross party lines for people they identify with and will vote for someone whose values they share. My opponents would always say to people, "She is really different from you. She doesn't believe what you believe, and you need to vote for me instead." I was always able to counter that with, "Here's who I am, and here's what I've done."

A Republican legislature passed Napolitano's legislative priority: all-day state-funded kindergarten. When she spoke at a hearing, the chairman told her, "Well, I don't know about this all-day kindergarten. I think the best all-day kindergarten is M O M." Her reply was, "Well, Mr. Chair, I can agree with the values of motherhood, but what if M O M had to W O R K?" The bill passed.

Republican Governor Rell works with a Democratic legislature that joined her in passing campaign finance and ethics reform laws.

The sixteen women in the U.S. Senate meet regularly for dinner and often work together on issues. Senator Susan Collins (R-ME) forges compromises across the aisle to gain support for her legislative priorities. The Congressional Women's Caucus, comprised of both House and Senate members and founded in 1977, has an impressive track record for collaboration on legislation benefiting women, including equitable pay, child support enforcement, promoting women's health, and protecting victims of domestic violence and sexual assault.

Congresswoman Pryce (R-OH) was selected president of her freshman class in the Congress in 1993:

> The freshman class always has to have their own signature on issues and make their own statement. I tried to lead this group to consensus on anything, and it was very difficult, very hard. We would meet through the night and into the next morning. The freshmen women, all Republicans and Democrats, met to do the same exercise and come up with an agenda and that took forty-five minutes. We ironed it out and got it done.

Playing by the Rules

One of the mysteries of the political process is how do you learn to play by the rules? One young woman said she would be scared to run for office because she might break one of the campaign rules "without even knowing it."

"My personal obstacle [to running for office] is the structure," said Lexi, a UVM student. "I like coordinating, but I don't know how well I would do in a formal political structure."

Political structures have rules, both written and unwritten. There are rules for getting elected, rules for passing a law, and rules for implementing a law. To play by the rules, it is necessary to be informed—and to be patient. Lexi's doubts may be due to her frustration over the complexity of the rules and her impatience with the time it takes to get something done. Many of the rules seem archaic, undemocratic, and so baroque that it is impossible to figure out how to draw a straight line from beginning to end. Newly elected politicians learn the rules from *Mason's Manual of Legislative Procedure, Robert's Rules of Order,* or Senate or House rules, only to discover that some lawmakers' greatest skill is circumventing the rules. What then? The answer is that it is necessary to learn both how to play by the rules and how to get around the rules.

My biggest surprise as a first-term legislator was that the rules of the political process are as important as the substance of an issue. Knowing the subject matter, the arguments on all sides, was important, but without knowledge of the rules, my favorite bill could easily get sidetracked or killed. The importance of knowing the rules became clear to me when I observed a legislator who had mastered the rules; he knew when to make a motion at a critical point to either pass or defeat a bill, which gave him inordinate power. I was determined to learn from him.

There are reasons for rules in a democracy: They provide a framework for civil debate, and they create a semblance of order out of what could easily become chaos.

Civility is sometimes abandoned in Congress and in some legislative chambers; but, generally, name-calling, fistfighting, and yelling are not allowed.

My impatience with the lengthy, complex legislative process was tempered when I learned that delay, even confusion, can sometimes be a friend. It takes a long time for a bill to become a law, with many traffic jams en route. It is easier to stop what some would consider "a bad law" than to pass "a good law." Democracy was not intended to be an impetuous process. That is why the Constitution required two separate Houses to approve bills. What one body may have approved in a moment of anger, passion, or chicanery (only to be on record, knowing the other body would not pass it) would get a fresh look in the other body. In

Nebraska, the only state with a unicameral legislature, legislators are more cautious, knowing they have the final word. The famous "separation of powers"—executive, legislative, and judiciary—that distinguishes the American system of government from all others created another bulwark against overreaching by any one branch of government.

Written rules can be mastered. Unwritten rules are not taught in class. "What's going on?" the novice asks. "Who's wheeling and dealing?" Every organization, not only political organizations, has its unwritten rules of procedure, established by custom, collusion, and creative problem solving, agreed on by a handshake, a nod, or even silence. They are set at the proverbial water cooler, the men's room and, increasingly, the women's room. The greatest frustration in maneuvering through the labyrinth of any organization is to not know what is going on. Experience and preparation help.

Few leaders like surprises. Speaker Norelli (D-NH) is no different:

> I try to be ultraprepared before I go to the floor. I put my ear to the ground. People come to me and say, "I've heard they . . ." and that usually means the Republicans are going to try [something]. So far, I was not surprised by anything parliamentary because I was really well prepared with the rules, with the citations.

Information is power in politics, information about process and information about substance. It is not easy to know everything in a timely fashion—before it happens—but it is possible to develop the skills. I learned my lesson about the importance of word-of-mouth rules when I attended my first meeting of the Joint Fiscal Committee that decides critical financial issues when the legislature is not in session. As the newly appointed chair of the House Appropriations committee, I was thrilled to be the first woman to be admitted into this elite club composed of the chairs of the House and Senate money committees.

Our first task was to elect officers. Nominations were made and seconded like clockwork. Everyone had been given a part but me. Finally, a legislator mockingly nominated me to chair the "social" committee. I fumed. Then I understood what had happened: There had been a meeting before the meeting from which I had been excluded. The key to learning the unwritten rules is to find out where the "meeting before the meeting" is held and barge in. If that is not appropriate, find a spy.

Playing with the "Jerks"

"We have to support each other in playing with the jerks," Amy Sheldon, a potential candidate, told me. Many politicians look and act like jerks when viewed from the outside but are transformed into colleagues on the inside.

The difference between looking at the "jerks" from the outside and negotiating with them on the inside is that most (not all) politicians are more nuanced than their caricatures. Politicians of opposing views respect and often like one another, if they keep their word, provide reliable information, and are friendly. Forming trusting relationships with colleagues, as I did with Cola Hudson, is one of the traits of successful legislators. Frequently, despite being polar opposites, they find enough common ground to move the question. I was one of two Democrats on my eleven-member committee when I was a new legislator. I had much to learn from politicians who had different opinions than I had. The most exciting times were when my liberal views and one of my colleague's conservative views came full circle; we laughed when we shook hands across the table.

Power Within the Power Structure

Legislatures, city councils, and even school boards can be unwieldy bodies. Who runs the show? When the thrill of being a newly elected legislator began to wear off, I realized that about fifteen people made every call. They decided who was appointed to key committees, what was on the agenda, whether a bill was likely to pass or not. This was "The Leadership." They were: the speaker of the House, the president of the Senate, the majority leader, the minority leader, party whips and deputy leaders, and the chairs of key committees. The most powerful chairs were those of the money committees; they had the power to tax and the power to spend. I realized if I were to have the greatest impact as a legislator, I had to become part of the leadership. In my second term, I was elected Democratic whip, and in my third term, I chaired the House Appropriations Committee, the first woman in either of those roles.

In 2006, a record number of women were elected to state legislative leadership positions, a total of fifty-eight—a 20 percent gain over the previous high of forty-eight and more than double the number in 2000. Women comprise 17 percent of all legislative leaders, less than their 23 percent membership in state legislatures.

When Norelli started her campaign for Democratic candidate for speaker in New Hampshire, she didn't think she had a chance because the majority party had always been Republican, and they elected the Speaker. On Election Day, her race for Speaker of the House changed; the Democrats woke up to discover that they not only controlled the House but they had swept the state—the U.S. Senate, the state's two congressional seats, the governor's office, and the governor's council. This had not happened since 1874.

How do legislators become part of the leadership? Committee chairs are appointed by the speaker of the House and the president of the Senate. Party leadership posts are won by election or appointment at legislative caucuses. The campaign for speaker is like an election campaign except that in this case the voters are legislators.

Being a woman was not a problem, Norelli said, but being liberal was. She said she earned people's trust by being fair with both Democrats and Republicans. She had no qualms about appointing women to a majority of leadership positions: a woman deputy speaker, a woman democratic leader, and half the committee chairs.

Vermont's speaker of the House, Gaye Symington (D), laid the foundation for her speaker's race by recruiting new House members. She had become incensed during a debate on repealing Vermont's civil union law. "We've got to get different people in here," she concluded.

U.S. House Speaker Nancy Pelosi was a prominent Democratic fundraiser in San Francisco long before she was elected to Congress. Helping other candidates get elected is a proven road to leadership. Success in a leadership role is not as clear-cut.

Speaker Norelli explained that many of the new New Hampshire members didn't run as traditional Democrats but came out of an activist movement spurred by the 2004 presidential campaign of Howard Dean. They don't necessarily fall into line. Neither do many of the newly elected Democrats in Congress. Building coalitions to enact legislation is a daily challenge. Not making too many enemies is another. "Leadership is a process of disappointing your friends at a pace they can absorb," Symington said.

In March 2007, Therese Murray (D) was elected Senate president in Massachusetts, a dramatic contrast to the prototype Massachusetts politician, Billy Bulger, who had been Senate president for 18 years and ruled with an iron hand. "We have a different style," Murray said. "They're not afraid of me. It's a different era. I communicate and am more inclined to share power. They [senators] feel a lot more comfortable walking into my office. I don't see the need for everything to be done top down."

Murray became qualified for the position when she chaired the Senate Ways and Means Committee, where she understood the budget and finances. "I ran for Senate president because the opportunity was there and I felt I could do a good job, not from the perspective of being a woman."

I asked Christine Quinn (D), speaker of the fifty-one-member New York City Council, how women in leadership made a difference. She replied,

> One of the things about women, gay people, or people of color—anybody who hasn't been in political leadership as long as others, you are mindful of the fact that people like you haven't always been there. You govern with the idea of, "How do I even things up? How do I do this in an inclusive and transparent way?" It's about bringing people into the system. If you haven't had that experience, it may not be ever present in your mind.

The significance of the positions these women hold is not to be underestimated. They reflect the level of trust and acceptance gained from their peers. They have more than one vote; they are at the rostrum, they wield the gavel. An example of the difference that a committee chair can make was played out one day at a Senate hearing on March 21, 2007. Former Vice President Al Gore was testifying on global warming before the Committee on Environment and Public Works, headed by the new chair, Senator Barbara Boxer (D-CA). The prior chair, James Inhofe (R-OK), who once stated that global warming was "the biggest hoax foisted on America," interrupted Gore's testimony with his own diatribes. He refused to let Gore answer his questions. "Would you agree to let the Vice President answer your questions?" Boxer asked. Inhofe replied that Gore could reply when he was finished talking.

Boxer raised her chairwoman's gavel high in the air, and said, "No, that isn't the rule. You're not making the rules. You used to when you did this. Elections have consequences. So I make the rules." The audience broke into applause.

The Juggling Act: Can Female Politicians Do It?

There is no script for women with children to follow who wonder whether they should step on to the political stage. When the curtain is raised, each woman performs differently, depending on her family situation and what works best for her. Many women, more than men, wait to launch a political career until the children are older, as did Speaker Pelosi (D-CA).

Of the eighty-seven women in Congress, seventy-one are mothers; they have a total of 186 children and stepchildren. Ten members have children under thirteen, which may be a record, "although no one has kept this particular statistic," according to an article in *The Washington Post*, "Mom's in the House, With Kids at Home."[1]

A small group of women in their twenties with young children is in office. One of them is Jessica Lappin (D), who took six weeks of maternity leave from her position on the New York City Council after her son was born. She regrets that there are not more women her age in office, "because they don't think they can manage it." She does:

There are millions of women in this country who have to work multiple jobs and raise their kids on their own who do it every day. Maybe that's not their choice, but they do it, and I think being in public office is so important, being at the table and making decisions that impact our lives. Yes, you make sacrifices. Yes, it can be hard. But I think it's worth it.

Sometimes called "The Mommy Council Member," Lappin has discovered that the public reacts differently to her as a mother than to her colleague who is a father. She described a female council member who had three kids:

> When she brought her kids to community meetings, people criticized her. "Hey don't you have child care, don't you know you can't just bring your kids everywhere?" I saw that when he would bring his kids to community meetings people thought it was great, it was sweet. They thought he was involved (with his kids) and this sensitive guy spending time with his kids. Total double standard.

Kirsten Gillibrand (D-NY), a first-term congresswoman, brings her three-year-old son with her to Washington, "So I can make his breakfast, take him to school, put on his sunblock and be home by 6 or 7 to make dinner and have bath time and book time."[2]

National Journal had a cover story in April 2007, "Member Moms," describing how congressional mothers coped. Three women share a house in DC: Representative Carol Maloney (D) of New York, Melissa Bean (D) of Illinois, and Debbie Wasserman Schultz (D) of Florida. The article called it "the feminine counterpart to the Animal House." Their families have remained in their districts. They go home every weekend and do a lot of mothering during the week by cell phone, BlackBerry, and e-mail. Their rule is the same as mine was when I was governor: whenever a child calls, no matter what meeting I am in—interrupt.

Congresswoman Wasserman Schultz, who has seven-year-old twins and a three-year-old, has become a role model for young women in politics. She explained,

I take every opportunity to talk to groups of young women who are interested in politics and leadership programs, to talk about my story and show that it can be done. I don't do it all perfectly. There are some things in my house that are not that neat. I think you have to recognize you can't do everything perfectly, and especially Type A women—they believe they shouldn't do something unless they can do it perfectly. I am one of those people, and I have to constantly have counseling sessions with myself, and sometimes I have to have outside counseling sessions. But I just keep my nose to the grindstone and not let the enormity of my responsibility, either as a mom, a wife, or as a member of Congress, overwhelm me.

She does not find it easy to leave her children each week. "Kids need their mom. I am the homework person more than [my husband] Steve is. That's not sexist. It's just the way it is. Plus, there is an emotional bond that only a mother can provide," she said. But she manages to be the leader of her daughter's Girl Scout troop by scheduling meetings when she is in Florida.[3]

So, why do it? She replied,

As a young woman I brought a different perspective because most of my colleagues were old enough to be my parents and grandparents. Instead of living those issues twenty years ago, I am from a generation of women who are living them now, who have been underrepresented in policy-making bodies. So that is my role; it is generational and gender. It can be a little sensitive to talk about this with older women mentors, but they are in a totally different place in their lives than I am now. It's important to have them here, but we also need a group of younger women to come in behind them, ready to step up.

Senator Mary Landrieu (D-LA) has kept her young family in Washington. She and her husband, Frank Snellings, have a house four blocks from the Senate. "It's the only way I can do this job and be a good mother to them," said Landrieu, who has two young children. "I put my children to bed almost every night, and they wake up to their mother's voice every morning. Nothing would separate me from that."[4]

Congresswoman Pryce (R-OH), a single mother, said: "My advice to women who don't want to become involved in public service because they have children is that it is not that hard to do both. You can juggle it. You may not have the most traditional lifestyle."

Senator McCaskill (D-MO) was a single mom for seven years before she remarried. Together, she and her husband have seven children, ranging from fifteen to thirty:

> There are several things about this career that are counterintuitive. One is that it's so difficult to have a family if you go into politics. I will give you that there are times it is, but there are many times that this career provides much more flexibility than a traditional nine-to-five job. Your bosses are the people. If I wanted to take a morning off to be the homeroom mother for the Valentine's Day party at my children's school, I did it. I also had to work nights and weekends sometimes, but ultimately you have the flexibility.
>
> When I ran statewide [for state auditor] I was single, I was divorced. My children were young, and that was hard. That was the toughest time because I couldn't afford help. My sister helped me with the kids. I've been blessed by having a close, supportive family, very involved in my career, very helpful to me. Now I'm blessed because I can afford to hire someone to do all the things that you've got to do if you are running a household but don't involve spending time with your family. I remember distinctly letting the housework go and the laundry go and not worrying if my kids were wearing something for the second time even if it had a little stain of ketchup on it.

Vermont Speaker of the House Symington (D) ran for office when the youngest of her three children was one. Now that she is speaker, her children are thirteen, sixteen, and eighteen, but family issues are

. . . the hardest part of my role. I deal with it in a number of ways. I remind my kids that if I weren't doing this job, I'd be doing another job. It's not as if it's a choice between my work in the legislature and being home making fancy meals all the time. This is just part of who I am, and I think they know that about me.

The accusation all working women fear most is being called a "bad mother." I was susceptible to that charge, sometimes uttered in my own voice. Living a political life can be considered selfish, even if it is for the well-being of others. I had to be a supermom, and my children had to be perfect. If anything happened to them, physically or emotionally, it would be my fault.

Texas Representative Van de Putte (D), mother of six, was asked when she ran by other women, "Who's taking care of your children while you're in Austin?"

"My husband."

"So he's babysitting?"

"No, my husband is not babysitting. My husband is parenting. I'm not babysitting my own children."

Congresswoman Wasserman Schultz (R-FL) has a thick skin. She has to because,

> Sometime ago, I did have a Republican woman opponent who had no chance of winning, but the whole theme of her campaign was that I was a bad mother. She had it on TV and in commentaries, saying that she was fifty-eight and I was thirty-seven years young and that I had twins and an infant, and she would spit out that there was no way that I could be a good member of Congress and a good mother. At candidate forums, I had one audience member say, "How are you going to do it, Debbie?" I have been doing it. My twins were born in 1999 when I was in the State House, and I was nine months pregnant on the last day of the legislative session when Shelby was born. So I said, "Let me tell you how I am going to answer that question if you would tell that it was OK to ask a man with young children the same question when he

was a candidate for Congress." The guy shook his head and said he probably wouldn't ask a man the same question.

She then said, "I'll be respectful and answer your question. I think it is really important that policymakers be living with the same situations as the constituents they represent. That makes me a better representative and makes me better able to understand the needs in my district. I got a standing ovation and it was a business candidate forum," she told me.

What About Husbands?

The easiest way to juggle family and career is to marry the right guy. When Michigan Governor Jennifer Granholm was asked about families by a group of women contemplating a run for governor, she replied, "I hope you all have married well. If it was not for my husband, I wouldn't be able to do it. We schedule things in for the kids, they have first priority."[5]

Women with young children were quick to acknowledge their husbands' willingness to share household responsibilities. Councilwoman Lappin was emphatic:

I'm lucky because my husband is amazing. He's a real partner, and he is a fantastic support system. He was my treasurer because campaign finance in New York is a serious undertaking; he made phone calls, he was out on the street, and he was really helpful.

I was surprised on the campaign trail that you get asked questions that you couldn't get asked in a job interview: "Are you married? Do you have kids? Do you plan on having kids?" I would answer people politely, and I would ask them, "Do you think that will make a difference?"

The thing that people used to ask me most is, "What does your husband think about you running?" I used to get asked that everyday, all the time. I don't think people would ask a male candidate, "What does your wife think of this?" The inference is, "Does your husband approve?"

Others also have supportive spouses.

"My husband is incredibly helpful," said Senator Klobuchar. "I go home for two or three weekends a month, and I've been home for all the recesses." She was bothered, however, when she learned that her daughter had a piano recital and "hadn't practiced because her dad hadn't made her. If I had been there, she would have been practicing every night."

Children learn self-sufficiency when mother can't bring the forgotten school lunch to school, several women noted. It is often mothers who miss their children more than children miss their mothers, said Gaye Symington (D-VT) reluctantly.

Some husbands are more tolerant than supportive. And, in some cases, a husband can become a liability for a woman who runs for high office, as Congresswoman Geraldine A. Ferraro (D-NY) discovered when she ran for vice president in 1984. Her husband's financial dealings became the source of much speculation and weakened her candidacy.

Women get more questions about male spouses than men get about female spouses, because husbands have, until recently, had more of a past to probe. Most female political spouses have admiringly stood at their husbands' sides, like Nancy Reagan, but their role is beginning to change as they take a more active part in their husbands' campaigns.

Still, the public is curious about male political spouses. What is it like to be married to a strong woman? Even recently, my husband was asked that question. The role is new, which accounts for some of the curiosity. The jokes about Bill Clinton's title, should Hillary become president, are a sign of amused confusion—first man, first lady, first laddie? The cover of the October 8, 2007 issue of *New York Magazine* had Bill Clinton's face morphed into Jacqueline Kennedy's with a black bouffant wig and a red sleeveless dress. The story was "The First: Female President, Male First Lady, Former President in the White House."

Bill Clinton's role in the campaign prior to the South Carolina primary was hotly debated. Some women wrote that Hillary could not be a true feminist if she needed her husband not only to defend her, but to lead the attacks on Barack Obama. In fact, in his endorsement of Obama, Senator Edward Kennedy said he disapproved of Bill Clinton's behavior. Was that fair? She countered critics that he only did what any spouse would do to defend their wives or husbands. Granted, a former president is not a typical spouse. Still, she found herself in a classic double bind, she could not leave him home or send him around the world or else voters would wonder whether her marriage was intact. When he campaigned for her, some voters questioned whether they would get two Clintons instead of one. On the plus side, he continues to draw crowds as no other spouse could have done. Once again, it was damned if you do, and doomed if you don't.

In the case of other women leaders, a male spouse is also under subtle pressure to prove that he is a man and a person in his own right. The hardest part is to learn how to share political life with a spouse. Tension in a political family does not only revolve around who does the grocery shopping, it is also created by the different world in which a politician lives. When I came home, dead tired, after a day in the governor's office, I would make an attempt to describe the day's myriad activities, highs and lows, but I seldom had the energy for a complete replay. I knew my answers were not satisfactory. I also knew that when we met people, the first eye contact was with me, and only seconds later did they focus on my husband.

Some men are exceedingly proud of their political spouses and discover that parts of the spousal job are fun. My former spouse (I am now remarried to another highly supportive spouse) was the first husband to break into the Legislative Wives Club in Montpelier and thoroughly enjoyed the women's company as much as they did his. Senator Klobuchar's husband

> . . . has the distinction of helping plan the Laura Bush luncheon. He is the only husband who has been consistently involved in the Senate spouse group. I knew things reached a mark of equality when Senator Claire McCaskill and I were driving out of the capital and she said, "Is that your husband?" because he was walking, carrying a big pink box, and it was lunchtime. I asked what he was doing, and he said he was going to [Virginia Senator] Jim Webb's wife's baby shower. Claire yelled out, "That is the sexiest thing I have ever seen."

How hard is it to be in political life without a spouse? The public has learned to accept that political women, like women in every line of work, may be single, divorced, widowed, or living with a partner. The women themselves may be more self-conscious of it. Vermont Representative Margaret Cheney (D) said she had a wonderful "picture of me and my three children" to put on her campaign literature. "It was mentioned to me that it reminded people that I am a divorced woman. It could be seen as a negative; obviously it wasn't, because I won."

She noted that combining politics and family was more difficult as a single mother: "I remember many people running for office having spouses at home helping them. That is especially true for men. It requires extra energy and a strong backbone."

Women Presidents

Hatshepsut was the only woman to rule as a female pharaoh of Egypt, for twenty years 3,480 years ago. Her mummy was identified on July 6, 2007, by a tooth and verified by DNA tests. She had disappeared for almost 3,000 years because of the vengeance of her nephew/stepson, Thutmose III, who ordered her images destroyed. Her temple in Thebes, Deir-El-Bahri, considered "one of the great architectural wonders of the ancient world"[1] reveals the amazing artistry of her genius and the vicious anger of those who tried to destroy her temple by using hammers and chisels to hack away images of her face and break her statues. Archeology saved her from anonymity. Only when piles of destroyed statues were unearthed from newly discovered pits in the 1920s and 1930s did her reputation begin to change from two contradictory perceptions: She had been either a "scheming, manipulative woman who lusted after power" or a "passive figure under the influence of her male courtiers."[2] Such gender-stereotypical assumptions about women rulers are found throughout history and continue into the twenty-first century.

Today Hathshepsut is regarded as an extraordinary ruler who enabled Egypt to become a world power (she may have led a military campaign herself) and is extolled for ruling over a period of great artistic creativity and innovation during long peaceful periods. There is androgyny in the statues and carvings that depict her, with some female and male symbols, including a false beard, the symbol of royalty.

It was sometimes necessary and often life threatening for women leaders to wear male attire. Joan of Arc, who saved France from the English during the Hundred Years' War, was burned at the stake in 1431, accused of heresy and witchcraft by both the church and the state. She was nineteen. Among her crimes was wearing a suit of armor, like a man. Today a woman no longer risks heresy when she assumes a traditional male leadership role, but neither is she accepted with equanimity. In 1920, the

Catholic Church restored Joan of Arc's reputation, as well as its own, by declaring her a saint. Ever since her execution, the story of the courageous "Maid of Orleans" has been frequently resurrected, most recently in the campaign of Ségolène Royal, the recent Socialist candidate for president of France.

Five English queens have held the throne and wielded power equal to that of any king, until the throne lost its glitter in the twentieth century. Today, Queen Elizabeth II, who was crowned in 1952, serves in a ceremonial role, largely supported by British sentiment for the "royals." Her predecessors were powerful: Queen Victoria ruled for sixty-four years (1837–1901).

Many believe that Margaret Thatcher was elected prime minister in 1979 without much fuss over her gender because the English had long ago become accustomed to female rulers. For two decades, Thatcher was the only woman to lead a major Western democracy. She was no feminist. "I owe nothing to Women's Lib," she said. And yet she once declared, "In politics if you want anything said, ask a man. If you want anything done, ask a woman," and added, "Any woman who understands the problems of running a home will be nearer to understanding the problems of running a country."[3]

The distinction of becoming the world's first female prime minister belongs to Sirimavo Bandaranaike of Sri Lanka, who was elected in 1960. Forty-four women have been elected leaders of their countries since then, ranging from unknowns, such as Jennifer Smith (premier of Bermuda, 1998–), to world stage leaders such as Indira Ghandi (prime minister of India, 1966–1977, 1980–1984), and Golda Meir (prime minister of Israel, 1969–1974). Ghandi's ascent to power was made possible by her father; she was the daughter of Jawaharlal Nehru, who was India's first prime minister for seventeen years after independence from Britain. She had to "show one is not merely a daughter but also a person in her own right. Of course, being a woman you have to work twice as hard as a man," she said.[4] When she first became prime minister in 1966, politicians called her a "dumb doll," who, they thought, would be easy to manipulate. They soon found out how wrong they were when she went to war with Pakistan. After her assassination in 1984, her reputation in India remains mixed; she is both revered for having forged India into a democracy and reviled for having threatened that same democracy during a period of emergency rule. Today many Indians look upon her as an incarnation of Shakti, the Hindu goddess of power.[5]

Golda Meir became prime minister of Israel at the age of 70. When David Ben-Gurion described her as "the only man" in his cabinet, she was amused that he thought this was the greatest compliment he could pay to a woman. "I very much doubt," she said, "that any man would have been flattered if had been said about him that he was the only woman in government."[6]

Not exactly a feminist, she nevertheless observed, "There is a type of woman who does not let her husband narrow her horizons." She was often torn about her conflicting responsibilities: "At work, you think of the children you've left at home, at home, you think of the work you've left unfinished. Such a struggle is unleashed within yourself, your heart is rent."[7]

A name of a new future female prime minister has emerged in Israel: Tzipi Livni. A *New York Times Magazine* cover story, entitled "Her Jewish State," described Livni, now the foreign minister, as a daughter of Zionist militants, an ex-spy "and a rising political star."[8]

Former Pakistani Prime Minister Benazir Bhutto was assassinated on December 27, 2007, two months after she had returned to Pakistan to campaign against General Pervez Musharraf, following seven years of self-imposed exile. After addressing her supporters, members of the Pakistan People's Party, at a large rally, she stood in the open sunroof of a car to wave at the crowd. An assassin fired several shots at her before blowing himself up. It was later determined, in a report released by Scotland Yard, that she died of head trauma sustained in the explosion. Her death shocked the country and the world. Her nineteen-year-old son, Bilawal Bhutto Zaraari, became head of her party, stressing the importance of following the "blood line." Her father had been executed in 1979, two years after he finished his term as Prime Minister. Bhutto served her country twice, first in 1988 and again in 1993; each time she was removed because of alleged corruption.

It is hard to tease out generalizations about these women, except to note that many of them have been called too tough ("Iron Ladies"—some ten women have earned that sobriquet) or too soft and easily manipulated by the men around them—again, the double bind. Some thirteen female heads of state have been called "Iron Ladies" or similar nicknames (Asian women are "Dragon Ladies"). Most famously, Thatcher was given the title by the Russians because of her staunch opposition to communism. Some Britons called her 'Attila the Hen.'

Corazon Aquino, known affectionately as "Cory," had a softer image. She came to power as the first woman president of the Philippines (the first Asian president) after the assassination of her husband. She is remembered for bringing democracy to her country following the dictatorial rule of Ferdinand Marcos. She said, "It has often been said that Marcos was the first male chauvinist to underestimate me." Struggling against violence throughout her term, she vowed, "As I came to power peacefully, so shall I keep it."[9] Today, a second woman is president of the Philippines, Gloria Macapagal-Arroyo.

Today's Global Leaders

Since 2005, three women have been elected to head their governments, all in unlikely places: Liberia, Chile, and Germany. What experiences did they bring to office, and what were the circumstances in their countries that enabled them to defy gender barriers?

Ellen Johnson-Sirleaf, President of Liberia

The new president of Liberia, Ellen Johnson-Sirleaf has been called both an "Iron Lady" and "Ma Ellen."

"Ellen, she's our man," shouted supporters of Johnson-Sirleaf on the campaign trail. Johnson-Sirleaf was elected president of Liberia after defeating a world footballer of the year, "the son" of Liberia. George Weah was enormously popular with the country's youth—half of the population is under thirty-five—and he should have won, had history been a guide. The country, founded mainly by freed American slaves in 1847 (Monrovia, the capital, was named after U.S. President James Monroe), had just emerged from a fourteen-year civil war during which 250,000 people were killed, out of a population of 3,000,000. The country was ready to heal the dreadful wounds of war and turn to a woman after looking at "what the men had done."

"We know that your vote was a vote for change, a vote for peace, security . . . and we have heard you loudly," Johnson-Sirleaf told Liberians in her inaugural speech.

"We recognize this change is not a change for change's sake, but a fundamental break with the past, therefore requiring that we take bold and decisive steps to address the problems that have for decades stunted our progress," she said.[10]

Cheering Liberians "expressed the hope that their new mother figure would take care of them. Perhaps Big Ma will do better than the Big Daddies who have so badly failed so many African Nations," wrote Trudy Rubin.[11] Johnson-Sirleaf compared Liberia to a sick child in need of care.

An African writer, Tonderai Munakiri, reflected on the euphoria African women felt at her inauguration:

> Women have been on the periphery of politics owing to our political culture, our patriarchal society, our value system. . . .
> The African culture has placed limitations over what women can and cannot do. It has made women observers and not players in the political system and has placed them in perpetual bondage where they remain accountable to men. . . . However Sirleaf's ascendancy gives all of us hope. . . . We hope the senseless loss of blood is gone by and that we shall never see stupid blood letting in Africa again. . . .[12]

The country did not give Johnson-Sirleaf 60 percent of the vote solely based on gender. They admired her credentials. She is a 1971 graduate of Harvard, a former World Bank economist, former U.N. staffer, and former finance minister. Her opponent, like most previous Liberian dictators, is illiterate.

Johnson-Sirleaf also has suffered. She was twice imprisoned in the 1980s by Master Sergeant Samuel Doe's junta and forced to flee into exile in Kenya and the United States. Her predecessor, Samuel Taylor, was forced from power in 2003 and was sent to a cellblock at the men's penitentiary while on trial at the International Court of Justice.

A less known credential, but one she spoke about with pride in Liberia, was that she was the granddaughter of a rural market woman. It was the market women, Johnson-Sirleaf said, whose support was stronger than the former militiamen and Taylor diehards who supported Weah. She talked about education to the women. "These were poor women who work in the markets, picking and selling vegetables. And they care about education for their children."[13] Grassroots women and market women were more than 50 percent of the electorate, "and I got over 90 percent of their vote. So clearly my victory's owed in large measure to the women of Liberia."

It is impossible to exaggerate the challenges she continues to face as the sixty-eight-year-old president of this plundered, war-torn country that was once one of the richest in Africa. Peace has come to Liberia because 15,000 U.N. troops are stationed there. Eighty percent of the country is illiterate, unemployment is at 85 percent, three-quarters of the population earns less than $1 a day, and half the children are not in school. Her goal, she said, was to enable the children to smile again.

What difference has gender made in how she governs? She has appointed women to positions never before held by women: ministers of finance, defense, sports and youth, commerce, and justice, and as chief of police and president of the Truth and Reconciliation Commission. Her criteria were competence and "no record of human rights abuses, inclusiveness as much as possible."[14] "The Iron Ladies of Liberia" is the title of a film about the women in her administration.

After her victory, she invited her defeated opponent, Weah, to join her government, a magnanimous peace gesture and hard to envision for an African male politician. Foreign investment has grown. She is pleased with the passage of a tougher rape law and refers to her teenage granddaughters as beneficiaries. The mother and grandmother roles give her great symbolic power that signifies change with an exclamation point! The road to implementing change, however, is rough.

When asked about her toughest moment, she talked about when "I was in prison after an attempted coup in 1985 with about 12 other so-called rebels, all of whom were killed." She also said that her childhood dream was to "wake up black. I was teased because of my [light] complexion. Of course, that was an impossible dream."[15]

Her dream now is to rebuild her country. "The biggest danger is that youth will become disenchanted with things, not wait for a new election [she has one six-year term] and become malleable to the next warlord or Big Man who comes along," said Donald Booth, the U.S. ambassador to Liberia.[16]

As both the Iron Lady and the Mother of Liberia, she said, "I represent the whole Zodiac of the Liberian contradictions, and I know the Liberian potential. If there is anybody who can bring change, it's someone whose life experience represents all the good and the bad."[17]

Michelle Bachelet, President of Chile

"Who would have thought, just five years ago, that Chile would have a woman President?" Michelle Bachelet asked her cheering supporters at her victory speech in 2005.

And who would have thought that this conservative Catholic country, the country in which machismo reigns, would have elected an agnostic, socialist pediatrician to lead their country, not long ago ruled by the brutal military dictatorship of Augusto Pinochet? Equally unexpected is that an electorate opposed to divorce (it was legalized only in 2004) would approve of a woman, long separated from her husband, who has two grown children from her marriage and a twelve-year-old from a subsequent love affair.

Born in 1951, she became the first woman in South America to be elected president without replacing a deceased or disabled husband. Gender was not a central issue in her campaign, according to freelance British journalist Justin Vogler, who lives in Valparaiso, Chile. She— like the president of Liberia—symbolized change; change away from a painful past, change away from a conservative Catholicism that many Chileans rejected, and change toward a new era of social justice. She is "also a symbol of healing in a country long divided by ideology, class and competing versions of a tumultuous recent history."[18]

A popular refrain during her campaign was, "Chile is no longer our fatherland—it's our motherland."[19]

Her life story, combined with her five-year experience as a cabinet minister, trumped macho tradition. It gave her an essential credential: authenticity. Bachelet's father, air force General Alberto Bachelet, was imprisoned after a 1973 coup that brought Pinochet to power; he died of heart failure after being tortured. She and her mother also suffered from torture in the infamous Villa Grimaldi torture center. They were later released and went into exile in Australia and then East Germany, where she began her medical studies. They returned to Chile in 1979. She became a pediatrician and also received a diploma in military strategy.

In Chile, she found an important mentor, Ricardo Lagos, the first left-wing president since the death of President Salvador Allende. He appointed her health minister in 2000 and defense minister in 2002, making her the first woman in Latin America to hold that post. Both her gender and her political affiliation signaled a new era of civilian control over the military.

She achieved reconciliation between the military and victims of the dictatorship, culminating in a 2003 declaration that "never again" would the military subvert democracy in Chile. Soon she became Lagos's hand-picked successor.

Bachelet did not hesitate to use her identity as a mother in her campaign; on January 4, 2005, she said,

> A president has to understand a country's needs. I am a mother and a doctor; I know the needs of my family and those of my country. Together we restored democracy and now I invite you to help pass another milestone. Make history and choose Chile's first woman president.[20]

Her rivals wanted to dismiss her as a lightweight without being accused of machismo. Her runoff opponent, Sebastián Piñera, used the slogan "Piñera can," which was thought to be chauvinistic. Like women everywhere, she was subject to gender stereotyping: "As a woman, they [the media] scrutinize your private life, look at your clothes and your hairstyle, that's to say, things that no one evaluates in a man, and in reality they demand more from a woman in politics than a man." Asked at a press conference if she had a boyfriend, she turned away.[21]

She mobilized women voters who came out in droves, breaking the tradition of voting like their husbands, according to Benjamin Witte, an American freelance journalist residing in Chile. On inauguration day, Bachelet dressed in a white suit and wore the Chilean red, white, and blue sash; thousands of women wore the same sashes. For the first time, they felt represented.

In her first official speech to the nation Bachelet reversed the usual order of address, "Thank you, women and men of Chile." She distinguished her presidency from her predecessors:

> You know that I never asked for power. I am willing to serve. . . . Today, Chile has a new government, led by a woman, which is the expression of a new era. Now is the time for happiness, for men as well, for young people and children, for seniors, and, of course, women.

Her first act was to appoint a cabinet that was 50 percent female; it was soon criticized for not having enough experience or ethnic diversity. Her agenda included guaranteeing the right of women to breast-feed at work and enabling girls aged fourteen and over to get free morning-after contraception pills. When the euphoria of her victory subsided, harsh critics emerged. A high school student strike, dubbed the Penguin Revolution because of the strikers' school uniforms, was allowed to go on for two weeks. This prompted questions about her leadership. An overhaul of the Santiago bus system, initiated by her predecessor, caused outrage and chaos. A year later, in an article, "Sex and Power in Chile," Marcelo Mendoza wrote that the political elites did not accept her. Their message, between the lines, was: "She is a woman, she acts like a woman, and women don't know how to exert authority." Yet the public gives her approval ratings of more than 50 percent, "especially remarkable given the bad press and setbacks that resulted from policies of the previous government of President Lagos," Mendoza wrote.[22]

Angela Merkel, Chancellor of Germany

A different set of circumstances faced Angela Merkel, a childless, once-divorced, remarried woman who was elected chancellor by the German *Bundestag* on November 22, 2005, the leader of a patriarchal country in which women were traditionally relegated to *"kirche, küche, und kinder"* (church, kitchen, and children). Like Johnson-Sirleaf and Bachelet, Merkel was vastly underestimated by leading male politicians, which was "something her rivals would later come to regret. . . . Merkel's 15-year rise to the chancellorship was improbable, accidental and unexpected."[23] Unlike her female counterparts in Liberia and Chile, she never identified herself as a feminist or proposed a women's agenda. It is difficult to ascertain what is most remarkable about her ascent: that she is a former East German, that she is a physicist, or that she is a woman:

> I have the impression that the fact that I am a woman—more than the fact that I am from the East, plays a big role for many people. For me personally, this is not the case. I know myself only as a woman. Naturally I know that there are no feminine habits for rituals of power. This will become more of a normalcy if this coalition succeeds in Germany.[24]

Despite downplaying gender differences, her gender is considered significant. This feminist context is fundamental for understanding Angela Merkel because she has no choice but to "run as a woman." According to Myra Marx Ferree, Merkel's very presence both rests on past gains and changes future opportunities for women in several ways:[25]

> Another behavior that some were willing to interpret as a "hint" of Merkel's feminist sympathies was that her closest and most trusted advisors within the party are women. . . . It is more than likely however that such a female-centered network represents less of a clue to her politics than an indication of just how untrustworthy as allies and confidants she has probably found her male colleagues to be.

... But having a feminist effect on the gender norms of politics does not require a woman to actually espouse feminist policies. It may be more telling to note that Merkel is well aware of the male norms and expectations that demean and attempt to exclude her. . . .[26]

Merkel is the daughter of a Lutheran pastor and studied physics because she wanted to avoid a profession that could involve communist indoctrination.[27] Her passion for freedom was born in East Germany, whose rule she viewed as "inhumane and lacking a future. Without showing it outwardly, she engaged in 'inner immigration.'"[28]

Merkel's first ministry was Family, Women, Seniors, and Youth, a typical female ghetto where she became known as Chancellor Helmut Kohl's *"Mädchen"* ("girl"). But unlike other female politicians, she used this position as a springboard to higher office.[29] Kohl was her mentor, and she was his brilliant loyal pupil for eight years in various cabinet positions, until his star sank under the weight of scandal. Shortly after Kohl was defeated in 1998, campaign finance irregularities were revealed, exacerbated by Kohl's stubborn secrecy. Merkel became the CDU (Christian Democratic Union) party's general secretary. Her gender became more of an asset than a liability because when male political leaders are tainted by scandal, women are given new brooms, or "'the moral capital' necessary to make a clean start."[30]

She became known as Kohl's *"Trümmerfrau." Trümmerfrauen* were the women who cleaned up the rubble in German cities after World War II and were given credit for Germany's economic miracle. Her rise was watched with skepticism, a scenario similar to what is facing Bachelet in Chile. Merkel has been far more successful than could have been anticipated. The media have been tempted to compare her to Thatcher as another Iron Lady, but the comparison is not entirely accurate.

When neither her party nor Gerhardt Schröder's Social Democrats won enough seats to form a majority in the *Bundestag,* both claimed victory. She demonstrated her consummate political skills when she won the negotiations that resulted in her being named chancellor. In return, Schröder's party would receive eight of the sixteen cabinet seats.[31]

Merkel had developed a reputation as a consensus builder, seeking gradual change, not only in Germany, but in Europe as a respected president of the European Council. In 2006, *Forbes* magazine named her the most powerful woman in the world, besting Condoleezza Rice, who came in second. Her favorability ratings in Germany remain unusually high.

The Women of Europe

Gro Harlem Brundtland

Scandinavians were, and remain, in the forefront of electing women leaders, both in their Parliaments and as heads of state. Finland was the second country to grant women suffrage in 1906 (the first was New Zealand, 1893), but the Finns also granted women the right to run for office. The first woman to be prime minister of Norway was a physician; Gro Harlem Brundtland was first elected in 1981 and then reelected two different times, serving February 1981 through October 1981, May 1986 through October 1989, and November 1990 through October, 1996. She established a global reputation as chair of the World Commission on Environment and Development for the United Nations, known as the Brundtland Commission, which produced a report called "Our Common Future" in 1987. That was when the term "sustainable development" was first used. She later served as director-general of the World Health Organization (WHO). She is now a U.N. special envoy for climate change. Her résumé appears seamless, but like most successful women, she had inner struggles managing her political and private life. She wrote in her autobiography, "Time with the kids was always in short supply. I missed them. So I did what I could to be free on weekends."[32] She sometimes felt discriminated against. "Of course I was vulnerable. A young woman in leadership was something new in politics. And such novelty had its price. Intuitively I felt that it was important to be strong and to show it. Not to be blinded by praise and expectations. Not to be paralyzed by criticism and unjustified attacks. That would be a way to break a woman."[33]

Ségolène Royal, Socialist Candidate for President of France

In 2007, after Merkel and Bachelet won historic victories, the French asked themselves if they would follow suit by electing Ségolène Royal, a socialist, unmarried mother of four as their next president. Her partner and father of her children, from whom she has since separated, François Hollande, was the Socialist Party leader and also had political aspirations. (Nicolas Sarkozy and his wife also announced their divorce six months after his election.) Her campaign strongly appealed to the women's vote, asking them to write "a new page in the history of France" by electing her as its first female president. "I need the women's vote," she said. "The entire world is watching you."[34]

Royal led a twelve-candidate field among young voters, but she lagged behind Nicolas Sarkozy with women older than sixty. In the runoff, she trailed Sarkozy by five percentage points among women. The simple explanation of the difference between young and older voters may be change versus tradition. It is difficult to determine what role gender played in her defeat. Some thought she did poorly in the debates, failing to reveal a command of the facts, a fatal fault for a woman, sometimes forgiven in a man. Although other recently elected women candidates represented change, Royal sent a mixed message; change as the first female president, but not change in policy. Some voters saw the election as a choice more between opposing political parties than between personalities; Royal promised to change France, "but softly," continuing France on its course, while Sarkozy proposed a bold new direction, reducing the role of the welfare state and revitalizing the economy.[35]

The *Times* of London on May 2, 2007, had a headline: "Dracula and Mary Poppins Fight It Out on Screen for the Last Votes." The article concluded, "To gain the upper hand, Ms Royal must exude a presidential authority that has been lacking from a shaky campaign in which even supporters have compared her nurturing, brisk style to that of Mary Poppins." Better than an Iron Lady? Probably not. French chauvinism played a role (the country gave women the vote as late as 1944), according to Maureen Dowd: "A Sarko adviser called Sego 'a very pretty gadget' who looked modern but had no real plan to move France out of malaise and into the future."[36] After her defeat, Royal was treated like a "heroine in a novel, not a Presidential candidate," observed a reader of the French press. One article began, "She likes clouds . . . "[37] and another, "Ségolène Royal: The Secret Wounds."[38]

Regional Trends: Women in Latin America

"At times of profound crisis, when the country faces dramatic situations, women appear and act with great strength and conviction."[39] The power of women has been evident with the Mothers of the Plaza de Mayo in Buenos Aires, who have been demonstrating regularly since the late 1970s, demanding an accounting of their disappeared sons and daughters. Their courage to challenge the dictatorship publicly and expose its brutality was an essential component in the downfall of the regime. The continent's most famous female politician without portfolio was Argentinean President Juan Perón's wife Evita who, through the Evita Perón Foundation, collected money from the rich—sometimes by thuggery—and gave it to the poor. After she died in 1952, Perón lost his working-class support and was forced into exile in Spain. In 1973, he was reelected, and his second wife, Isabel, was his vice president. She took power after her husband fell ill in 1974 but was an ineffective leader and in 1976 was overthrown in a military coup, ushering in a bloody period in Argentine history known as the "Dirty War."

Violeta Chamorro, with strong support from the United States, defeated the Sandinista leader Daniel Ortega to become president of Nicaragua from 1990 to 1997, after her husband, Joaquin Chamorro, was assassinated in 1978 by the Somoza dictatorship. Women have served as interim heads of state in Dominica, Bolivia, Haiti, and Ecuador[40] Mireya Moscoso was elected president of Panama in 1999. Portia Simpson-Miller is the first female prime minister of Jamaica.[41]

"Women in Latin America are rising in top positions at a time when voters across the region are searching for fresh faces to chart new economic and political models," explained an article in *The New York Times*.[42]

Many Latin American countries have a higher percentage of women in their legislatures than the United States because they enacted quotas.

Argentina was the first country to enact a gender quota law; today the legislature is comprised of 39 percent women. Costa Rica boasts the same figure. Ecuador moved from 15 percent to 25 percent and Honduras from 5.5 percent to 23 percent in recent elections, both as a result of quotas. The newest political star in Latin America is Cristina Fernández de Kirchner, elected president of Argentina in October 2007. She is being compared to Hillary Clinton because she is a fifty-four-year-old senator, the wife of the now former president (as of December 11, 2007), and a lawyer.

On America's Borders

Both Mexico and Canada have a higher percentage of elected women than does the United States at 16 percent. Mexican women did not win the right to vote until 1947 and to run for office until 1953. Today, 24 percent of the members of Congress are women.

Canada has a representation of 21.1 percent in the Parliament; the highest province is Manitoba with 31.6 percent. A record number of women hold leadership positions: In the Senate, Marjory LeBreton is leader of the government, Céline Hervieux-Payette is leader of the official opposition, and Rose-Marie Losier-Cool is Senate Deputy Speaker. Karen Redman is Official Opposition Whip. The Governor General of Canada is also a woman: Michaëlle Jean.

Canada has had a female Prime Minister, Kim Campbell, who was elected leader of her Progressive Conservative party before the 1993 election but was defeated months later in the election.

"Do women in Canada make a difference?" I asked Senator Claudette Tardif.

"Absolutely. We deal with different issues and move them to the top of the agenda—children, education, gun control and health care."

Weary of War: Women in Rwanda

The ability of women leaders to bring about change has influenced elections in another African country devastated by genocide in 1994 that left more than 800,000 people dead: Rwanda. The result is an improbable statistic. Women in the Rwandan Parliament comprise the highest percentage of women of any country in the world—48.8 percent. The runner up is Sweden at 45.3 percent, followed by Norway at 37.9, and Finland at 37.5. The United States ranks sixty-ninth out of 187 countries, according to the Inter-Parliamentary Union. One explanation for the high number of Rwandan women in Parliament is that so many men have been killed. This is partly true, but not entirely. The country turned to women because it was sick to death of war. The women, who had suffered so much, were no longer going to stand by. Women became active in postgenocide politics

> because they were subjected to sexual assault and other torture, including rape, forced incest and breast oblation. Women who survived the genocide witnessed unspeakable cruelty and lost husbands, children, relatives, and communities. In the aftermath, 70 percent of the population was female.[43]

Rwandan Senator Odette Nyiramilimo, a physician, told me why Rwanda had such a high percentage of women in their Parliament:

> That is because of the end of genocide. They created different women's organizations; they were very strong in helping the orphans and to integrate families. Women were very active in building houses. For the first time Rwandan women were in positions to help the country.

Nyiramilimo referred to the International Women's Conference in Beijing in 1995 that had passed a resolution declaring that all decision-making bodies should be one-third comprised of women. Rwandans took it seriously. (Note that Title One of the Rwandan constitution establishes a commitment "ensuring equal rights between Rwandans and between women and men without prejudice to the principles of gender equality and complementarity in national development.") Why did women get so much support?

"We see today that women are working really hard on creating lasting peace in the country. I think women are very trusted by the men in this country in such a way that even the president of the Supreme Court is a woman. Half the judges are men, and half are women." The head of the commission on genocide is a woman, Nyiramilimo added.

Still, what inspired so many women to run?

"Women were mostly worried about the survival of their children. We had to do it. It was human rights issues." She sought to assure me that there were also men in the government. And Nyiramilimo is very optimistic about the country's future:

> The country is developing tremendously. We have security. It is a country where you can walk at night wherever you want. We are preaching a lot of unity and reconciliation, trying to forgive but not forget what happened. Lots of Rwandans talk of genocide as past history and go ahead to live peacefully together.

Every female head of state knows she is gaining membership in a club whose rules were designed by and for men. Some were given membership through family names, others by their own determination. Many represented change and were believed to be less corrupt than the politicians who preceded them. Some were able to play by the rules while continuing to maintain their female personas and introduce a gender-influenced agenda.

Whether they acknowledged or denied gender differences, their very presence at the helm showed that women could be in command in countries that had never before elected women leaders.

The question that follows is: If these countries—historically and culturally perceived to be far more patriarchal than the United States—elected women heads of state, why are many Americans still questioning whether a woman can be elected president of the United States?

Being the Leader

"When you're running for a legislative seat, voters feel they can take a chance, you're just one more," Mary Hughes, a consultant, told a group of "may run" Democratic female candidates for governor at a Washington, DC, training session in June 2007. "When you run for governor, it's intense, it's tough, and it's not like anything you have experienced before," she told the women who already were in office: lieutenant governors, speakers, a secretary of state, a secretary of finance, two congresswomen, a state senator, and a state auditor.

I nodded because I knew what she was talking about. It had been hard to train for the high jump from a legislative to an executive role because the bar was not raised gradually. Suddenly, it was under my chin. Not only had I to jump higher to get myself over the bar, I had to jump higher than my male opponent, Attorney General John Easton. My credentials needed to be spelled out; his were assumed. This assumption has not changed for women who run for executive offices today—we haven't come as far as we think.

"The issue of competence is one that men seem to get an advantage on. For a man, either because he comes from an executive background, or just because he appears to be competent, there's an assumption that men know how to run things and that women are compassionate and understand your feelings, but may not have executive ability," Dotty Lynch, former political editor at CBS News, told me. What has changed is that there are more portraits on the walls showing women governors, CEOs, and college presidents than there had been when I first ran for governor in 1982. It makes a difference. "We found that once you got a woman governor, it was a lot easier for the next one," Lynch added. Twenty-four women have been elected governor in their own right. The all-time high serving at one time was nine, reached in 2004. Twenty-five years ago, the only woman whose picture bore the plaque "governor" was Ella

Grasso (D) of Connecticut, who served from 1975 to 1980 and has the distinction of being the first female governor elected in her own right. The daughter of Italian immigrants, she had been secretary of state for twelve years and served two terms in Congress before being groomed for governor by long-time Democratic Party chair, John Bailey.

The first female governors were Nellie Tayloe Ross (D-NY), elected in Wyoming in 1925, and Miriam ("Ma") Ferguson (D-TX), elected in Texas in the same year—both as surrogates for their husbands. Lurleen Wallace (1967–1968) was elected to fill in for her term-limited husband, George Wallace (D-AL).

In the southern part of Vermont, a few people had heard of Ella. "You want to be another Ella Grasso?" a group of men asked me when I handed them my brochure at a Bennington restaurant. I was delighted they made the connection. No one in Vermont ever mentioned the other two female governors who had preceded me, Dixy Lee Ray of the state of Washington (1977–1981) and Martha Layne Collins (D) of Kentucky (1983–1987). We were the first wave of women governors; no polling had been done about us; there were no do's and don'ts. As I listened to the results of the latest research based on successful governors' campaigns, there were some pointers I wish I had been given; most others, we had followed by instinct. The good news was that the consultants confirmed what we had experienced: Yes! Women running for governor face gender stereotypes—both when they campaign for the job and when they are in the job. Instead of being surprised by this as we often were, the consultants advised women to be prepared, to be positive. The title of the presentation was "Strategies for Managing Gender Stereotypes, Maximize Benefits, and Minimize Burdens." We knew we had some burdens to minimize when we saw the results of our first poll. When the pollster listed my credentials, side by side with my opponent's, without mentioning either of our names, I came out ahead as the more qualified candidate for governor. When our names were mentioned at the outset, followed by our respective credentials, he came out ahead. As with the auditioning violinists, we had to figure out how to get the voters to listen only to the music. I had chaired the House Appropriations Committee; nevertheless, he fit the male stereotype as more qualified to manage finances. That

We Are the Men We Wanted to Marry
GLORIA STEINEM (1934–)

Gloria Steinem, the most well known and most photographed feminist of the women's movement, spans across a generational divide: She was a spokeswoman for the second wave of the women's movement (1960–1970) and is an icon for young women today.

Her early life in Toledo, Ohio, was difficult. Her parents divorced in 1944, and she was left with the responsibility to care for and support her mentally ill mother and sister. She graduated from Smith College and defined her own career as a writer and feminist. She married for the first time at the age of sixty-six, but her husband died three years later.

Her writing first drew public attention with a magazine story that appeared in *Esquire* in 1963, "I Was a Playboy Bunny."[1] In 1971, she cofounded the National Women's Political Caucus, and the next year *Ms Magazine* appeared on the newsstands. It was a revolutionary publication in its time, filled with stories about the women's movement. I looked forward to each copy.

Steinem received much press attention because she defied the stereotype of the unattractive feminist:

> Since she could not be caricatured as ugly, the press and many of her detractors trivialized Steinem as glamorous and sexy . . . Steinem

could simultaneously evoke indisputable sexuality and feminist courage. The notion that all feminists are homely or fat and certainly frustrated could hardly hold firm in the face of such evidence.[2]

Steinem herself was concerned that her looks not detract from the seriousness of her message and began to dress down, often wearing jeans and a T-shirt. When she turned forty she said, "This is what forty looks like." It was repeated with each new decade. (I used it myself.) Less well known are the words that followed: "We've been lying for so long, who would know?"[3]

I first heard her speak at the 1977 First National Women's Conference in Houston where she roused the crowd of 17,000 cheering women. She came to Burlington, Vermont, to speak at a fundraiser for my 1983 gubernatorial campaign. My older brother was concerned that her presence would label me a feminist, an indication of how sensitive the issue was. Steinem drew a large crowd and helped establish my base of support. She told the women that the stubs in their checkbooks reflected their values. "Get out your checkbooks," she urged them; most had never before written a check to a candidate.

Steinem said her political awakening occurred during the 1972 McGovern campaign:

> The truth is that I haven't thought about politics, at least not in the conventional sense that I would have five or six months ago, since I woke up to the fact that my own position, and the position of women in general, was political in the deepest sense. I'm told it's called the Feminist Realization.[4]

This realization sparked a sea change, she noted, for herself and other women:

> If it weren't for the women's movement I might still be dissembling away. But the ideas of this sea-change in women's view of ourselves are contagious and irresistible. They hit women like a revelation, as we had left a dark room and walked into the sun. . . . Greatly simplified . . . Women are human beings first, with minor differences from men that apply largely to the single act of reproduction. We share the dreams, capabilities and weaknesses of all human beings, but our occasional pregnancies and other visible differences have been used to create an "inferior" group and an elaborate division of labor. This division is continued for a clear if often unconscious reason: the economic and social profit of patriarchy males as a group.

> The odd thing about these deep and personal connections among women under patriarchy is that they often leap barriers of age, economics, worldly experience, race, culture—all the barriers that, in male or mixed society, seem so improbable to cross.[5]

Today, Steinem noted, women are becoming the men they had once wanted to marry. "Once, women were trained to marry a doctor, not be one."[6]

This was a symptom of her generation, and the system in which she came of age:

> In my generation, we were asked by the Smith vocation office how many words we could type a minute, a question that was never asked of then all-male students at Harvard or Princeton. Female-only typing was rationalized by supposedly greater female verbal skills, attention to detail, smaller fingers, goodness knows what, but the public imagination just didn't include male typists, certainly not Ivy League–educated ones. Now computers have come along and "typing" is "keyboarding." Suddenly, voilà!—men can type! Gives you faith in men's ability to change, doesn't it?[7]

information became the basis for our first television advertisement, in black and white, listing my credentials and his, mentioning my name at the end, to give voters the chance to focus on my credentials before my gender. We did what I heard the consultants advise this crop of future governors to do: State your credentials to prove your competence.

Gender stereotyping is not malicious; both men and women are prone to it because we have all grown up in the same culture in which men are given the benefit of a doubt and women are given the burden of proof. That doesn't mean women can't win or can't govern successfully, it only means that female candidates have to be aware of the gender differences and make conscious adjustments for them.

My campaign manager, Liz Bankowski, was one of the first women to run a major candidate's campaign. We knew we were taking a chance when we sat in the office of David Garth, a high-profile political consultant who believed he was doing us a favor by giving us the benefit of his wisdom: "If there is one piece of advice I have to give you, it's never hire a woman as your campaign manager." Minutes earlier I had introduced Liz as my campaign manager.

Whoever runs a woman's campaign, male or female, has to be sensitive to gender issues, to understand not only how they affect the campaign but also how they affect the candidate. It is important to have a person in the room who can be the interpreter, who helps the candidate avoid paranoia and keep a grip on reality, and most importantly to know when to make an issue about sexism, when to ignore it, and when to have a good laugh.

Without having a playbook in hand, we knew from the start that our biggest challenge was to be "gubernatorial." I had to look like a governor, and speak and behave like a governor, if I were to become a governor. That model of a governor was being cast in a new mold—not male as all Vermont governors had been, but not entirely different from them either. Male governors are what the voters knew. It was also what we knew.

The voters were prepared to make some adjustments for gender, but they were not prepared to go into the unknown and unpredictable. It was a difficult teeter-totter to balance—to simultaneously follow tradition and break with it. Each woman who is in a position that few women have occupied before—whether it is a new CEO, college president, governor, or candidate for president—has to balance that equation. The public gets excited by the prospect of the "new" promised by gender and race, but that excitement gets tempered if the candidate veers too far from the familiar. I could not constantly weigh every decision and every item of clothing to determine whether it would assure the voters or unsettle them. What I learned to do was to rely on my own instincts, to talk about what I knew and believed, to trust the people close to me to tell me the truth, and to remind myself, whenever I faltered, why I was running.

There are some things no consultant or pollster can do for a candidate. I had to believe I could do the job, and I had to understand why I wanted to do it. Politics is as brutal as most people think it is; it is like competing for the Olympics, testing both physical and emotional stamina almost to the breaking point. The only way to rationalize this decision and feel it is something normal people do is to have a sense of purpose embedded somewhere in your soul. Each candidate goes through that process differently, understanding why she wants to run, what she wishes to achieve, and how much pain and glory she can sustain. Time to think is never found on a campaign schedule; it should be. The passion, the purpose, the "Why am I doing this?" need to be reinvigorated at regular intervals, both while running for office and while in office.

Political consultants are loath to tell candidates to refresh themselves, that it is important to have a life, even if sporadically, outside of politics. I restored my balance and energy during the time I spent with my family and with my nonpolitical friends who loved me no matter what I did or did not do. They were nonjudgmental, and they knew who I was because they had known me for a long time. Politics depicts the candidate in a one-dimensional snapshot in time. The portrait cannot, because of strict editing, be complete. Family and friends provide the larger context in which politics takes place—the real world in which life goes on, in which someone has to do the shopping or there will be nothing to eat for dinner. The biggest question on my children's minds when I came home was not be how to reform education but how to do their homework.

Under the hot political klieg lights, answers have to be simplified, right or wrong, good or evil, yes or no, even when we know that most of life is not etched in black and white. It is important to retrieve the nuances, to stimulate the imagination, and to know what other people are doing for fun. Whenever I could, I went to movies, art exhibits, and concerts and read novels. None of the special studies and reports, with their charts and graphs, provides the same insights into the human condition as do the creative arts. I can understand why Abraham Lincoln loved going to the theater.

How did I establish my credentials and assure the voters that I could do a good job as governor and be reelected twice? Despite increasingly sophisticated polling, no one knows exactly why people vote the way they do. (Drew Westen's book, *The Political Brain,* claims to have scientific evidence that voters make emotional decisions.) We make our best guesses, based on past experience and a look into the future through smudged glasses.

The steps I took before running for governor could be seen as a calculated plan or as serendipity. They were not completely either. I ran for a leadership position in my second term in the House because I wanted to have more input into the agenda. That position led to a seat on the Appropriations Committee, which led to chairing that committee. These were crucial decisions that I could make because there had been a Democratic speaker for the first time in Vermont legislative history. Under Republican leadership, I would not have received these appointments.

Timing, as always in politics, was key. As I listened to Mary Hughes tell the aspiring governors that the office of lieutenant governor is not the best position from which to run for governor because the position has no clout, I reflected on my decision to run for lieutenant governor. I sensed that the voters had to become familiar with me, and I had to learn how to run a statewide campaign. I would not be the first female lieutenant governor; Consuelo Northrup Bailey of Vermont, a Republican, had been there first in 1954. She never aspired to be governor. I did. My ambition crystallized during my apprenticeship under Republican Governor Richard Snelling. Perhaps there is no stronger motivation to run for office than to have to listen to someone else's speeches in polite silence and think about what you would say instead. I learned both how to do the job and how not to do the job from my predecessor, who did not know he was my teacher.

Now I was a teacher for this new class of governors. I was also a student—there is always more to learn about winning elections and governing. There, on PowerPoint, were three challenges that women faced:

1. Insider versus outsider
2. Consensus management versus decisive leadership
3. Hard issues versus soft issues

My own experience generally corroborated these findings. The difference was that I had never thought in PowerPoint. It was back to the teeter-totter on all three.

Insider versus Outsider

Historically, women are considered outsiders, which is positive when voters are looking for an antidote to corruption or want change, as was the case in Liberia and Chile. This is not so good if they question how a woman would run the government or deal with the legislature. Is she so far out of the mainstream that she is locked out of the existing power structure, which includes having access to funds to finance a serious campaign?

- *Advice:* "Slay a dragon, solve a problem, start a movement. People must define you as an outsider with a willingness to stand up for them."
- *Conclusion:* "Demonstrating both is key." I knew that if women are immigrants, new to the political landscape, it is better to be a legal than an illegal immigrant, carrying the right credentials. The immigrant status generates excitement, particularly among women, but—to carry the metaphor one step further—it's important to speak the local language without too strong an accent.

Consensus Management versus Decisive Leadership

Voters expect women to be more collaborative, inclusive leaders who are positive, but they ask, "How good would she be in a crisis?"

- *Advice:* Be decisive in a crisis; go out there alone—before a raging fire, a flood, an accident—command the microphone, show you are in charge.
- *Conclusion:* Do both.

Women are judged differently from men, both when campaigning for the job and after they win. "Ah, now it's all over," my staff and I believed the morning after the election. "We've proven we could do it, no more gender issues." Not so. The question changes from "Can a woman win?" to "Can a woman govern?"

I resonated with the "slay a dragon" advice. I took on the ski industry and called them "crybabies" when Killington balked at obeying environmental regulations. I got a positive response and learned what the consultants confirmed: The public wants to know that you can stand up and fight.

The issue of decision making is more fundamental than a question of style; it is a question of substance. Whom do you listen to, and whom do you ignore? How much is any executive swayed by what she already knows and believes to be true, and how much is she open to new and unsettling ideas? It is comfortable to stay in place with the people, information, and opinions that are familiar. These are often the people who are closest to a governor, staff and special interests who have access and want to please the governor. Whatever the outward style, the inner process has to be based on reaching out to people who do not have a seat at the table. How is this done? The best way is to step out of the governor's office (all those speeches and ribbon cuttings can be educational), bring new people into the office, and do more listening than talking.

The art of politics is to develop a political "ear" much like a musical ear. It is different from putting your finger in the air to feel which way the wind is blowing at a particular moment. It means being aware of the larger, more sustainable themes that define people's hopes and fears and developing the capacity to connect with them by trying on their shoes for size. As Congresswoman Shea-Porter (D-NH) said, "My ears were close to the ground as a grassroots person."

Hard Issues (Quantitative) versus Soft Issues (Qualitative)

This is where gender stereotypes are most frequently played out. Voters believe women are already good on education, health, and the environment. They don't think women are good at the issues historically related to toughness and finances: crime, jobs, economy, taxes, and security.

- *Advice:* Do both soft and hard issues.
- *Conclusion:* Talk about them in the same sentence. Don't talk about education without mentioning education finance; don't talk about the environment without talking about science. In talking about security, to be credible a woman can't use the "shoot 'em up" language a man might use. Talk about cooperation, safety, and preparedness. Talk about facts and recite figures. I knew the consultants were right when I recalled that I always saw my audiences pay special attention when I inserted numbers into my speeches; voters are still surprised when women demonstrate such knowledge. Financial experience and law enforcement experience give female candidates credibility on traditionally male issues.

The two issues that fueled my campaign were the environment and education, "soft" issues on which I had credibility and that were also important to Vermont voters. Once elected, I spent much time on the economy, on keeping and creating jobs (a must for any governor), but it was more difficult to present my credentials on that "hard" issue. Was it all about gender? Probably not. But it was reassuring to know that gender may have played a part.

Gender is not the only lens through which female candidates for governor are viewed. Party and what a candidate stands for, and against, are clearly more important for voters. The purpose of this presentation was to alert candidates to what they will face because, for many women, gender bias had not been a visible deterrent until they aimed for the top. Neither had they experienced the level of press scrutiny and public questioning before. The Girl Scout motto was the message: Be prepared.

There is cause for caution about drawing too many conclusions about female candidates for governor because the pool is so small, and the women are different from one another.

Time selected five of the best governors in America and three of the worst. Two women made it on the "best" list, Janet Napolitano (D) of Arizona and Kathleen Sebelius (D) of Kansas. Kathleen Blanco (D) of Louisiana was relegated to the worst list for her response to Hurricane Katrina, a dragon she did not slay.

Both Napolitano and Sebelius are Democratic governors in red states. Both were cited by *Time* for tight fiscal management without raising taxes or cutting education. How did these governors deal with the toughness issue? In 1998, Napolitano was elected attorney general as one of the "Fab Five" women who were elected to all five constitutional offices, after a series of scandals. She is the third female governor of Arizona.[8]

She had proven herself on the toughness scale, but she also found that she had to be feminine to ensure people liked her.

"I was a lawyer. I was a litigator. I had dark suits, and I used legal terms." Friends told her she didn't need to look and sound like a lawyer. "I went through a process of adjusting myself to that. As governor, I think people want a very human connection with that person who happens to be in that chair and they don't always want you behind the podium looking stern."

Governor Sebelius believes her election as insurance commissioner helped provide her with the right background on one of those hard issues: economics.

"It turned out to be a very good place to be. It helped me develop financial credentials. The other piece is that it allowed me to be a consumer champion, a great asset when I ran for governor." She explained that in her final year as commissioner, Blue Cross/Blue Shield applied to be taken over by a for-profit company:

I decided that was not going to be good for Kansas so I blocked the takeover. They sued me, and I ended up winning the suit in court. It turned out to be an enormously popular decision and frankly an effective decision because the company is doing extremely well and still providing great coverage to people. I guess my dragon was that I got to take on the big bad corporate boys and keep that company safe and secure in Kansas hands.

The dragon for Governor Rell (R) of Connecticut was corruption. She was catapulted into the governor's chair after nine years as lieutenant governor when Governor John Rowland was forced to resign because of corruption. She was sworn in July 2004 and underwent surgery for breast cancer six months later, ten days before she was to give her first State of the State speech to the legislature:

I said to my doctor, "I have to give a speech in ten days," and he said, "Sure, we'll talk." I said, "You don't understand, the people of Connecticut are counting on me. I've told them we are going to turn this state around. They need to see me strong right now. They can't see me as being weak, ineffective, whatever." He continued to say, "We'll talk," and in the meantime I wrote the speech. I said, "I promise you this, the speech will be short"; seven minutes, I think it was.

She received kudos for her courage and was elected in her own right two and a half years later with 63 percent of the vote.
Democratic pollster Geoff Garin found, for example, that a female candidate who has survived breast cancer gets equivalent respect from voters as a man who has suffered a war injury.[9] Rell acknowledged her good timing.

I think what the state was ready for at that very moment was somebody who was going to come in and say, "Everything is going to be OK." I'm reluctant to say they needed a mother, but in a way, that's what it was. I know that sounds very simplistic, but that was the message I delivered on the day I was sworn in. We are going to restore faith and integrity, and we are going to remember exactly what we are here for, and that is to serve the public.

When Rell ran for governor, she did so "with no contributions from lobbyists or PACs or anyone who had direct business with the state of Connecticut. It was very difficult to do."

In Massachusetts, Jane Swift became another Republican lieutenant governor who suddenly found herself in the governor's chair in April 2001 when Governor Paul Cellucci resigned to become ambassador to Canada. She was thirty-six when she became the first governor of any state to give birth while in office—twin girls. She already had a two-year-old. Her brief time in office was controversial. She had a three-hour one-way commute from her home to the capital (Massachusetts does not have a governor's mansion) and held an important meeting from her hospital bed after giving birth. The press zeroed in. Swift said:

> The great surprise to me, maybe this was naïveté, was the degree to which society was so conflicted about the choices that women made about work and family. [In politics] you hear more from people who disagree with your choices, and that's true on every issue as a politician, than you do from people who agree with you.

It is hard to untangle the roots of Swift's unpopularity. Was she a young, inexperienced governor who was unprepared for the job or did the public focus unfairly on her efforts to combine motherhood and governing? After Mitt Romney announced he would challenge her in the Republican primary, she decided not to run again.

How much gender bias do women governors experience? When Governor Rell announced she would run for governor,

> I did detect a lot of, I can't even think of the word I want to use, I don't want to say chauvinistic, but patronizing. I heard this a lot, "I'm surprised she's going to. We figured she was just a short-termer, that she was going to fill in the vacant slot and that she

would probably just go back to being a homemaker." So I kind of chuckled at it, and the more they said it, the angrier I became. I thought, "Well, I've done a good job in two-and-a-half years, think what I could do in four."

Governor Sebelius experienced little gender bias:

Kansas has a long tradition of electing women. I'm the second governor to be elected; Nancy Kassebaum was the first woman to be elected to the U.S. Senate. You probably get points for being a woman. They assume you come to the job without a lot of the special interest baggage that a lot of men have. On the flip side, we confirmed this in Kansas, are you tough enough? In the dark room with the boys, can you get the deal done, can you move things along? That characteristic may be more difficult for women to demonstrate without being seen as too harsh. There is a tipping point for women that doesn't exist for men.

In her first campaign, she applied a lesson learned at "the Girl Governor School"—if media coverage is biased, push back:

I did not have a primary; they did, so it was five men and me. The men were introduced by their backgrounds of what they had done and said, but the description of me was that I was insurance commissioner and that I wore a bright green suit and I had nail polish on my toes. I had sandals on. We went right back to the reporter whom I knew well and who had a ten-year-old daughter. My press secretary, who was a woman, said to him, "John, I cannot believe you, as the father of a daughter, would write this kind of an article," and walked through it with him, and frankly, he was stunned. He had never thought about it, he never wrote that again.

What about hard issues and soft issues? The hard issue of taxes was a challenge for Governor Jeanne Shaheen (D) in New Hampshire who was elected in 1996 and reelected twice. She became a U.S. Senate candidate in 2008. When she first ran for governor, she didn't feel any gender bias; being a woman was "helpful because I stood out. I think there was a different, very subtle, assessment of the job I did as governor because I was a woman. For example, on taxes."

Shaheen had taken "the pledge" that all New Hampshire candidates for governor must take to become serious contenders: not to enact an income or sales tax.

> I think there was a feeling that I couldn't mean what I said about taxes. I think there are different expectations for women than for men in executive positions. I think everything from the language that we use, to the way we make decisions, to the way we build consensus because I'm not out there saying I did this all by myself and I did it by beating people over the head.

How is the job of chief executive different from a legislative position? Governor Napolitano gave an answer in a 2004 speech at the University of Virginia. "Legislators," she said, "have a certain degree of latitude to choose issues they tackle. When you're governor, the issues choose you. And therein lies the test of leadership that shapes the public's perception of its leaders."

Napolitano told me that when she took office she planned to reform the Arizona education system's budget management. She prepared to modernize the state's economic base and bring prescription drug price relief to our senior citizens:

> I didn't choose to be an expert on wildfires in western forests. But in my first year in office, wildfires destroyed nearly 200,000 acres of forest in Arizona. I didn't choose to be America's most knowledgeable governor on petroleum pipelines . . . and I never expected to know much about hostage negotiations. But in January, prison inmates took two correctional officers hostage.

Like those of other women office holders, governors' backgrounds vary. Sebelius came from a political family; her father, a Democrat, had been governor of Ohio, and her husband is the son of a Republican Kansas congressman. The others did not have such family credentials, but all had run for prior office. What they share is an enthusiasm about public service. "There's a sense of energy and joy. I think that we aren't doing a good job of communicating that to the next generation of women. Campaigns are fun too. That's why you get campaign volunteers. They [campaigns] are a way to unite people from different places in their lives with one common purpose," Napolitano said.

Sebelius also has some advice for young women looking to get into politics:

> I do think there are lots of women I see, young women particu-
> larly, who are way too hard on themselves in terms of thinking
> they are not up to the job, whether it's an entry-level political
> position, or a corporate job, or the willingness to apply for a
> job. We have to do a better job of getting young women more
> comfortable with risk taking and stepping out through the door
> that may not be all the way open but may be partially open. I am
> always telling folks that I see men, dumber than my desk, willing
> to stick up their hands and say, "Pick me, pick me," and have no
> qualms about putting themselves out there and very competent
> women who say, "No, I need to take three more courses."

Napolitano also has advice for the next generation of leaders: "Get some experience, and don't do anything stupid that will keep you from being able to run."

The good news about women who have been elected to the highest position in their states is that they are powerful role models. Parents have named their babies after them, and young girls are thrilled to discover their portraits in State Houses. The greater the number, the fewer the stereotypes until one day, the same expectations will exist for women as for men. We are not quite there yet.

A Woman President in the United States?

Whenever the question, "Is the country ready for a woman president?" is posed, it implies American voters are on the road to a place called Gender Equality, but the time and place of arrival are uncertain.

The timetable cannot be set because there are no specific conditions that have to be met; there are only gut reactions that come from the culture, like ether. The question itself is interesting: No one has ever asked—except possibly in a prehistoric matriarchy—"Is the country ready for a man to be leader?" When a woman makes a serious run for president of the United States, gender is inevitably an issue—because she would be the first. "Make History," Hillary Clinton's campaign website stated; "by electing a woman president" is unstated but is understood. Other women made history before her, simply by putting their names on the ballot. Between 1872 and 2004, twenty-one women ran for president, but "none of these women could have been self-deluded about winning, but most had an audience to reach, a message to send, or a point to make about the value of the candidacy itself. A number of them enjoyed enthusiastic national followings."[1]

Victoria Woodhull was the first, followed by Belva Lockwood. They both campaigned as feminists for the party they had organized, the Equal Rights Party. One hundred years after Woodhull, in 1972, Shirley Chisholm, the first African American woman elected to Congress, campaigned for the Democratic nomination and received 151.25 delegate votes, a record thus far. Why did she run? In her memoir she wrote,

> I knew I could not become President. But the time had come when persons other than males could run for the presidency of this country. Why couldn't a woman run? Why couldn't a black

person run? I was angry that everything always, always rebounded to the benefit of white males.[2]

Chisholm angered some black voters when she was asked whether racism or sexism was more of a handicap, and she flatly answered: sexism.

The first woman to be nominated was Margaret Chase Smith of Maine at the Republican convention in 1964. In 1999, Elizabeth Hanford Dole began a campaign for the Republican nomination after having served in the cabinets of four presidents but abandoned the effort after having trouble raising money and gaining traction.

Geraldine A. Ferraro set off political fireworks that lit up the sky for women when she became the Democratic nominee for president, Walter Mondale, chose her to be his running mate in 1984, a decision that was influenced by feminists, including Betty Friedan. People continue to debate whether Ferraro was an asset or a hindrance to the Mondale campaign, which ended in a victory sweep for Ronald Reagan; no woman has been nominated since.

The first African American woman—and still the only one—to serve in the U.S. Senate, Carol Moseley Braun, announced her candidacy for the Democratic nomination in 2004, one of ten candidates. She gained visibility through debates and free media but was not viewed as a viable candidate. What made her run for president after she lost her reelection bid to the Senate, where she had been criticized for campaign irregularities?

For starters, she had just returned from being ambassador to New Zealand in the Clinton administration. "New Zealand was on its second woman Prime Minister when we came back home and women were not even talked about in the 2004 campaign," Braun said. The defining moment came when her ten-year-old niece, Carol, had her social studies book out and told her, "All the presidents are boys." "I said, 'Sweetie, girls can be president, too.' She looked at me as if I said people can go to Mars. And I thought, if I've got one contribution to make in the public arena, this is it. That's why I did it."

I asked her the same question they had asked Shirley Chisholm, "Do you think it's more of an issue to be female or black, or both?"

Whether they mitigate favorably or unfavorably frankly depends a lot on the circumstances. There are some circumstances in which being both black and female is a positive thing. Black women are trained from childhood to be independent and not to look for approval for what we do. I think it is a real strength and a real help. That has made a difference for me in taking on challenges, being a pioneer, going down paths that haven't been trodden before.

And what about being a woman candidate? I asked. "Being a woman makes you more practical in terms of public policy. Women, whether conservative or liberal, have a reality check on the way things work in the real world."

Braun believes the dual stereotypes she had to face illustrate the problem with running in a white male-dominated field:

Frankly, the downside expresses itself in terms of role stereotypes. Women run into the stereotype of being female, weak, and malleable—controlled by men, indecisiveness. A recent study found that men who express anger get rewarded for it, whereas women who express anger get penalized for it. Similarly, being black has its own minefield, which again, back to stereotypes, of being lazy, shiftless, criminality, sexuality. So you wind up where you are viewed on one hand as being lazy, shiftless, and oversexed, and on the other hand, where you are earth mother, warm, fuzzy, and people come up to you in public and put their arms around you as opposed to shaking your hand.

Braun is optimistic that race and gender are being transcended:

What was so exciting about the presidential campaign was that big burly farmers in the middle of Iowa would come up to me and say, "I think you are right on the issues." New Hampshire was so comfortable. For me, what was edifying was that all that suffering had not been in vain because people were prepared to listen to a candidate who had something to say, who was also female and black.

As for the media, Braun believes she fared better than her foremothers:

> I talked with Shirley Chisholm before she died, and I think I got a better shake than she did. I wasn't marginalized like Mrs. Chisholm or in outer space like Mrs. Woodhull. They may not have paid me a lot of attention, but at least they hadn't relegated me to the loony fringe.

If somebody had told Braun when she was running that the next time, two of the top candidates for the Democratic nomination would have been an African American and a woman, would she have believed it?

"Uh-huh, I would. I was out there, and I saw how people reacted and listened to what I had to say. The public is way ahead of the political class on a lot of this stuff."

Still, she believes both still have the potential to be a deterrent:

> Look at the kind of foolishness Hillary had to go through. Were she a man, her qualifications and her political infrastructure would have made this a slam dunk, and there wouldn't be a debate. As it is, she's got to talk about keeping her husband on the porch. And stories about how many hairstyles she has had. And her cleavage. Can you believe that? Barack has to navigate too, but so much ground has been plowed on the issue of race. But quite frankly, gender is more intractable than race.
>
> A girlfriend of mine once said, race is something that just happens out there, it's outside of you, but gender happens in the home, that has to with your relationship to your mother and father. Gender is much closer to the bone as a social construct.[3]

How big is the gender barrier for a woman running for president today? The question is best answered by looking back. In the 1930s, one-third of Americans said they would vote for a qualified woman for

Remember the Ladies
ABIGAIL ADAMS (1744-1818)

"Remember the ladies," Abigail Adams wrote to her husband, John Adams, in a letter while he was busy working with Jefferson on the Declaration of Independence at the Second Continental Congress in Philadelphia in 1776. Students today are surprised to discover that women's rights were discussed early in American history. The exchange between John and Abigail Adams did not turn into a public debate because it was taken for granted by the Founders that only men of property would have the right to vote.

Abigail Adams compensated for her lack of a formal education and travel by becoming an avid reader and correspondent. Historian David McCullough writes of her in his biography of John Adams:

His marriage to Abigail Smith was the most important decision of John Adams' life, as would become apparent with time. She was in all respects his equal and the part she was to play would be greater than he could have possibly imagined, for all his love for her and what appreciation he already had of her beneficial, steadying influence.[4]

Regardless of his love for her, or her influence on him, Abigail Adams remains a footnote in history to her husband, who became the second president of the United States.

Her famous admonition is found in this letter:

. . . and by the way in the new Code of Laws which I suppose it will be necessary for you to make I desire you would Remember the Ladies and be more generous and favorable to them than your ancestors. Do not put such unlimited power into the hands of the Husbands. Remember all Men would be tyrants if they could [a line from a poem by Daniel Defoe, also familiar to her husband]. If particular care and attention is not paid to the Ladies we are determined to foment a Rebellion, and will not hold ourselves bound by any Laws in which we have no voice or Representation.

That your Sex are Naturally Tyrannical is a Truth so thoroughly established as to admit of no dispute, but such of yours as wish to be happy willingly give up the harsh title of Master for the more tender and endearing one of Friend.[5]

When Abigail Adams wrote that women should not be bound by laws made by a government that granted them no representation, she echoed the arguments made by the patriots who fomented the revolution against the British, a strategy she undoubtedly thought would resonate with her husband. The words "naturally tyranni-cal" were no exaggeration because women were denied most rights of citizenship: Married women could not own or inherit property (which included the clothes on their backs) and did not have custody of their children after divorce; they were legally invisible.

John's reply to Abigail could be interpreted either as a serious insult or an attempt at humor—or both. Because of their relationship, some historians are more forgiving than others.

He wrote on April 14, 1776:

> As to your extraordinary Code of Laws, I cannot but laugh. We have been told that our Struggle has loosened the bands of Government every where. That Children and Apprentices were disobedient—that schools and Colledges were grown turbulent—that Indians slighted their Guardians and Negroes grew insolent to their Masters. But your Letter was the first Intimation that another Tribe more numerous and powerful than all the rest were grown discontented—This is rather too coarse a Compliment but you are so saucy, I won't blot it out.

> Depend upon it, We know better than to repeal our Masculine systems. Altho they are in full Force, you know they are little more than Theory. We dare not exert our Power in its full Latitude. We are obliged to go fair, and softly, and in Practice

you know We are the subjects. We have only the Name of Masters, and rather than give up this, which would completely subject Us to the Despotism of the Petticoat, I hope General Washington, and all our brave Heroes would fight. I am sure every good Politician would plot, as long as he would against Despotism, Empire, Monarchy, Aristocracy, Oligarchy, or Ochlocracy.[6]

Serious or not, "I cannot but laugh," is a response every woman has feared when-ever she has the courage to speak out: The ultimate affront is to be not taken seriously. The claim that women are the real bosses because they are the power behind their husbands is also a familiar story, which placates few.

After Abigail received John's reply, she wrote to her friend Mercy Otis Warren and recounted her request to her husband and his reply. She concluded,

> So I have help'd the Sex abundantly, but I will tell him I have only been making trial of the Disinterestedness of his Virtue, and when weigh'd in the balance have found it wanting.

> It would be bad policy to grant us greater power say they since under all the disadvantages we Labour we have the ascendancy over their hearts.

president. Between 1958 and 1969, more than half did, according to Gallup polls. By the 1970s, majorities of two-thirds to three-quarters said they would vote for a woman.[7] The numbers have moved from 33 percent to 87 percent over time. The positive response to the question, "Is the country ready for a woman president?" has jumped sixteen points in the last ten years. As with most polls, the answers depend on how the question is framed.

An August 2007 *Newsweek* poll showed a significant disparity between those who claimed they would vote for a female commander in chief (86 percent) and whether they believed the country was ready for one (only 58 percent). A similar gap was found for an African American candidate: Ninety-two percent said they would vote for one, but only 59 percent thought the country was ready. In a head-to-head match up, Senator Clinton beat Senator Obama 56 to 33 percent in the summer of 2007. By January 2008, Clinton's national lead had narrowed: she led Obama 41.6 to 33.6 according to Real Clear Politics which provides the average polling numbers.

Why do voters think they are likely to vote for a black or female president but that their friends and neighbors aren't? One theory is that voters do not want to express personal discrimination based on race or gender but, given some distance, they acknowledge it in others. The good news is that the numbers have steadily improved. The numbers go way up for both women and African Americans when the word *qualified* is added, Dotty Lynch, a political analyst, observed.

The sobering news is that it is hard to place too much credibility in these numbers because voters are not always truthful with pollsters or even with themselves. As Braun described, everyone has grown up with gender and race stereotypes. That does not mean they cannot be overcome, but *overcome* is the operative word that is not on a white male candidate's "to do" list. There is no way that a woman candidate for president can avoid the "hard" issues; a governor must act decisively in emergencies to protect people in her state, but the president is the commander in chief who defends the country against all dangers, domestic and foreign. The title "commander" speaks for itself.

Senator Clinton had to reach a threshold to achieve the credibility to be commander in chief. "To be the first woman, it has to be proved, where it is assumed in men, right?" asked Ann Lewis, senior advisor to the Clinton campaign and a seasoned political advisor to both Presidents Clinton and Carter.

Polls in 2007 indicated that Senator Clinton began to overcome the toughness barrier and she emerged from the early debates as "presidential." Asked whether she would be an effective commander in chief, 58 percent of registered voters answered "very/somewhat likely."[8] No other woman has come this far, yet a substantial number continue to question how she would handle an international crisis: Forty-two percent are confident, 52 percent are uneasy. When Ferraro was in a vice presidential debate with George H. W. Bush, she was asked what she knew about "throw weights," hitting a tender spot in her résumé. Senator Clinton positioned herself early for such questions by getting a seat on the Senate Armed Services Committee, the first clue for many observers that she would run for president.

Her homework paid off, according to the primary endorsement she received in *The New York Times* on January 25, 2008. "It is unfair, especially after seven years of Mr. Bush's inept leadership, but any Democrat will face tougher questioning about his or her fitness to be commander in chief. Mrs. Clinton has more than cleared that bar, using her years in the Senate well to immerse herself in national security issues, and has won the respect of world leaders and many in the American military. She would be a strong commander in chief.

Clinton continued to have to pass particular scrutiny among male voters. In every category, more women than men believed she would do a good job. (More women than men preferred Obama as well, but the gap is narrower.) More women (82 percent) than men (68 percent) believed she would be a strong leader. Her strongest support came from younger unmarried women (54 percent). Married women and white women were the weakest, 39 percent for each. Why were these women not as excited as might have been expected by the first qualified female candidate for president?

Dotty Lynch compares this phenomenon to Jewish reactions when Senator Al Gore chose Senator Joseph Lieberman, an orthodox Jew, as his running mate. Everyone thought Jews would be thrilled. Many were not, because if he ran and lost, it would bring out anti-Semitism. "Some fear if she lost, it would bring out antifeminism, and she would wind up hurting the cause."

When I asked Ann Lewis, senior advisor to the Clinton campaign, why some women were not responding more enthusiastically to Clinton in the primary, she replied. "I don't do psychology. I chose politics a long time ago because I like to count votes. I saw the same dynamic take place in 1999–2000 [Clinton's first Senate race]. It takes women longer to be immediate and enthusiastic supporters." *The Wall Street Journal*[9] quoted Clinton advisors saying that professional women are "less inclined to see things in black and white, and seek more information before deciding."

A *Wall Street Journal*/NBC national poll taken in early November showed that 52 percent of nonprofessional women had a favorable impression of her; women who identify themselves as professionals were at 42 percent positive and 44 percent negative.[10]

Ellen Malcolm, founder of Emily's List, told me in June 2007, that Clinton does well with working women and single women but less well with the "latte" women:

> It is bizarre. It is not at all what we thought would happen. I never thought she would be the frontrunner, or the toughest and more experienced in the race. It says something about all of us. I think some of us have a very uncomfortable relationship with power. We want women to have power in the abstract, but when we see it up close and personal it makes us uncomfortable.

In New Hampshire and Nevada Clinton had more support from women than Obama. He captured the women's vote in the Iowa caucuses, 35-30 percent and did equally well with African American women in South Carolina. Clinton had an edge in the state with white women.

Television entrance polls in Nevada showed she received 51 percent of women's votes, to Obama's 38 percent. Older women were more supportive than younger women, leading to the possible conclusion that mothers have experienced "the struggle" which their daughters have not and therefore understand that the bar is higher for a woman candidate. But the women's vote is more complex. Income may have been as big a factor—or bigger—as gender in the Democratic primary.

The socio-economic gap is a big factor, explained Michael Dimock, associate director at the Pew Research Center for People and the Press. "And this gap is much larger among women than among men: the women who don't have a college degree favor Clinton two-to-one. The college-educated women are more evenly split."

Lower income women may feel that a female candidate is more likely to place priority on their concerns than a man. They are the ones who are more dependent on government assistance than upper income women, in areas such as child care, education and health insurance.

How much was the women's vote affected by Hillary Clinton's show of emotion on the eve of the New Hampshire primary? The media went wild with "the moment," showing the video again and again—her eyes welling up and her voice quavering in response to a question from an undecided woman asking how 'did she do it?' She replied, "I couldn't do it if I just didn't passionately believe it was the right thing to do." It seemed like a "just us girls" moment which permitted her to open up. Many saw her emotional response: *The New York Times,* for example, carried the headline on January 8, 2008, "On Eve of Primary, Clinton's Campaign Shows Stress." The article began to write her political obituary, as did all the pollsters and political pundits who had her running behind Obama by double digits. Two days later (January 10) the paper saw it differently. "Message of Experience and a Wet-Eye Moment, Won the Primary Day." A lot of women saw it differently too. "I think women got as mad as I was, seeing Hillary trashed," said Myra Dinnerstein. Others rallied behind her because of the possibility that her campaign for President might be over if she lost in New Hampshire. Because she was the first serious female candidate for President, they wanted her to stay in the race.

Cheryl Hanna, a Vermont law school professor, was not excited by Senator Clinton's campaign because "It's hard to see her passing the girl-friend test," which sounds like the female equivalent of the "Do I want to have a beer with this guy?" test, perhaps not the best litmus test for the presidency. An article in the November 2007 *Atlantic* by Caitlin Flanagan was entitled "No Girlfriend of Mine." She was angry with her because, among other reasons, when the Clintons left the White House, they gave their cat, Socks, to Betty Currie, President Clinton's assistant.

Hanna does not give Clinton points for courage "because she got there on her husband's coattails." Hanna raises a point of contention often brought up by women; she resents that Bill cheated on Hillary and that she stayed with him. "She should have thrown his clothes out on the White House lawn."

What is it about Hillary's decision to forgive Bill and repair the marriage that infuriates some women and not others? There are parts of the Hillary Clinton story that touch such sensitive spots in people's psyches that they jump as if electrified. Possibly his infidelity brings out the fear and pain that other women have experienced, and they don't want to see the drama played out in a public figure. Or, worst of all, they suspect she stayed in the marriage for the wrong reasons, not because she loved him but because she needed him to fulfill her political ambitions, confirming the suspicion that "she will do anything to get elected." Inquiry into the Clintons' marriage reached new heights in *The New York Times* on May 23, 2006, when a front-page story concluded, after interviewing more than fifty people, that the Clintons spent fourteen days a month together.

Some women who have climbed the success ladder rung by rung object to Clinton's candidacy because she didn't get there by herself. She is there because of her marriage to Bill. Yes and no. She is brilliant in her own right and could have made it on her own I believe, but there is no doubt that her marriage to the former President has given her enormous visibility, evidenced by his major role in her candidacy.

On December 9, 2007 *The New York Times* ran a front-page story, "Clinton Proudly Talks of Her Scars While Keeping Her Guard Up," by Mark Leibovich. The article describes Hillary Clinton's display of powerful emotions at her best friend's, Diane Blair, memorial service in 2000. It concludes "When he (Bill Clinton) spoke of Mrs. Blair, Mr. Clinton wept. 'I felt about her as I have rarely felt about anyone,'" he said. His wife, Diane Blair's best friend, held steady in the front row."

The article brings up the age-old question: Can women cry? I wonder, if she had shed real tears, would the story have been the same?

Many women believe that gender has nothing to do with it. "I would gladly vote for a woman, but not Hillary," is a frequently heard comment. Governor Sebelius said this was not a sexist attitude in Kansas. "It's a visceral reaction, they just don't like her, they can't warm up to her." Her high negatives back these statements up. What do her negatives mean? It is impossible to separate out who Clinton is as a person and who she is as a woman. She cannot shed her gender. But the voters can alert themselves to how gender affects their perception of her. Her stands on issues, her experience, her personality, her toughness, her femininity, her coldness, her warmth, her decisiveness are all debated and should be. But for better or worse, "like" and "dislike" are filtered through a gender lens that makes voters see qualities in women that they don't like, while similar qualities in a man may be acceptable or even admirable. We are beginning to know what a congresswoman, female CEO, mayor, and college president look like. We don't yet know what a female commander in chief should look like or, more importantly, act like. "More than any other figure, Hillary forces us to acknowledge that the path to power for American women is not all that clear, more an odyssey than a march," concluded an article in *Mother Jones*.[11] Can gender stereotyping be measured? Experiments have proven that scientists, professors, and musicians are believed to be either better or worse depending on their gender. Remember the auditioning violinist hidden behind a curtain that covered her feet? That's when the judges listened dispassionately to the music. Can we put a woman running for president behind a curtain? Not easily. Not for long.

What can we do to judge her fairly? A July 2007 study by Catalyst— founded in 1962, this nonprofit organization works with corporations to place women in leadership positions—"The Double Bind Dilemma for Women in Leadership: Damned if You Do, Doomed if You Don't"[12]— concluded that gender stereotyping is

> . . . one of the key barriers to women's advancement in corporate leadership, it leaves women with limited, conflicting and often unfavorable options no matter how they choose to lead.

Women leaders are perceived as "never just right." If women business leaders act consistent with gender stereotypes they are considered too soft. If they go against gender stereotypes, they are considered too tough.

The study concludes that the solution does not lie in women changing their leadership styles—in fact women's and men's styles are often similar—but "organizations have to change their norms and culture."

The double-bind is not a new discovery. What is interesting is that it continues to get confirmed. Deborah Tannen, who wrote *Talking from 9 to 5* in 1994, recently told me:

What it boils down to is our image of what a good politician is, or public speaker, or public official, or any person in authority and our image of what a good woman is, are at odds, whereas, for a politician and a man, they are the same. It doesn't mean every man fulfills that, or even aspires to it. But if he wants to aspire to it, he is aspiring both to being a good man and being a good public figure. Things like being self-confident, don't hesitate, be decisive, speak loudly, be the center of attention—all those things, if a woman does them it comes out differently than if a man does.

And, yes, she sees this happening to Hillary:

That's the double bind. I think it happens to Hillary every minute of the day. If she doesn't, then she's not a good candidate. If she does, then she's too aggressive, she's too scripted, not soft, and not feminine. Often people don't think of it in terms of women and men. They just think, "I don't like her." They don't know why. "She just rubs me the wrong way."

"Is this a subconscious reaction?" I wondered. "I'm not sure subconsciously. I would say automatically," she said.

Kathleen Hall Jamieson, Director of the Annenberg Public Policy

Center at the University of Pennsylvania, attributes Clinton's high negatives to the pillorying she has received from political talk radio show hosts Rush Limbaugh and Sean Hannity. "She is now at the point that a candidate is at the end of an election. It is no surprise. She has been the object of an election-like campaign since 1993. That's nothing to do with gender. That could be done to a man or woman just as easily." Columnist Ellen Goodman commented on the public radio talk show "On Point"[13] that all the talk radio hosts are male, as are almost 100 percent of the listeners and callers.

The author of *Beyond the Double Bind,* who tracks press coverage of some presidential candidates with her students, Jamieson said the last time they looked at a woman presidential candidate was Elizabeth Dole. "The press was still disproportionately focusing on what she wore, her age, the fact that she didn't have children, and things such as jewelry and voice."

Stereotyping has been reduced, "but is still sitting there" since Jamieson wrote her book because "women have run for offices, have won, and been successful." With Dole's race, "what happened was the run for the presidency was so short lived that we never got past the first stage of gender filtering." Clinton's sustained race is enabling her to move beyond stereotypes.

> They have made her out to be a cartoon stereotype demon, and she's a complex, articulate, competent individual. . . . When somebody can say, "I've met Hillary Clinton, she came to my part of the state, and she did very well, I've talked to her, she isn't that stereotype," that's the ultimate rebuttal.

Still the stereotype persists, Jamieson said in an interview on *Bill Moyers Journal*.[14] He asked if the old argument that you can't be caring and tough is still used against women. She replied:

> At one time there was actually an argument that if women became educated, they would become infertile . . . And the residue of that is a language that suggests that women in power cannot be women and be in power. . . . Hillary Clinton certifies herself as

being tough enough to be president, competent enough to be president, these attacks say that she can't be president because she's not actually a woman. And you can't trust someone who is inauthentic. So underlying this and underlying the vulgarity and underlying the assertions of raw sexual violence is deep fear about a woman holding power.

During Jamieson's interview, gross sexual Internet clips about Clinton were shown on the screen. The extent to which coarse language has entered the mainstream was exemplified by a clip showing a woman in the audience at a John McCain campaign event asking "How do we defeat the bitch?" McCain made no objection to her characterization of Clinton.

Gender is still "underplayed and overplayed," she observed. About Clinton's 2002 vote on the war in Iraq, Jamieson said:

> The position she took on the war has gone a long way toward solidifying her as commander in chief. If she had taken any other position, she would have been vulnerable to the gender critique on defense. She cannot apologize for her position. You've got to understand, there are still residual stereotypes, the perception that inconsistency in women or men is still undesirable in politics. It would be catastrophic for her to say she was wrong.

Jamieson described Clinton, Obama, and New Mexico Governor Bill Richardson as "unknowns" because they are different. "It's not gender, it's the unknown."

Inconsistency was the charge aimed at Clinton during an October 30, 2007 Democratic primary debate in Philadelphia. Most of the questions were targeted at Clinton by her six competitors and moderator Tim Russert. The game was "knock down the front-runner." Were they harder on her because she was a woman? Was Clinton more vulnerable to the charge of inconsistency because of the gender stereotype that women can't make up their minds? This is a difficult question to answer. Later Clinton stated that she had not been attacked because she was a woman, but because she was ahead. What became clear is that when women fight back, they become "unattractive." On public television, Mark Halperin of *Time* commented after the debate, "She got a little shrill, a little hot I thought, and that was unattractive." Those adjectives—shrill and hot—are never used when describing a man. Her campaign responded to the debate attacks by calling this "the politics of pile-on." Some male and female columnists promptly charged that she was using the gender card by playing the victim—not good for a commander in chief. Two days later she was scheduled to visit her alma mater, Wellesley, to launch "Students for Hillary." She told the 1,000 women who had been lining up since 6 A.M. that the all-women's college "prepared me to compete in the all-boys club of presidential politics." Was she again using gender to her advantage, as charged by some? I don't think so. She was telling the truth. The presidential primary is an all-boys club. When she said she "liked the kitchen," referring to the Truman quote, "If you can't stand the heat, get out of the kitchen," one commentator sniped that she was using a female metaphor. Cokie Roberts observed on National Public Radio that in some cases gender is an advantage, but it is a disadvantage as well. She quoted a poll that pitted Clinton against Giuliani. She had 56 percent of the women's vote, while he had 51 percent of the men's vote. Going head to head with Giuliani, she won.

Gender can also be an asset. "Once you pass that threshold [credibility to be commander in chief], gender is an asset," Clinton advisor Ann Lewis said. Women comprise 59 percent of the Democratic primary voters. Lewis wants to get it up to 60 percent.

"My goal, from the beginning, was to build a component of women where we build around networks that women have built over the last twenty years," said Lewis. She mentioned organizations ranging from Emily's List to advocates for breast cancer research to book clubs. Seeing Hillary Clinton as the leading candidate "is reaffirming and energizing for women. They see this campaign as one in which they are clearly included." In the primary, Celinda Lake, a political analyst, believes gender is working for Clinton because of the "huge gender gap" that she has accumulated.

The Nation (June 19, 2007) headlined a story: "What Women See When They See Hillary," which concluded that Clinton didn't have a woman problem, she had a feminist problem. Some believe that a feminist agenda would move forward more quickly if a more progressive man were elected, dismissing the impact of a woman in the White House.

"You expect more of a woman," said Medea Benjamin, founder of Code Pink, an antiwar group. Elizabeth Edwards, campaigning for her husband, John, claimed he would be stronger on women's issues. Barack Obama touted his feminist credentials in early December, stressing that he was brought up by a single mother and is married to a strong woman, an effort to woo women away from Clinton. Is it fair to expect more of a woman than a man, or is this reverse sexism?

Clinton's challenge was summed up by columnist Ruth Marcus:

> Any woman in the post-Sept. 11 world faces an extra hurdle in convincing some voters that she's strong enough to be commander in chief. Clinton has an extra challenge of appearing simultaneously formidable and likeable, commanding and not cold, smart and approachable."[15]

During a debate, a question was asked of both Obama and Clinton:

> Whenever I read an editorial about one of you, the author never fails to mention the issue of race or gender, respectively. Either one is not authentically black enough, or the other is not satisfactorily feminine. How would you address these critics and their charges if one of you should end up on the Democratic ticket in '08?[16]

Clinton responded:

> Well, I couldn't run as anything other than a woman. I am proud to be running as a woman. And I was excited, that I may, you know, be able, finally, to break the hardest of glass ceilings. But obviously I'm not running because I'm a woman. I'm running because I think I'm the most qualified and experienced person to hit the ground running in January 2009.

Anna Quindlen wrote in her *Newsweek* column:

> And every time Clinton is described as calculating or ambitious, you realize that such words are never used for male politicians because for them both traits are assumed and accepted. Old habits die hard. . . . When we imagined a woman president we imagined a new day, a new strategy, a new vision and new tactics. Even when we said it was unfair to hold women to a higher standard than their male counterparts, in our hearts we did. . . . But with Senator Clinton's candidacy, the brand new is the same old, revolution and throwback simultaneously. . . . The fantasy was that the first woman president would be someone who would turn the whole lousy system inside out and upside down. Instead the first significant woman contender is someone who seems to have the system down to a fine art.[17]

Another double bind? We expect a lot from a woman running for president; she has to change the rules of the political game, while playing by the rules, if she wants to win. And she is "In It to Win" as her website stated at her announcement. That distinguishes her from every woman who has ever run for president of the United States; they admittedly wanted to push the conversation forward, make it easier for the next woman, but they never expected to be elected. Neither did they have the credentials. Clinton did precisely what women of her generation had to do, she worked hard to have deep roots in the male political establishment. The irony is that Senator Clinton is the first woman to be qualified for the presidency, to have the requisite experience, intelligence, and judgment to be "presidential"; but having reached this threshold, she is considered by some to be too qualified, too scripted, too "same old," or too much of a politician, carrying the baggage the word implies.

How does she achieve the balance that the governors were advised to achieve: outsider versus insider? By the definition of gender she is an outsider. By temperament and experience, she is an insider.

To succeed, the formula has to be just the right mix, not too much of one ingredient or another. Even if the right combination is achieved on the balance scale, it does not work the same way for a woman as it does for a man.

Imagine that Barack Obama were Betty Obama. Would she be taken as seriously with two and a half years of experience in the U.S. Senate? A woman, no matter who she is, has to present her credentials before she can be taken seriously.

Senator Clinton's biggest hurdle with liberal Democratic voters is her vote on the war in Iraq. She has moved away from that position, but she has never apologized. I agree with Jamieson; an apology would sound weaker coming from her than it did from Senator Edwards.

Small wonder that Senator Clinton cultivated the military, in part to avoid the difficult relationship Bill Clinton had, but more to demonstrate that she has a grasp on national security. The television series about a fictional woman president entitled *Commander in Chief,* which premiered in September, 2005, had some of its most exciting scenes in the Situation Room when actress Geena Davis, playing President Mackenzie Allen, gave orders to the Joint Chiefs of Staff. At the time I believed the show would provide a preview to the real president, but the series did not last long enough to have that impact. The public needs to get used to making the gender switch from male to female commander. It can be done, as Golda Meir, Margaret Thatcher, and the thousands of female officers serving today in the military have proven. It is not yet automatic. Clinton's vote in the Senate on September 26, 2007 in favor of declaring Iran's Revolutionary Guard a terrorist organization may have been a further effort to assert her "toughness" credentials, but it also may have alienated some voters.

The press's view of Clinton has changed, according to Helen Thomas, veteran Washington reporter, who started out as a copy girl in 1942. "As first lady she was very antipress. After her health care plan debacle— which was written by candlelight, she's learned that she has to reach out to people. She has a real leg up; she's accumulated a lot of capital, and garbage as well."

It seems as if every aspect of Hillary Clinton's life has been ransacked, leaving little chance that a new drawer can be pulled out and its contents dumped on the floor. A small sampling of the stories in the summer of 2007 included two lengthy biographies; a review of the Clinton White House years, *For Love of Politics—Bill and Hillary Clinton;* articles on her Wellesley classmates and about letters saved by an old "sort of" boyfriend; a story entitled "Hillary's Mystery Woman: Who Is Huma? (Huma Abedin, her assistant who accompanies her on her travels); articles on her all-female personal staff (Hillaryland); a story on sports, "Hillary Finds Her Inner Jock"; an analysis of Hillary's faith; and innumerable articles about Bill, including a *Newsweek* cover story with a photo of him whispering in her ear, "The Bill Factor." Stories also have analyzed her laughter: Is it sincere, and does she or does she not have a sense of humor? Is it a cackle?

The top story of a week in late July 2007 was about cleavage. On July 20, 2007, *The Washington Post* described how she looked while speaking on the Senate floor (not a word about what she said) written by fashion writer Robin Givhan. Clinton:

> . . . was wearing a rose-colored blazer over a black top. The neckline sat low on her chest and had a subtle V-shape. The cleavage registered after only a quick glance. No scrunch-faced scrutiny was necessary. There wasn't an unseemly amount of cleavage showing, but there it was. Undeniable.

One blogger on DailyKos.com had this headline: "The Boobs at *The Washington Post.*" Miss Laura wrote, "*The Washington Post* is reporting—and maybe you should sit down before reading this—that Hillary Clinton has breasts." She asks, as many did, "This is news? Even fashion news?"

The good news was that there was push back. Clinton advisor Lewis thought the article outrageous enough to send out a fundraising letter to female supporters.

An example of the extent to which Clinton's words are analyzed is her August 9, 2007 statement before the AFL-CIO Democratic Presidential Forum, when she said she would be the best president. "For 15 years, I have stood up against the right-wing machine, and I've come out stronger, so if you want a winner who knows how to take them on, I'm your girl."

This statement, and her nod to being "your girl" got a huge response on the blogosphere and not all of it positive. Here is a sample of comments:

> Blogger: "A rare sighting of Hillary the human being. We're sure people will get on her for describing herself as a 'girl' but come on, don't you think she could stand to cut loose like this a little more often?"
>
> Blogger: "You're my girl, Hillary! You hold the hopes & dreams of billions of women worldwide, if you can be President of the U.S. All of us can do anything! You go girl!!!!!!!"
>
> Blogger: "GIRL? Did she say GIRL? Honey you haven't been a GIRL for over 40 years!!! I thought the feminist movement that you were and are a part of 'screamed in the streets' not to be called girls but women. Just another flip flop by the GIRL."
>
> Blogger: "Hillary isn't anyone's 'GIRL,' she is for a socialistic country, she would put this country in extreme danger."

"I'm your girl," made headlines because it achieved two things: The words made people smile (people like girls); and it showed she could "take them on," be tough and be feminine in one sentence.

The blogosphere is not always so evenhanded. Ellen Goodman, columnist for the *Boston Globe,* observed that the blogosphere is not only an outlet for liberal young people. Half of the 96 million bloggers are women, but of the 1,200 political bloggers who came to the Yearly.Kos convention in Chicago in 2007, the majority were men. Is it any surprise that Hillary got only 9 percent in most online-activist polls while garnering more than 40 percent in traditional polls?[18]

Vermont Representative Rachel Weston (D) reported that when elected officials and candidates gathered at the YearlyKos convention, there were three women among thirty-two men.

To get a better sense of Hillary Clinton as a presidential candidate, I interviewed her in her Washington Senate office on June 7, 2007. I had known Hillary Clinton as a governor's spouse when my terms as governor overlapped with Bill Clinton's, as well as during my service in the Clinton administration. And, yes, dear reader, I endorsed her for president.

Clinton said:

> I always was interested in working in politics in political campaigns and doing policy and public service. That was always part of who I was. But I didn't think that I would ever personally run for office.
>
> I thought that the roles that are available for someone like me are so diverse. I started off doing advocacy for the Children's Defense Fund. Jimmy Carter appointed me to Legal Services Corporation. I became chairman of that. I created organizations that advocated for children and families. . . . I chaired the American Bar Association Commission on Women. I considered all of that small "p" politics.

Her commitment to public service and working on Bill Clinton's campaigns often prompted remarks about her running as a candidate:

> We had a partnership where I could help him in his campaign and help him with the work he did in the governor's office. People talked to me about running all the time, and I said repeatedly, "You don't have to run for office to make a contribution in politics." That would be my first point, because not everybody wants to run for office, but there are so many ways that women can influence the political process and the policies that affect their lives.
>
> I didn't seriously ever think about running for office myself until after the 1998 election when Daniel Patrick Moynihan [New York Democratic senator] announced that he wasn't going to run. It was within minutes of being revealed that Charlie [Congressman Rangel, D-NY] called me. They were worried that Giuliani would run and win because of his strengths. They were trying to recruit somebody.

At first, she knew her presence was being requested because she was a former first lady. "I was fully aware that it wasn't because I was so evidently the person who should be senator, but because they needed somebody with a high profile to run against Giuliani," she said. "I said, no, no, no, I'm not interested."

More people asked her to run, but

> I kept saying no, I didn't think that I could do it, or didn't want to do it. I had many reasons. I did think I wanted to live in New York. That was something I had talked about with Bill and with close friends. I thought we'd have his library in Arkansas, and we would get an apartment in New York.
>
> There were a couple of turning points. I had people come to see me who wanted to set up a new foundation on women's issues around the world; they wanted me to be the first person to run the foundation. The more I thought about it, I realized I would be spending all my time talking with people in Congress and the administration about why we should care about women's health and education. Maybe I should think about running for office. I've urged countless women to run for office.

Still, as is the case with many women, the old "the time isn't right" scenario played itself out for Clinton over a period of months:

> Every time I was on the brink of saying I wasn't going to run, something would happen that I would take as a sign that I should reconsider. I got a letter from a priest who ran the local boys' Catholic high school, who wrote me and said, "I hear from the press that you are thinking about running for the Senate. We don't always agree on every issue, but I think you would be a great senator." My gosh, that was so touching.
>
> Then I went with Chelsea to New York and had a woman encourage me while I was at the *Dare to Compete* event.

In 1999, there was a screening of an HBO film, *Dare to Compete,* celebrating the role of women in sports. Clinton was the guest speaker. A high school student, Sofia Totti, whispered in Clinton's ear, "Dare to compete, Mrs. Clinton, dare to compete."

> That really affected me because I had told so many other women to go out and do it, and I thought maybe I'm not doing it because I'm afraid to do it, then what right do I have to tell other women that they should do it? That's pretty hypocritical. So that was March or April, and around May or June, I thought maybe I should put my toes in the water. I wasn't even sure that I would be any good at it or knew how to do it. There is such a big difference between standing on the sidelines, even in a very big, up close and personal way, and crossing that line yourself.

Clinton formed an exploratory committee and in July 1999 announced her candidacy from Senator Moynihan's farm in upstate New York.

> There were lots of bumps along the way, lots of problems. My dual role as first lady was often a real quagmire for me politically. But I just kept persevering. I really liked campaigning for myself. I had to learn to stop saying "we" and start saying "I." That was a big change. I found out that I really liked it. I wanted to continue to campaign and do the best I could. So it turned out well.

Now, however, she was running for president and was noticing changes in how she was being treated by colleagues, the press, and the public. I asked her to explain the differences.

> I can only speak from my personal experience. I think it is both a novelty that people are digesting and trying to come to grips with. It is the same double standard that women in public life have had to contend with—that wonderful image that Ginger Rogers did everything that Fred Astaire did, going backwards and wearing high heels. I think the judgments about my hair and my clothes and whether I look tired—I look at my fellow candidates, and they all have bags under their eyes. I am the only one dissected

over whether I do or not. But that's unfortunately inevitably part
of the landscape. You just play the hand you've got.

There are many more plusses to being a woman candidate.
There is an excitement that particularly young women and girls
feel. There's hope that older women express to me, like the
woman in New Hampshire who said to me, "I'm 95, I was born
before women could vote, and I don't want to die before I see a
woman in the White House."

Clinton said that kind of emotional response to her campaign is
more uplifting than unnerving. In fact, it keeps her focused. "There is
a tremendous amount of emotion invested in my candidacy and in me
personally, which I take very seriously. So there are, like anything else in
life, upsides and downsides, but the upsides far outweigh any challenges
that come with being a woman."

I asked if women bring something different to politics, and Clinton
said she believes they do.

I don't know if it's been verified, but I've seen enough evidence
of women making a difference on the issues that are addressed. I
know that women in the Senate have made a tremendous difference in addressing women's health issues. If it hadn't been for
women like Barbara Mikulski, there wouldn't have been clinical
trials as early as they did on women. I think that women often
try to be more collegial. We've had a good bipartisan relationship among women in the Senate. . . . We often vote along party
lines, but we try to find common ground. I have worked with
some of my Republican colleagues on women's health initiatives,
on kinship care in the foster care system, on Alzheimer's. The
decisions we have to make for ourselves, our children, our elder
relatives, the care giving falls predominantly on women, and I am
very conscious of that.

One of the best small bills that I have passed with Kay Bailey
Hutchinson [R-TX] was to end discrimination against military
widows who historically had to give up their pension benefits

when they [re]married. A lot of women in their 40s, 50s, and 60s wanted to move on with their lives but also didn't want to give up—not just the monetary benefit—but what they saw as the last link with their first husband.

And, how does she see her presidency differing from that of her husband's?

> We are different people. We share many of the same political and policy decisions. But we work differently. We make decisions in a different process. The times have changed. There is a lot I would like to continue that worked so well in the 90s, but we are in a new century with new challenges and new threats to America's future.
>
> But I will certainly rely heavily on him because I don't know anybody who is more able to look at the world, sum it up and synthesize it, and come up with assessments and practical ideas about how to deal with problems. He's probably the most popular man/president in the world right now, so I would certainly use him to deal with problems.

Her security man was beginning to hover, signaling that time was up. As for advice to young women, and young people in particular, Clinton is direct:

> Please care about politics because everything in our life is going to be affected by the decisions of political leaders, and if you don't get involved and you don't even vote, then you leave it to those that oftentimes don't understand the importance of investing for the future, of solving problems that are going to affect you in how you work and how you live.

In an e-mail follow-up with Clinton I asked her how she copes with criticism and attacks and what advice she would give women thinking about running for office but who are deterred by negative campaigns.

Well, first I'd say that public office is not for the faint of heart! The rewards of public service, however, far outweigh the negatives. I try to focus on the positive and to think about what a public life allows you to accomplish. If you really want to make a change in policy, as you know, you have to be in the arena. I'd urge any woman who is considering a run for office to remain focused on her goals. Politics is not always easy or fair or kind, but it can be noble. It is a way to improve your community and serve your country. Thirty-five years ago, as a young lawyer, I was motivated by a desire to help children and families in need. That still serves as a source of strength and inspiration today as I run for president.

And I asked her if she sees the need to balance between being as tough as a man and as soft as a woman:

I don't know that I accept the premise of your question. (And to be honest, I never really think about it!) Being a woman is part of who I am as a mother, wife, daughter, senator, and now candidate for president. I just try to be myself. This is a moment of profound challenge for our country, here at home and around the world. I really believe that we must be smart and tough, compassionate and strong. And being tough means a lot more than tough talk; it means actually setting goals for our country and working to achieve them, from global warming to global competition, rising demands for energy to rising cost for health care. I really think all of us—women and men—have to strive to do the best we can in our families, careers, and lives.

From my observations of Hillary Clinton, the one word that comes to mind is *resiliency*. After her health care plan failed, Clinton was at a low point in her life. She was assailed from every side, from "Why did she take this on in the first place?" to "How could she have done it so badly?" She was going through great uncertainty about how to define her roles as first lady and as a person. Everybody gave her advice, but only she could reinvent herself. She did it by going back to what she cared about and knew about, children and families, and sat down to write *It Takes a Village to Raise a Child,* which remained on the bestseller list for months. Both she and the voters felt comfortable when she went back to a traditional female subject and role, as wife and mother. She spread her wings again slowly, traveling widely while attending to the accepted duties of a first lady, planning menus and standing by her husband's side.

On September 5, 1995, during the U.N. Fourth World Conference on Women in Beijing, she emerged fully as a woman in her own right once again. The drama of the moment was electric. She spoke before thousands of women from almost every country in the world. As a delegate, I, along with many others, was getting soaked in the pouring rain covered by plastic ponchos that enterprising vendors had miraculously produced. We were riveted. It was as if the sun had suddenly broken through. We forgot the pelting rain, the wretched cold, and the mud rising over our shoes. We only heard her voice booming through the loudspeakers: "If there is one message that echoes forth from this conference, it is that human rights are women's rights—and women's rights are human rights."

That line was preceded by:

> It is a violation of human rights when babies are denied food, or drowned, or suffocated, or their spines broken simply because they are born girls.
>
> It is a violation of human rights when women and girls are sold into the slavery of prostitution.
>
> It is violation of human rights when women are doused with gasoline, set on fire, and burned to death because their marriage dowries are deemed too small.
>
> It is a violation of human rights when a leading cause of death worldwide among women ages fourteen to forty-four is the violence they are subjected to in their own homes.
>
> It is a violation of human rights when women are denied the right to plan their own families, and that includes being forced to have abortions or being sterilized against their will.

Every woman understood her. Clinton had addressed the most sensitive issue of the conference: How was the United States going to confront China's human rights problems, without giving offense to China, and give support to women everywhere? The White House and the State Department had not wanted her to attend the conference. It was too risky, they feared. She proved them wrong

After Beijing, she realized her impact around the world and kept up a travel schedule that was even more adventurous than that of her role model, Eleanor Roosevelt. She continued that pace almost until the end of Bill Clinton's presidency. She was the featured speaker at the World Economic Forum in Davos, Switzerland, in 1997 when I was ambassador. We had skied together, happily at the same pace, making wide turns, with the guidance of an instructor. The next day she spent time in her hotel room, preparing for her speech. That night, true to her reputation, she gave a flawless talk, without notes. Her brilliance was once again confirmed. She had to accomplish two goals for this well-heeled influential crowd of corporate CEOs and political leaders: tell them what they did not want to hear, that the world was changing, and the benefits of globalization were not being shared equally; and assure them that the United States remained their strongest ally. Her intelligence was on full display, something *The New York Times* later noted in its endorsement: ". . . we are hugely impressed by the depth of her knowledge, by the force of her intellect and by the breadth of, yes, her experience." Klaus Schwab, founder of the conference, announced after the applause stopped that he hoped she would run for president.

During the hard months of the unraveling of the Monica Lewinsky affair, when she perused the Swiss newspaper headlines, she said with surprise, "They're even writing about it here." Her resiliency was tested to a degree that few women had yet experienced. Discovering an affair is not a new experience; doing so in public is. Political life makes many demands, but the cruelest may be that there is no time or place to deal with emotional shocks; no time to express anger, no time to grieve, no time to heal away from the public eye. Debates will continue about whether she did the right thing, but there is no question that she has emerged whole and that the marriage, from what we know, remains intact as well.

Her public resiliency is evident in her ability to maintain her sense of self, and often her sense of humor, against the barrage of right-wing mockery and caricature that was aimed at her from the start.

Celinda Lake, political consultant, observed, "In some ways, because she didn't have so much likeability they could go after her without paying a price. She [more than Bill Clinton] was really their target."

Although many shake their heads over what they believe are unfair attacks, some of it seeps into the public's consciousness and contributes to her negatives.

Her ability to be a survivor, rather than a victim, is part of her story— possibly the first woman president, a leader who put up with the right-wing political machine. She extracts the positive from the negative: "I am stronger for it, I have learned from my mistakes," she said when she unveiled her new health plan, receiving more attention for it than her competitors had for similar plans.

Her story makes her candidacy both exciting and daunting. It would be too easy to conclude that voters' questions about her candidacy are purely gender based. She, like all of us, is unique; some gender stereotypes apply, others do not. The questions voters want to have answered are, "Who is she? What does she stand for?"

The public got more of an answer during the early televised debates where the consensus was that she emerged as an experienced, strong leader who could be president. In a later televised debate from Philadelphia, it was concluded that she had stumbled. She acknowledged that she had not been at her best. With her inevitability shattered, her lead began to narrow. Super Tuesday gave her victories in three delegate-rich states— California, Massachusetts, and New York—but Obama had a string of triumphs in the primaries and caucuses that followed. As this book goes to press in February, 2008, Obama has gained momentum with his message of "change," which has challenged her message of "experience". He and Clinton are locked in a tight race for the nomination, fighting for each delegate to the Democratic convention.

The issues of race and gender make good stories as well. Which is more of a barrier? Who should achieve the Presidency first?

There are no good answers to these questions, but they are reminiscent of the days of the struggle for women's suffrage when there were sometimes acrimonious debates about which disenfranchised group should get the right to vote first. Gloria Steinem pointed out in a *New York Times* column (January 9, 2008) that "Gender is probably the most restrictive force in American life, "and that women's right to vote was won half a century after it was granted to African Americans." One conclusion is that both women and African Americans have experienced centuries of struggle. Judging by large voter turnouts in the Democratic primaries, the country seems more poised than at any time in our history to write a new chapter for both.

Women Helping Women Get Elected

When I launched my first statewide campaign for lieutenant governor in 1978, I did what every candidate did—I went to Washington to raise money. After wearing out some shoe leather, I discovered that no one in Washington was interested in a woman running for lieutenant governor from Vermont except one organization—the bipartisan Women's Campaign Fund, founded four years earlier. (All the labor PACs—a traditional hunting ground for Democrats—were interested only in Senate and House races.) They sat me down, gave me advice, and provided me with my first part-time campaign consultant; Audrey Sheppard arrived at our tiny one-room Burlington campaign office one week later, flip chart in hand. We were launched!

Today, the Women's Campaign Fund has been reconstituted as the Women's Campaign Forum by its energetic thirty-two-year-old director, Ilana Goldman. It is one of several Washington, DC-based organizations that help pro-choice women get elected.

Emily's List, founded by Ellen Malcolm in 1985, is the fundraising behemoth, distributing $41 million in 2006 for female candidates who meet their criteria—viable pro-choice Democrats. The acronym stands for "Early Money Is Like Yeast," based on a close race in Missouri when Lieutenant Governor Harriett Woods lost her Senate bid; many attributed her defeat to lack of funding, both early and late.

The forerunner of these organizations, the National Women's Political Caucus, is less active today—raising $34,000 in 2006—than when it was founded in 1971 by the mothers of the feminist movement: Bella Abzug, Gloria Steinem, and Betty Friedan. It is bipartisan, supports pro-choice women, and has several state chapters.

The White House Project, founded by Marie Wilson, former president of the Ms. Foundation for Women, has determined that the best way to get a woman in the White House is to fill the pipeline. It runs

A Unique Partnership
SUSAN B. ANTHONY (1820–1906) AND
ELIZABETH CADY STANTON (1815–1902)

Susan B. Anthony and Elizabeth Cady Stanton spent all of their adult lives campaigning to give women the right to vote. They did not live long enough to see their dream realized.

Anthony and Stanton formed a unique partnership, complementing each other's skills. Stanton was the writer, the idea person, and Anthony was the strategist. Anthony traveled tirelessly throughout the country by train and by horse-driven coaches to give speeches to any group who would listen while Stanton stayed home.

Even their backgrounds were different. Anthony, a Quaker, had a supportive father who favored her cause. She never married. Stanton had to oppose both her father and her husband, who did not understand or approve of her passion for women's equality. She found time to write while housebound with seven children. Her husband was often away. It was her housekeeper, Amelia Willard, who freed her, one of the countless women throughout history who made it possible for other women to leave the house. Stanton wrote: "But for this noble self-sacrificing woman, much of my public work would have been quite impossible."[1]

Of her partnership with Anthony, Stanton wrote:

In writing we did better work together than either could alone. While she is slow and analytical in composition, I am rapid and synthetic. I am the better writer, she the better critic. She supplied the facts and statistics, I the philosophy and rhetoric, and together we have made arguments that have stood unshaken by the storms of thirty years.[2]

Anthony wrote to "Mrs. Stanton" about her difficulty in writing a speech for the teachers' convention:

So, for the love of me and for the saving of the reputation of womanhood, I beg you, with one baby on your knee and another at your feet, and four boys whistling, buzzing, hallooing Ma, Ma, set yourself about the work, Now will you load my gun, leaving me only to pull the trigger and let fly the powder and ball?[3]

Stanton replied five days later: "Your servant is not dead but liveth. . . . Imagine me, day in and day out, watching, bathing, dressing, nursing and promenading the precious contents of a little crib in the corner of the room. I pace up and down these two chambers of mine, like a caged lioness longing to bring to a close nursing and housekeeping cares. . . . [4]

Stanton encouraged Anthony's public speaking skills: "I will gladly do all in my power to help you. Come and stay with me and I will write the best lecture I can for you. I have no doubt a little practice will make you an admirable speaker."[5]

The pivotal event in the early women's rights movement was the Seneca Falls convention of 1848, when 100 women gathered. Stanton was the driving force behind the convention that produced "The Declaration of Sentiments," based on the Declaration of Independence. The women simply substituted "all men" for "King George,": "We hold these truths to be self-evident: that all men and women are created equal. . . . The history of mankind is a history of repeated injuries and usurpation on the part of man toward woman, having in direct object the establishment of an absolute tyranny over her."[6]

The only resolution that was first defeated and then narrowly adopted was, "Resolved, That it is the duty of the women of this country to secure to themselves their sacred right to the elective franchise."

Many feared that asking for the vote would jeopardize their other demands. What the women and men who signed the Declaration did not anticipate was the ridicule they would receive. In dismay, many who had signed the Declaration asked to have their names removed.

Stanton gave her first speech at Seneca Falls:

> I should feel exceedingly diffident to appear before you at this time, having never before spoken in public, were I not nerved by a sense of right and duty, did I not feel the time had fully come for the question of woman's wrongs to be laid out before the public, did I not believe that woman herself must do this work; for woman alone can understand the height, the depth, the length, and breadth of her own degradation.[7]

In November 1872, Anthony was arrested in Rochester for illegal voting. She defended herself:

> Friends and Fellow-Citizens—I stand before you under indictment for the alleged crime of having voted in the last presidential election, without having a lawful right to vote. It shall be my work this evening to prove to you that in thus doing, I not only committed no crime, but instead simply exercised my citizen's right, guaranteed to me and all the United States citizens by the National Constitution beyond the power of any state to deny. . . . It is we, the people, not we, the white male citizen; but we, the whole people, who formed this Union.[8]

campaign training sessions for women who are contemplating a run for offices from city council on up.

Republicans have their pro-choice organization, WISH (Women in the Senate and House), which does recruitment and training and is headed by Pat Carpenter. The Republican pro-life group is the Susan B. Anthony List, chaired by Marjorie Dannenfelser, formed in 1992 to counter the newly elected pro-choice women in Congress. They support women and men.

All of these organizations raise money and offer training programs for women candidates on the assumption that women running for office have less access to traditional political networks than men. They are significant political players because they tailor their advice to women, help them raise money, and welcome them into a club where like-minded women believe running for office is normal, even heroic.

There is consensus that the chief barrier to electing more women is disarmingly simple: No one has asked them to run. Some women may cling to the old-fashioned idea that you don't dance until you are asked. Boys don't wait to be asked, even though they often are by their old boy network. But if nobody asks a man to run, he is likely to decide for himself, or "self-identify." Women are less likely to think of themselves as qualified and are more likely to be uncomfortable by the seeming arrogance of declaring their own candidacy.

In an effort to help women identify themselves, Vermont Secretary of State Deborah Markowitz organized one-day sessions for *potential* candidates. She found them by asking local people, "Who are the active women?" Many were surprised by the invitation.

"I think it's a big step for them to have someone say, 'Hey, I think you'd be great as a candidate.' Then women start thinking about themselves differently. That's the most important piece of it, the invitation," Markowitz said.

A study on low-income women's community involvement revealed the same pattern. Most people get involved in community action "in response to personal invitations" that "came from friends, neighbors or others needing help with specific community activities."[9] Emily's List's answer to "the ask" was a short video entitled, "Consider Yourself Asked," featuring female officeholders who extol the rewards of public office. The

Women's Campaign Forum spread the net wider in the summer of 2007 by initiating the "She Should Run" program, urging both the Democratic and Republican political parties to recruit and support 1,000 women to run for office, up and down the ballot. The campaign asked their 70,000 members to "nominate your friends and family members. Can you think of a 'PTA mom' who should run for school board? A community leader who should run for city council?" By November 2007, they did it. Women from all walks of life were nominated—lawyers, teachers, businesswomen, mothers, and community activists. Nominators represented an equally wide range—former candidates, donors, party leaders, and community leaders. Goldman discovered, "There is a sense of honor for these women that people see them that way, they never thought of it themselves. The proof will be in the next year or two to see how many of them actually run."

The Women's Campaign Forum issued a report in 2007, "Vote with Your Purse," which revealed that women represent only 27 percent of individual contributions to candidates, party committees, and PACs. When women do give, they prioritize female candidates; women gave 30 percent of their contributions to female candidates, while men gave them 17 percent. Why do women give relatively little? In the old days, the excuse was that women did not have their own checkbooks; this is not so today.

Ilana Goldman of the Women's Campaign Fund perceives another reason: "I have to think there are women who are passionate about social change, who are incredibly capable financially, who are putting their dollars into charity because then they know where their money is going, like giving $50 for breast cancer research. They don't know that their $50 to a future governor or senator could mean $15 million dollars in appropriations for breast cancer research." Her message is simple: "Put your money where your politics are."

Emily's List is ready to write big checks for the candidates they support. What has changed for women since the organization started in 1986, I wondered?

Emily's List founder Ellen Malcolm explained,

> I think it's an absolutely different dynamic in many places of the country. Voters are used to seeing women win and serve in office.

If you go to California, there are now seventeen Democratic women in the Congressional delegation. Two of the women are senators. The gender stuff disappears when you see all these women running over and over again.

Emily's List has expanded its focus from national and statewide elections, to include legislative races, Malcolm said:

We have to control the pipeline, and we have to control redistricting. One of the most painful mistakes I have seen after the 1990 election when we had redistricting, are the stories women legislators would tell, "I was in the Senate, and my seat mate was on the redistricting committee, and I thought he would take care of me, but now I'm sitting in a Republican seat." The women were the first thrown overboard.

National redistricting will occur in 2012; states redistrict every ten years. Because of gerrymandering, redistricting has been used as a tool by both parties to create safe seats.

Incumbency remains the biggest obstacle, not only for women, but for all challengers. "In any one year you might have twenty-five to thirty-five open seats, and 40 percent are Republican. In any election, we may only have fifteen possible seats, and we put everything but the kitchen sink in to win those," Malcolm said.

The other big piece is to get out the women's vote. "In '94, when we lost the Congress, we lost because college-educated women stayed home because they were mad at the Democrats." The assumption is that if women voted in proportion to their numbers in the population, they could determine the outcome of many elections.

Former Ohio Speaker Jo Ann Davidson, now cochair of the Republican National Committee, explained, "We have an Excellence in Public Service Leadership program in nineteen of our states, which are for Republican women but not affiliated with the RNC. About 1,200 to 1,300 women have gone through the program."

What impact do these candidate training sessions have? Jessica Riegel's blog described her experience in the "New York Go Run" session sponsored by the White House Project. During her interview for the program, she was asked,

> "Do you think you want to run for political office?"
>
> "Well, um, no," I said, "but I definitely want to be involved somehow, whether policy work or writing about it." An OK answer. Spinning tough questions is smart politics, right?
>
> "It's so interesting," Lindsay (the interviewer) said. "Because whenever I ask young women who are so involved and interested in politics whether they would actually want to run themselves, most of them say they'd rather do behind-the-scenes stuff."
>
> Whoops. I guess my response wasn't that original, or effectively spun. I tried to save it, quickly sputtering, "'But maybe someday."
>
> But the reality was I could not picture myself at a mahogany desk with stars and stripes behind gleaming white teeth and stiff bobbed hair. I could not picture myself knocking on strangers' doors, or making fundraising calls, or forming a quick, coherent answer to reporters' jabs.
>
> As much as I loved learning about policy and wanted to make a difference in my community—and hey, I watch C-SPAN for fun—it bothered me that I couldn't trust myself to make the pressing decisions demanded by a political career. But it bothered me even more that I couldn't put my finger on why I felt I wasn't capable.

In addition to learning the nuts and bolts of campaigning and listening to inspiring leaders, Riegel wanted to gain "more insight into why I couldn't picture myself running":

> Liz Krueger, New York State Senator, called herself an accidental politician. "You have to know why you're doing it," Liz said. "You have to believe you can change your government and community."

Jessica wrote "A young woman from Atlanta described the opposition she faced from community members who said she couldn't get anywhere since she was not part of Atlanta's black elite. She wanted to know how to break into the club. "I have decided that I'm not going to let them pass me the torch," she said, "I'm going to take it from them."

> Peggy, a leadership trainer and treasurer of the Minneapolis Board of Education, was here to talk about power. When she said that word, the participants gave what she called an expected reaction: Ick. I attribute that reaction to the bitch complex: while the assertive man is a good leader, the assertive woman is a bitch. We don't want to be seen as aggressive, bossy or otherwise "unfeminine," we hold back. We speak our mind—but not too loudly. When editing articles for my high school newspaper, I often found myself tip-toeing around suggestions. I coated criticism with a sugar tone and prefaced every critique with "this could be really stupid, but." But I knew I wasn't stupid, and it was frustrating that I didn't trust myself. Throughout the weekend other women shared similar stories. They too cringed when other women played down their strengths, and cringed even more when they did it themselves. Together, we worked through our fears of having authority, learning to embrace it.
>
> The word "politician" connotes (besides corruption and such) a square chinned, gray-headed, slick parted white man in a suit. And that's, more or less, who's elected President. Girls of my generation (I'm 17) are told they can be whatever they want. But that message is not enough.
>
> Why can't politicians look and act like normal people? Well, they can. The women I've met this weekend are proof. But we at The White House Project knew that. It's another thing entirely for voters to feel confident that the woman who looks like their next-door neighbor, who jogs in the morning, who loves horror movies, spills coffee, organizes clothing drives, schleps her kids to soccer practice and orders take-out, is responsible, intelligent and driven enough to represent them.

Changing the face of political leadership is, to me, The White House Project's most important mission; we need to shift our perception of what a leader looks like.[10]

Finding a Public Voice

Women and girls have come a long way since the 1970s, thanks to their education, role models, and the encouragement of their mothers and fathers. That's why it is hard to understand why so many women still apologize before they speak. They drain the blood out of their arguments by prefacing their words with, "This could be really stupid, but . . ." or "I'm not sure about this, but . . ." and "I don't know if this is right, but . . ." and finally "You may not agree with me on this, but . . . " How can we strike all apologetic or tentative clauses?

Recognize the pattern in yourself and others. Rehearsing helps but is not always possible. I find that, after all these years, I still have to watch myself, substituting the words "I will" for "I would like" or "shall" for "may."

Deborah Tannen, a linguist who has done research on how women and men converse, observed that women are sometimes viewed as lacking in confidence not only by the words they preface their remarks with but by their rising intonation, using a high-pitched voice, sounding as if they are asking a question rather than making a statement. She calls the phenomenon "butterfingers." For those who remember playing hopscotch, if you make a mistake in the game and say "butterfingers," it doesn't count against you. "If you say it first—that you were totally off base—they can't use it against you because you said it first." The other habit girls and women exhibit is saying, "I'm sorry," too much. Often it's not an apology. It is a way to ward off criticism. "You always have to tell women to speak up," she added. An irksome, almost universal experience for women in leadership and management positions is to present an idea or observation in a conversation or at a meeting and then listen to a man present the exact same idea a few minutes later. "What a great idea Jim had," someone will say. It's as if the woman's remark had never been made. Instead of feeling angry or stupid and remaining silent, a better strategy is to say, "I'm so glad that Jim agrees with me." The same holds true for interruptions: Push back. Make a point of it: "I haven't finished," or simply, "Please don't interrupt." Often the interrupter is unaware of what he is doing; he is simply accustomed to controlling the conversation.

When Riegel noted that others said "Ick" to power, she had spotted a common female reaction. Arianna Huffington, cofounder and editor in chief of the *Huffington Post*, made the same observation:

> Women still have an uneasy relationship with power and the traits that are necessary to be a leader. There is this internalized fear that if they are really powerful, we are going to be ruthless or pushy or strident—all of those epithets that strike at our femininity. We are still working at trying to overcome our fear that power and womanliness are mutually exclusive.[11]

Carol Gilligan, a psychologist, said the challenge for young women is to:

> ... really say what you think and feel without losing your connection to other people—knowing your experience, not giving way to false authority, being in touch with what you know to be real and to be true, and what you care about, what you stand up for, what you call an inner voice. That has to be nurtured, educated, developed, then heard and listened to so that if it gets distorted in the public realm, in the media, you don't get caught in that distortion.

"You've talked about developing your inner voice and what I'm saying is, take your inner voice and make it your public voice," I said.

"We're saying the same thing. Your public voice should be in line with your inner voice," she noted.

Some young women writers, Verlyn Klinkenborg[12] observed, also hesitate to use their voices. "'Why not,' I asked, 'be as smart and perceptive as you really are? Why not accept what you're capable of? Why not believe that what you notice matters?'" The women responded, "Won't that make us seem too tough, too masculine . . . won't the world punish us for being too sure of ourselves?"

That fear and the fear of public speaking become deterrents for women when they contemplate running for public office. They fear not only *how* they will say something, they are anxious about *what* they will say.

Most often, women overprepare.

Former Vermont legislator Kinney Perot was so nervous about her first candidate debate that she turned down a dinner invitation from the Democratic House leader. "Sorry I have this debate tomorrow night, and I have to get prepared. Do you have any advice for me?" she asked anxiously. She expected to hear important details about a new formula for school funding or an explanation of the milk pricing program.

Instead he said, "Sit up straight, pull your chair closer to the table than you normally would, look straight ahead, don't nod when your opponent speaks, and speak up."

She was hard on herself afterward, certain that she had done badly. To her surprise, the sound system had failed half way through the televised debate. Her body language had conveyed her message. She won the election.

Nonelective Politics

Elective politics is not the only way to create change. Some people need privacy, but that does not mean they are accepting of the status quo. It is important to make a distinction between being an elected politician who is out front and being a political person who has opinions, expresses them, envisions change, and is willing to work to bring it about but who remains in the background. No one would get elected to office without voters, contributors, volunteers, advisors, and on up the line to campaign managers. I am quite certain that my career would not have been as successful without Liz Bankowski, my campaign manager.

"I'm not an out-front kind of person," said Bankowski. "I would not seek the public forum, I'm more introverted than extroverted, and I'm happy to work behind the scenes.

"It's never crossed my mind to run for any office. I mean it's unthinkable to me. It's shocking to me when people suggest that." She has discovered that she's good at what she does—getting other people elected. After leaving my administration, she became a vice president for ice cream entrepreneurs Ben & Jerry.

Her first campaign was a state legislative race that she managed for Julie Peterson against former Vermont Lieutenant Governor John Burgess, "who was a shoo-in for the seat." The campaign team of five women called themselves "the termites" because they worked quietly, going from door to door:

> The powers that be, or the mainstream, didn't pay much attention, saying, "Who are they, anyway?" That's the story throughout politics, people get comfortable and think everything is fine, and then the "Who are they anyways?" have their moment. Everybody I've always worked for has been an outsider in the process.

One of the ways to have an impact that is sometimes as powerful as serving in elective office is to work in an appointed position in city, state, or federal government. Women governors are slightly more likely to reach out to other women because that is their network but a recent study "Unlocking the Cabinet" by The Women's Campaign Forum shows that women and Democratic governors do better than their counterparts, but not by much, only by four and three percent respectively. The average for cabinet-level appointments made by governors is 31 percent. The top state is Washington (52 percent). Three states—New York, North Dakota, and West Virginia—are at 50 percent. New Hampshire and Texas are at the bottom at zero percent. I was shocked to see that Vermont ranked near the bottom at 17 percent, a sharp drop from my administration when 45 percent of top positions were filled by women.[13]

Working *for* an elected official is one step removed from being *the* elected official: That layer lowers the heat. The big difference between making a mistake as an elected official and working in government in an appointed position is that when a mistake is made, in some cases nobody else has to know. I asked Karen Meyer, a member of my cabinet, what the rewards were. "Being around power. I'm willing to admit it is intoxicating, even if you don't have it yourself, having access, being thanked." Kathy Hoyt, my chief of staff, explained, "These jobs are incredibly exciting. I love policy, I love programs—getting to affect so many people's lives." The women in my administration created a different culture. For outward appearances, we governed like those who had governed before us. We could not announce that we were different because we were women. But we knew who we were. Between "us girls," we knew we were different because all of us were doing our jobs for the first time, "playing it until we were making it," Hoyt said. There was an excitement, a joy, in that experience. We understood one another as no one else could.

An example of how women, situated in strategic positions, can make a difference was the enactment of a Family Court system in Vermont, an old idea whose time had come because Representative Amy Davenport (D), chair of the House Judiciary Committee, Gretchen Morse, Secretary of the Agency of Human Services, and advocates for children's services had joined forces.

Did these women, and the elected women I have written about, make a difference only because they were women? No. They were similar to the men before them roughly 85 to 95 percent of the time. They made a difference because they brought other life experiences to their jobs. This leads to a different ranking of priorities and, sometimes, a different way to achieve them.

Women have brought subjects such as domestic violence into the public forums that were once thought to be in the private sphere A fight between spouses was long thought a private, family affair, as was child abuse and sometimes even rape. Such assaults are crimes today because of women's advocacy and female lawmakers and the men who joined them.

Where Do We Go from Here?

Imagine a Congress that is 50 percent female and representative of the population of African Americans, Hispanics, and Asian Americans. Would this Congress have reformed immigration laws, dealt with climate change, provided universal access to health care, and not supported a guns-blazing, American-cowboy foreign policy? The answers to these questions would remain difficult, but the debate and the outcome would certainly be different from the stalemate we have today. How do we take the step from *imagining* a democratically elected leadership structure that reflects the face of America to making it a *reality?*

The simple answer is to inspire more women and people of color to serve in government at all levels, in elected and appointed positions. The question is "How?" Elected women have offered some clues by telling their stories. Most of them got the urge to get involved in politics when they were young, by being active in their communities. Others were fired up by a popular movement, such as feminism, civil rights, or the environment. How meaningful are these pathways for today's generation?

Community Service

Each generation complains that the next generation does not know what they knew at their age; that young people are indifferent, that they have no sense of responsibility and no time to give to the community. They cover their ears with iPod earpieces, and their mouths are attached to their cell phones when their fingers aren't text messaging—and sometimes even when they are. Is that an accurate description? Not completely.

One contrary indicator is the number of college students who participate in community service projects—something my generation rarely thought about. Many college graduates want to work for nonprofits, such

The Second Sex
SIMONE DE BEAUVOIR (1908–1986)

The Second Sex, published in 1949, provided the philosophical foundation of the modern women's movement for intellectuals by defining woman as the "Other." In 1971, de Beauvoir was among the 300 French women who signed a manifesto announcing that each had had an abortion, then illegal. *Ms Magazine* later staged a repeat, publishing the names of hundreds of women in America who had had abortions. De Beauvoir lived much of her life in the shadows of her partner, the French philosopher, Jean-Paul Sartre.

The following is an excerpt from *The Second Sex:*

> The terms masculine and feminine are used symmetrically only as a matter of form, as on legal papers. In actuality the relation of the two sexes is not quite like that of two electrical poles, for man represents both the positive and the neutral, as indicated by the common use of man to designate human beings in general; whereas woman represents only the negative, defined by limiting criteria, without reciprocity.
>
> She is defined and differentiated with reference to man and not he with reference to her; she is the incidental, the inessential as opposed to the essential. He is the Subject, he is the Absolute—she is the Other.[1]

as Teach for America, the Peace Corps, and AmeriCorps, if their college loan payments don't prevent them. The spirit of giving back to the community is stronger than ever; what is missing is the connection between community service and politics. Quite the opposite; community service is a "friendly, morally pure alternative to the messy, dirty, compromise filled world of politics."[2] Service learning is a form of pedagogy rather than a prelude to activism; its purpose is to develop students' ability to be caring and foster their personal growth, but there is little emphasis on changing institutions through political participation, such as voting or lobbying:

> Service clearly meets young people's need to express idealism, hope and engagement. But service, particularly when it is understood as individual action to meet individual needs, does not address systems of power. That is the role of politics.[3]

I have spoken to "Alternative Spring Break" students at the University of Vermont who spend their break not drinking on the beach but rather teaching in poverty-area schools, helping the homeless, or volunteering in New Orleans. I praise them for their social concern, but I ask them to take the next step: to analyze the root causes of the wrongs they are trying to right. I talk about politics, but I often have the impression that this part of my talk does not arouse much interest in them. It is enough, they believe, to give a few hours to a worthy cause. That is where they see results: gratitude for a hot meal, a child learning to pronounce a new word, or a simple chat with a woman who lives alone. The challenge for schools, universities, religious groups, and volunteer groups is to seize that spirit of community service and develop it into full participatory citizenship, with all its risks and rewards. That means integrating community service and political action, teaching young people what they can do to create systemic change.

Where Has Feminism Gone?

Does this new generation of women care about the issues as much as my generation, which became politicized in the 1970s? When I am asked why I ran for office, I explain I was inspired by two revolutions—the feminist movement and the environmental movement. I believed the feminists when they told me that we could do anything—have children and change the world. There was so much to be done; we were on the cusp of change, and our participation would make a difference.

"I'm a child of these movements," Donna Brazile, political commentator, told me in an interview. She secured her reputation as an activist by organizing Washington rallies to make Martin Luther King's birthday a national holiday. She discovered, "I had all these bridges. I would bridge my student politics to the civil rights movement, my civil rights movement work to congressional politics. . . . "[4]

Claire Giesen, director of The National Women's Political Caucus, said:

I don't see that same sort of passion among young women as there was in our generation. I will sound like an old fart! Many young women take their freedoms for granted. The recent Supreme Court ruling on pay equity [the Ledbetter case] makes me so damn mad. I have known pay inequity. I think young women live in denial. They don't want to know. I think sometimes the movement embarrasses them. On issues like choice, they don't think it can ever be taken away. I don't think they have a consciousness on the issues that were so real to us.

Most young women are turned off by the word *feminism.* It is passé because the world has changed. The passions of feminism have faded, but its negative connotations have not. My twenty-year-old step-grand-daughter, Lizzy, a junior at Dartmouth College, is atypical of most college students. She sees feminism as a moral issue and is puzzled by her friends who abhor the term *feminist,* fearing it would label them as aggressive, man-hating, and possibly lesbian.

An academic colleague with two young children expressed anger at feminism's promise "that you can have it all. We feel we were lied to," she said.

To understand what young women think about feminism and politics, I talked with each of the authors of *ManifestA.*[5] They define the term: *ManifestA* "was created to fill a gap in the lives of young women like me, who yearn for a connection to feminism." Jennifer Baumgardner and Amy Richards are both in their early thirties and both mothers of young children.

Baumgardner explained that the third wave of feminism (the first wave was the suffragist movement; the second wave, the feminist movement)

. . . has more of a sensibility about feminism. It engages with pop culture a lot more. The second wave was not responsive to the needs of poor women, not representative enough of women of color. It was responding to this critique. A third-wave organization would start out diverse as opposed to do outreach to become diverse.[6]

Rory Dicker and Alison Piepmeier make a similar case in the introduction to their book of essays on feminism:

> Feminism is not simply about women's issues but is a broad based political movement that seeks freedom for all those who are oppressed. *Catching a Wave* is a call to action for all of us who have benefited from feminism's gains . . . we believe that political engagement and activism are crucial components of a feminine consciousness in the twenty-first century.[7]

Baumgardner said,

> The popular media was not considered serious enough [by second-wave feminists] not a political thing, but it's a way we get messages and the way we live our lives, so it's a feminist concern. The second-wave women were pioneers in critiquing and analyzing popular culture, the way it pictured women in a one-dimensional way or the way they were left out. I think the younger feminists are more likely to be creating pop culture than they are to be critiquing it.

Baumgardner quoted a line from the singer and songwriter, Ani DiFranco, "Every time I make a move I make a women's movement." In their essay, "Who's the Next Gloria? The Quest for the Third Wave Superleader," the authors say they do not need a Gloria, as in Gloria Steinem, because they are

> . . . feminists who are rooted in their communities, who were nourished by a feminist culture (one that taught them they were as good as the boys), and who know that they are entitled to both rights and responsibilities. Each woman identified an injustice and took steps within their own power to solve it. No need to kiss any frogs or wait for the next superleader to solve it.[8]

Richards said,

> I think there is more feminism integrated into their lives from day one. I think they live more equal for a longer period of time. I think the realization that things aren't as great as they thought they were sets in later, because you can graduate from high school and go to college and get a decent job, and you are not going to be economically beleaguered because your male counterparts are usually not in better jobs. You can keep your name when you get married.

"When does the light go on? How do they express that?" I asked.

> The most common scenario is when a woman has a kid or a woman gets a job and thinks, "This isn't as equal as I thought it was going to be." So the first is questioning, "Is it just me?" which I understand did go on in the 60s and 70s. "Oh! It can't be just me. It must be a systemic problem." Now it's less about books and more about the Internet. "Oh, is there a blog addressing this?"

"There is more a sense of the individual needing and owning their own power," Baumgardner explained. "And therefore the traditional ways of looking at movements are not as forceful as they once were . . . trying to understand how power works rather than to join groups."

Baumgardner lumps political groups into her analysis:

> I've done a little with political groups like NOW. And talk about irrelevant . . . they are basically jokes. They are not power brokers. They don't have a good relationship with the media. At one point, if you were a mom growing up in Fargo, North Dakota, NOW was where you went for feminism.
>
> I think we need to look in an honest and savvy way at what the conditions are in the current time.

What About Abortion?

The one consistent rallying cry for most feminists has been the preservation of *Roe v. Wade*, providing access to safe and legal abortions.

Richards and Baumgardner may not be typical of their generation, but their more complex view of the divide between pro-choice and pro-life women distinguishes them from their mothers.

"I don't think you could try to make abortion illegal and call yourself a feminist. But I think you could say taking a life has extreme moral repugnance around it," Baumgardner explained.

Richards said,

> The language has changed from reproductive rights to reproductive justice.
>
> Historically we were fighting for one choice, for abortion to be legal or illegal. That made more people clear about what they were fighting for. But today supporting choice is so much broader than that. When you are supporting choice you are supporting women who have abortions for fetal abnormalities. Today when someone is asking, "Are you pro-choice or are you not?" you're expected to take so much into consideration. If you are a disability rights activist, you are saying, "I don't know if I support that." I don't see it as backpedaling on the issue, I see it as a natural evolution in how much more complex the issue has become.

Baumgardner said,

> When women of my mother's generation hear women of my generation speaking in more emotional terms about having an abortion, they feel really scared, like, "Oh, my God, they are identifying too much with the fetus."
>
> The emotional is allowed to be there now. I think of the deprivation of the previous generation where that wasn't allowed, out of desperation.

She added that now "You can have a child with very little social stigma. It's hard to do financially, but there is no stigma in being a single mom. That doesn't mean they should or want to be, but they *can* be."

Baumgardner said young women today have a lot more freedom. "They are taking advantage of the freedoms that were hard-won. Part of freedom is not doing things the way you were told to do them." Both women believe that young people are political, but they express their politics differently. Richards noted that young women who support an organization that funds breast cancer research "think they don't have to get involved in politics as it used to be defined—a much more traditional way. In more and more people's minds they are politically engaged."

And how do they define political?

Richards said,

> A lot of college kids are involved in banning sweatshop labor, and they lobby their university to stop doing it. And there is a national organization that gives them tips on how to do this. I see young people frustrated by the military recruiting letters that go out, and they counter that by writing letters to their schools, and they see that as entirely political.

"That is healthy, but we also need people who are going to increase the minimum wage, and that happens in Congress," I interjected.

> That connection is important to make, but it's about taking those issues and show both their *out* of Washington world and their *in* Washington world. They see it is so bureaucratic down in Washington, so they'll just circumvent it by applying to these other organizations.
>
> I think young people get really frustrated with people telling them, "Well, you weren't there in 1960, this is how it has to happen because that is what worked then." In the Kennedy era, I think it felt more like change was possible because you did all of those things that made a difference. You marched on Washington,

you sent letters, and you spoke out. You voted—that proved to turn the tide. That changed people. Now you don't see that happening so you become disillusioned that that is not the right way to solve these issues. It gives you the impression that their minds are made up and that it doesn't really matter. Dealing with young people, I don't think they realize how long political change takes. I think you are dealing with a short attention span.

And their advice for young women?
Baumgardner said,

If you have a complaint, or something just does not make sense, or something frustrates you, the solution is out there. The truth is out there. You as an individual probably can figure it out by believing you can, by making phone calls, by asking questions. The tools of social change are pretty tedious, but they are actually available to all of us.

That is the challenge, to convince young people not only that the tools of social change are available but also that they must be used by more women if we are to change the policies that frustrate them.

The conversations gave me pause—why aren't we reaching young women and getting them more involved in elective politics? What is wrong with the political system that participation does not seem worth the effort? And what is wrong with contemporary feminism? If they knew more about the women's suffrage movement—in which women labored for 100 years to gain the right to vote—would they cherish it, rather than dismiss it? Although more young people have voted in the recent primaries than in the past, young people continue to have the lowest voter turnout of any age group.

The conversations also gave me hope—these women are living in a different time; inevitably their views will not be like ours. Their concern about social justice shows that they want to create change just as much as my generation did. We have to do a better job of telling them how and why they can keep their idealism alive and create change in their time, in their way. One way is for other women to tell them why it is worthwhile to enter the fray, to be the one wielding power, rather than reacting to it.

We also have to prove to them that elected officials are addressing what they most care about. Congresswoman Tammy Baldwin (D-AZ)was excited about her first bill-signing ceremony that was "the reauthorization of the national breast and cervical cancer early detection program, which provides cancer screening for low income uninsured women—over a billion dollars—to save lives." More people need to know that this is what "politics" means.

We have to assure women that "the power of the vote changes policy," said Congresswoman Shea-Porter (D-NH). "You can make laws that protect people and punish wrongdoers. If you are interested in helping people you have the opportunity to do that every day [as a Congresswoman]."

"Senator Susan Collins (R-ME) recalled that she obtained funds for a mentoring project in a rural school in Maine. "As a result, far more students are going to college—students' lives have changed."

More rapists were put behind bars because of a bill sponsored by Congresswoman Carol Maloney (D-NY) that required processing the backlog of DNA-related rape cases.

We also must do a better job of revealing that politics is fun. "You know what we are missing with younger women; we are not sharing with them the joy of these jobs. These jobs are tremendously fulfilling. I think we emphasize the downside and forget the upside, which is at least equal, or greater," said Governor Janet Napolitano (D-AZ).

The case for getting involved in politics was made by Senator Klobuchar (D-MN), "They [young people] have to do it. Otherwise I don't know how we will get change in this place, unless we have throngs of people and young people saying we are not going to keep going on the track we are on because there won't be anything left for us, including our world."

One common denominator for elected and appointed women is that they are seen, they are heard, and when they speak, people listen because they have titles in front of their names: councilwoman, state representative, congresswoman, senator, mayor, and governor. They have legitimacy. That is what Teddy Roosevelt called the "bully pulpit."

I discovered my bully pulpit the day after I became governor-elect: My phone calls were returned within hours.

After her election, Vermont lawmaker Rachel Weston (D) found that her bully pulpit opened new doors. At twenty-five, she was asked to give speeches and serve on boards and was invited to conferences. One day she had been a recent college graduate with an MA in public administration; the next day, she was an elected official—someone to be taken seriously.

What can we do to enable more women of all ages to envision themselves, as Riegel described, sitting in front of the American flag, behind a mahogany desk and running for office, competing for a government appointment, or working for other candidates and causes?

How to Get There

What needs to be changed to make running for public office more accessible and desirable for women and other political outsiders? The simple answer to making politics more desirable is to enable women to realize that they can hold on to their ideals and to nurture the belief that change can happen. Michigan legislator Shanelle Jackson (D) knows how hard and how important that is. "Some people get the dream sucked out of them. I'm not going to let them do that to me."

Education, the culture, and laws have to change to open the doors wider to the halls of power and to reprioritize the decisions that are made within those halls to achieve a government that more accurately reflects the will of the people.

Make Public Office a Civic Virtue

Public office does not have to be a lifetime commitment. I campaigned nine times for election (lost one) and served for sixteen years. I loved serving in elective office, but I was ready for new experiences.

The Founders had not envisioned that congressional representatives and senators would be elected for a lifetime. The Congress was supposed to be the "people's house" with frequent turnover. President George Washington hoped to set an example by declining to seek reelection after having served two terms. The country pleaded with him to reconsider, but he said in his Farewell Address in 1796, "Satisfied that if any circumstances have given peculiar value to my services, they were *temporary*. I have the consolation to believe that while choice and prudence invite me to quit the political scene, patriotism does not forbid it" (italics mine).

"There is a fullness of time when men should go": This quotation from Thomas Jefferson was used by John Warner (R-VA) when he announced his retirement at the age of eighty after serving five terms.

In Roman times, holding political office was a form of civic virtue. The most famous exemplar of this was Cincinnatus, who was plowing his field when he learned he was appointed dictator to defeat an enemy; he accomplished his mission in sixteen days and returned to his farm. His statue is found in Cincinnati, Ohio, with the inscription, "With one hand he returns the fasces, symbol of power as appointed dictator of Rome. His other hand holds the plow, as he resumes the life of a citizen and farmer."

When I decided not to run for a fourth term, some thought it was a sign of defeat. "What made you quit?" someone asked me recently. I didn't quit; I went on to serve six years in appointed positions in the Clinton administration and then to academia and nonprofit work, where I happily remain.

Most people knowingly scoff when a politician who decides not to run again announces, "I want to spend more time with my family." Some actually do. Congresswoman Pryce (R-OH) announced after our interview that she would not seek reelection. The assumption was that she would face a tough race and was not up to the fight. She thought otherwise. This was the right time in her life to make a transition. Her five-year-old daughter was now in school and could not travel back and forth to Washington; her father had Alzheimer's disease. "Most people have chosen to say to me, 'Congratulations.' Sixteen years is a long time. I will find new ways to stay involved in Ohio."

Just as there is great excitement when entering politics, leaving may be exciting too. Even the prospect of a life after politics may be liberating.

"Do not always think about the next election, that gives you freedom. If I get defeated, somebody just as good will get elected. I have a life. I have six kids and one grandchild. At the end of the day, if it's all about power, it's kind of sad," observed Texas state senator Van de Putte (D).

Turnover in the House of Representatives in the first 100 years was 43 percent. Most members served one or two terms. Today roughly 98 percent run for reelection. State legislatures have a higher turnover rate, averaging 25 percent every two years. States like Pennsylvania and New York are on the low side, 10 to 12 percent; California, Michigan, and Maine are on the high side, 35 to 40 percent, City council seats turn over frequently, and many local appointed and some elected positions beg to be filled.

Term limits have been enacted by eighteen states; some have been repealed, and others are being modified. They create more turnover but remain controversial because they deprive the voters of the opportunity to make the decision whether to keep someone in office or not. The best term limits are voluntary. If more people would follow the counsel of George Washington and Thomas Jefferson and consider public life a civic duty, more people would have an opportunity to serve, creating a more representative democracy. A *New York Times* "political memo" on September 10, 2007, asked whether lifetime tenure for Supreme Court Justices should be reconsidered, a radical concept to some, an attractive idea to others.

Inaugurate a Bipartisan National Campaign to Elect and Appoint More Women

First, demand that political parties recruit and financially support female candidates, setting a minimum goal of 33 percent.

Both major parties have the right language in their platforms: Democrats endorse "full and equal access of women and minorities to elective office." Republicans support "vigorous recruitment and training and campaign support for women candidates at all levels to give women an equal role."[9]

The rhetoric is right; the action is missing. Many countries have included quotas in their constitutions, including Iraq and Afghanistan, which have 25 percent quotas for women. Quotas sometimes sound better than they are because they often are ignored if they are voluntary. By setting a clear goal, however, quotas elevate the gender issue and create an incentive to nominate and elect more women.

The United States—to the surprise of many—does have a voluntary quota system in one area: electing delegates to the Democratic National Convention, roughly 50 percent. At the 1920 Democratic Convention (the year that women got the vote), delegates doubled the size of the national committee by deciding that "one man and one woman hereafter should be selected from each state."[10] Republicans followed in 1924. After the 1968 convention, the Democratic Party formed the McGovern-Fraser Commission to reform the delegate selection process. The commission recommended that racial minorities, youth, and women be represented in state delegations "in reasonable relationship to their presence in the population of the state."

Republicans did not adopt that mandate, but convention delegates in both parties have become increasingly diverse.[11]

What has been the effect of this requirement? I saw it firsthand when I spoke to the executive committee of the Democratic National Committee in 2007. Sitting at the table were African Americans, Hispanics, Asians, and an equal number of men and women. They looked like the face of America, so different from the overwhelmingly white male members of Congress and state legislatures.

Seek Commitments from Gubernatorial and Presidential Candidates to Appoint 50 Percent Women to Top Positions

Can it be done? France did it. President Nicholas Sarkozy recently appointed seven women to his fifteen-member cabinet. Did he do it to prove that he was more of a feminist than his former opponent, Ségolène Royal? Regardless of his motive, he has included more women and more minority women in his cabinet than anyone in French history.

How can American women achieve gender equity in elected and appointed positions? Women of both parties have to demand more equal representation by forging coalitions among women's organizations and civic groups. What do women have to offer in the negotiation process? Their vote and their campaign contributions. Women voters have clout—they vote in larger numbers than men, and they have the potential to contribute as much or more money to campaigns as men. They cannot settle for more rhetoric. The time has come for action plans with time lines and numbers.

Ask Women to Run

The Women's Campaign Forum is off to a good start by asking friends and neighbors to ask women to run. The next step is to think strategically and mentor women to run in winnable races by targeting open seats.

The people who ask candidates to run are most often political party leaders, part of the good old boy network. In the past, women have been nominated in sacrificial races against strong incumbents. This is changing as women have proven their electability. The good old boys club is a network that acts like an informal "prenominating committee" composed of the men, and sometimes women, who ask the people in their circles to run. When they forget to include women, it is not because of gender bias or memory loss; it is because they fail to identify women who would be good candidates. This nonelected "prenominating committee" may be skeptical that a woman, a person of color, or a gay or lesbian person can win. Women are sometimes told, as Congresswoman Linda Sanchez (D-CA) was, that it isn't their turn. She ran and won without their permission. Once a nontraditional candidate is a winner, as Congresswoman Carol Shea-Porter (D-NH) was in 2006, the party, which had once ignored her, is fully behind her. Few party leaders could have predicted that State Representative Alisha Thomas Morgan (D-GA), an African American woman, could get elected to the Georgia legislature from a predominantly white district. Candidates should be identified by coalitions of women's and civic organizations that would spot women who do not fit a traditional political profile but may defy the odds because they understand the needs of their constituents.

Encourage Community Participation

U.S. Speaker of the House Tip O'Neill (1977–1987) is remembered for the saying, "All politics is local." And so it is. Involvement in community and volunteer organizations is important in and of itself. It is also good preparation for running for office at all levels. There is no prerequisite in politics to start at the local level before running for higher office, but for many it is a good place to start. Seats on school boards, planning commissions, zoning boards, and city councils may demand much time, but they provide an opportunity to make a contribution. The cohesiveness of a community depends on the engagement of its citizens as volunteers, activists, and candidates.

Educate Girls to Exercise Power

It all begins at home. A common background for many elected women is that a father, a mother, or both, told her "she could do anything." As Loretta Sanchez (D-CA) said, her father believed she could be "Madame Curie in a spaceship." Families remain the best role models and mentors.

These women acquired confidence at an early age and were more likely to become politically engaged if current issues were discussed at the dinner table. Girls may get better grades than boys today and are more eager to go to college, but they still are more reticent to express their divergent opinions and declare their readiness for leadership. These skills need to be taught and practiced in a safe home or school environment.

Teach Citizenship

Civics and current events courses and debating have been taken out of the classroom and stored with the dinosaurs in the Museum of Natural History. It is time to bring them back and make them come alive with interactive teaching and the creative use of technology. Mock U.N. sessions, Congresses, legislatures, and elections, which some schools have held, are exciting and interesting. Programs like Girls State and Boys State should be held in each state. The women's suffrage movement and the civil rights movement must be part of every American's education so that students understand that there was a time, not so long ago, when girls and boys like them were humiliated and died for their freedom, not only on the battlefield but in marches, demonstrations, and prisons.

The biggest challenge is how to teach students to be informed about current events. We can not simply bemoan the fact that newspaper readership is declining and young people do not feel informed enough to vote or believe that their vote will make a difference. We have to learn how to develop the lifelong habit of knowing what is going on in the world and the most basic democratic privilege—voting. Students should be given opportunities to debate and defend their positions and develop their oral skills. It's time to dust these skills off and restore them to their proper places—the classroom and, if not there, clubs and civic organizations.

Some teachers include "class participation" in their grades. A student who does not speak up should be tutored, just as she or he would be for deficient writing or reading skills. Speaking well is like playing a sport; it requires practice and the courage to assert yourself and to say what you think.

Community Service and Politics

Service learning programs have provided an enriching experience for many students in high school and college. They should be developed further to educate students about the underlying political dynamics that foster social change. The seeming political purity of academia often makes professors consider politics too crass, and possibly too dangerous, for the classroom. That divide between public policy and politics must be bridged as part of an American citizen's education.

Campaign Finance Reform

New York City has one of the best campaign finance laws, matching campaign contributions with public funds by a ratio of six to one for contributions of $176 or less.

"We hope it will help grassroots candidates," Speaker Quinn (D) explained. Several states have some form of public financing, including Arizona, which passed a Citizens Clean Elections Act in 1998 and provides full public funding for candidates who raise sufficient seed money in $5 contributions.[12] When State Representative Kyrsten Sinema (D-AZ) was asked how she felt about raising money, she replied,

> I'm a clean elections candidate. So we only have to raise seed money, which is $3,600. The way you get the money is by teaching voters about the clean elections system and getting them to give a $5 contribution to the state. It's a great way to run a campaign because, instead of spending your time on the phone dialing for dollars, you are spending your time in front of the voters' houses, going door to door.

The cost of campaigns is a deterrent for women and other outsider groups. Amy Richards, co-author of *ManifestA,* said,

> For women to run, I think that you almost have to remove the extent of money that is necessary because I think that really intimidates women. The money is huge. I think that women want to feel like they aren't going to disappoint somebody if they do that. And running for office is a real gamble. I would like to win, but I could also lose.

Yes, you could lose. But the person who contributes to your campaign knows that, and she or he is taking a gamble too, hoping that by betting on you, it will improve your chances of winning and their opportunity to have a voice.

Asking for money from relatives, friends, and strangers is not fun. I have not talked to a politician who enjoys it. Several women have been surprised to discover that raising money, particularly in smaller amounts, is easier than they had anticipated. People actually *want* to contribute to a candidate who they believe will make a difference. Their contributions make them part of the process; they have a good time at fundraising events where the food is not great and the liquor is stingy, but the conversation is ever so lively. (New Jersey State Senator Nellie Pou (D) raises all her campaign money at fundraisers.) They are realists; they know the process of financing campaigns is flawed, but they also understand that this how it works. Most citizens—except for a few large donors and some (not all) political action committees—expect nothing specific in return. What they may ask for is a phone call returned, an e-mail answered, or fifteen minutes of time. That access is valuable, but it only requires an ear, not a soul.

Large contributions are a different matter because the line between access and favoritism may disappear. Money has long played a role in elections. Only 800,000 property owners, out of a population of 4,000,000, could vote during the early days of the Republic. Campaign finance reform originated in the Congress in 1971 with the Federal Election Campaign Act. The most recent effort was the McCain-Feingold Act, which prohibited unregulated contributions, or "soft money," but was weakened by a recent Supreme Court decision.

A coalition of organizations, including Common Cause, Public Campaign, Public Citizen, and Public Agenda, advocates public financing. I am on the advisory board of Just $6, Americans for Campaign Reform, a bipartisan organization that supports public financing of federal elections. Campaign finance reform—if it were to be successful—would provide the greatest incentive for more average Americans—the bottom 99 percent of us, as Congresswoman Shea-Porter (D-NH) puts it—to run for office.

Establish a Mentoring Bank

Women often do not know where to turn for advice when they consider running for office. How-to books, campaign training programs, and the Internet provide valuable information, but none of these sources describes what it is *like* to run for office and serve, otherwise known as the inside scoop.

In states that have a high percentage of elected women, role models are more accessible. In states with few female elected officials, it is much more difficult to contact someone who is able to share the realities of political life and prepare the person for what to expect when she holds her first press conference. A mentoring bank would ask present and former elected officials, at all levels, and other prominent women in the community to agree to be listed as mentors. The bank could ask every elected woman to make a pledge that if she decides not to run for reelection she will recruit a woman to take her place. That is why Vermont Representative Helen Head (D) decided to run: "Two former female representatives asked me to run, and then I called my predecessor, Susan Wheeler, then Gaye Symington, and Madeleine Kunin. All encouraged me."

Teach Negotiating Skills

Politics is not confined to the halls of Congress; it exists in academia, in the corporate world, in science, and in the nonprofit world. But the word is rarely printed in raised letters, sensitive to the touch. Politics is power, deciding who has it. Negotiations about the apportionment of power take place in friendships and marriages and between nations. They take place between workers and managers.

Several studies have shown that one reason women continue to make lower salaries than their male counterparts, at all levels, is that they fail to negotiate for their raises and benefits as effectively as men. Instead of bargaining for a higher starting salary, they are more likely to accept the offered low salary. In a study of Carnegie Mellon master's degree graduates, only 7 percent of the women, but 57 percent of the men, negotiated their salaries. Those who did raised their salaries by an average of $4,053.[13] That conclusion was confirmed by a study in which a group of volunteers were given $2 to $10 for their time. Men asked for more money at eight times the rate of women.[14]

The power to negotiate depends on the confidence and skills of the individuals doing the negotiating. Negotiating means risk taking; the offer may be rejected. The job offer itself may be withdrawn. A woman who negotiates for a higher salary cannot be intimidated by authority. Neither can she allow herself to feel "unladylike" or ungrateful for asking for more money.

When I got my first part-time teaching job after my fourth child was born, I was so grateful to be employed that I didn't object when they asked me to teach three classes of first-year English with fifty students in each section. I had little choice, and that is sometimes the case for women. But it is not always true. The best outcome of negotiation is winning; the most likely is compromise, which is better than nothing.

Change the Political Culture through Outreach and Training

Women make up 23.5 percent of state legislatures across the country—once we stop using decimal points, we will know we have achieved a critical mass. The average is not the norm. Percentages range from the highest—37.8 percent for Vermont and 35.8 percent in New Hampshire—to the lowest, 8.8 percent in South Carolina. Three states have two female senators: Washington, California, and Maine. And four states have never elected a woman to either the Senate or the House: Mississippi, Iowa, Delaware, and Vermont.

New Jersey proved in 2007 that change is possible. The state legislature ranked 43rd in the nation in the percentage of women in 2004. The Rutgers Center for American Women and Politics decided to do something about it by training women to run. Today, New Jersey ranks 15th. How did it happen? "This is a classic example of preparedness meeting opportunity," explained Debbie Walsh, the Center's director. "When open seats became available, women were ready to run."[15]

In some states it is more difficult than in others to break the gender barrier because of the political culture. Some states have a more traditional view of the role of women, not only in politics but in society. This appears to be the case in the Midwest and to a greater extent in the South. Historian Anne Firor Scott explained that the South was slow to develop a suffrage movement because "many of the early suffragists were abolitionists; the idea of woman's rights was anathema in the South."[16] The image of the Southern lady persists in some ways "not as a complete prescription for a woman's life, but as a style which as often as not was a façade to ward off criticism of unladylike independence or to please men."[17]

Why the disparities? Part of the answer is that running for public office appears to be contagious. Washington not only has two female senators, it also has a female governor and a high percentage of female legislators and government appointees. Arizona, New Hampshire, and Vermont have had women governors; they also rank at the top in the percentage of women legislators. A silent mentoring process is going on in those states that have a history of electing women. It becomes the norm, rather than the exception, when their portraits hang on the walls.

It is time for women's portraits to be hung everywhere. Will it make a difference if they are, not only for women, but for all the citizens of America?

Ilene Lang of Catalyst cites proof that the Fortune 500 companies with the highest percentage of women in senior leadership outperform the companies with the lowest. Why? Because they not only look different, but they think differently, and they value collaboration and innovation.

It may just be that this is what America needs to bridge our divides and create change. Women will not have all the answers, but they are sure to inject new talent, ideas, and optimism into a political system desperately in need of all three.

Acknowledgments

My husband, John W. Hennessey Jr., urged me to write this book, assisted me with research and editing, and encouraged me every step of the way. He is the most enthusiastic supporter of women in leadership I know.

I am grateful to my former student, and now legislator, Rachel Weston, who assisted with interviews and research and became an important sounding board. Melissa Kalinen, a future officeholder, assisted with interviews and research and provided important feedback. I appreciate the work of Emily Bishop, a former student and research assistant, and Dzeneta Karabegovic, translator. I thank all my former students in my seminar "Women, Politics, and Leadership," who provided the motivation for this book.

I thank the University of Vermont for having provided me with the time and space to write this book and give special thanks to the staff of the Political Science Department, Carol Tank-Day and Candace Smith, for rescuing me from many computer crises. I thank Professor Lynne Bond of the psychology department for giving me helpful comments, and Professor Caroline Beer for providing information on women in Latin America.

I am grateful to the Vermont Studio Center in Johnson, Vermont, which enabled me to have two weeks of uninterrupted time to finish the book.

The Eagleton Institute for the Center for American Women in Politics at Rutgers University was a great resource for information and contacts. All the women who made themselves available for interviews deserve special thanks; without them this book would be an empty cover.

Resources

American Association of University
  Women
1111 Sixteenth Street, NW
Washington, DC 20036
Phone: (800) 326-AAUW (2289)
helpline@aauw.org

Catalyst
120 Wall Street, 5th Floor
New York, NY 10005
Phone: (212) 514-7600
Fax: (212) 514-8470
info@catalyst.org
Offices are also in San Jose, CA; Zug,
  Switzerland; and Toronto, Canada.

Catalyst is a nonprofit research and
advisory organization working globally
with businesses and the professions to
build inclusive environments and expand
opportunities for women and business.

The Center for American Women and
  Politics
Eagleton Institute of Politics
Rutgers University
191 Ryders Lane
New Brunswick, NJ 08901-8557
Phone (732) 932-9384
Fax (732) 932-0014
www.cawp.rutgers.edu

The Center for American Women and
Politics (CAWP) is the best resource for
information about women in politics,
past and present. Its website is rich with
facts and research. The site includes a
complete list of "Web Sites of Interest."

EMILY'S List (Washington, DC)
1120 Connecticut Avenue NW, Suite
  1100
Washington, DC 20036
Phone: (202) 326-1400
Fax: (202) 326-1415
www.emilyslist.org

EMILY'S List (San Francisco, CA)
100 Spear Street, Suite 1510
San Francisco, CA 94105
Phone: (415) 658-0700
Fax: (415) 658-0707

EMILY stands for Early Money Is Like
Yeast. It supports pro-choice Democratic
women at the state and federal level with
campaign funds and training programs
and getting out the vote.

Feminist Majority Foundation (East
  Coast)
1600 Wilson Boulevard, Suite 801
Arlington, VA 22209
703-522-2214
703-522-2219 (fax)

Feminist Majority Foundation (West
  Coast)
433 S. Beverly Drive
Beverly Hills, CA 90212
310-556-2500
310-556-2509 (fax)
www.feminist.org

Girls Inc.
120 Wall Street
New York, NY 10005-3902
Phone: 1-800-374-4475
www.girlsinc.org

Girl Scouts of the USA
420 Fifth Avenue
New York, New York, 10018-2798
Phone: (800) 478-7248 or
    (212) 852-8000
www.girlscouts.org

Girls State Program
7100 Connecticut Avenue
Chevy Chase, MD 20815
www.girlsnation-auxiliary.com

Girls State and Girls Nation are
sponsored by the American Legion
Auxiliary. The website lists states and
dates with Girls State sessions and
is maintained by the National 4-H
Conference Center.

**National Council of Women's
    Organizations**
1701 K Street NW, Suite 400
Washington, DC 20036
Phone: (202) 293-4505
Fax: (202) 293-4507
www.womensorganizations.org

The National Council of Women's
Organizations (NCWO) includes more
than 200 member organizations. They
support policies that address girls' and
women's economic, legal, social, and
physical well-being.

National Organization for Women
1100 H Street NW, 3rd Floor
Washington, DC 20005
Phone: (202) 628-8NOW (8669)
Fax: (202) 785-8576
www.now.org

National Women's Political Caucus
P.O. Box 50476
Washington, DC 20091
Phone: (202) 785-1100
Fax: (202) 370-6306
info@nwpc.org

The National Women's Political Caucus
(NWPC) is a multipartisan grassroots
organization dedicated to increasing
women's participation in the political
process by recruiting, training, and
supporting women who seek elected and
appointed offices.

PLEN
1001 Connecticut Avenue, NW, Suite
    900
Washington, DC 20036
Phone: (202) 872-1585
Fax: (202) 872-0141
www.plen.org

PLEN, Public Leadership Education
Network, is a national consortium of
women's colleges that places women
students in public policy internships
with research, government, and advocacy
organizations.

Susan B. Anthony List
1800 North Kent Street, Suite 1070
Arlington, VA 22209
information@sba-list.org

The Susan B. Anthony List trains
pro-life and political activists to run
grassroots campaigns to end abortion.
The candidate fund supports pro-life
women candidates.

Wellesley Centers for Women
Wellesley College
106 Central Street
Wellesley. MA 02481
Phone: (781) 283-2500
WCW@wellesley.edu

Wellesley Centers for Women brings together an interdisciplinary community of scholars engaged in research, training, analysis, and action, looking at the world through the eyes of women.

The White House Project
434 West 33rd Street, 8th Floor
New York, NY 10001
Phone: (212) 261-4400
Fax: (212) 904-1296
www.thewhitehouseproject.org

The Project is a nonpartisan, nonprofit organization that aims to advance women's leadership in communities and sectors—up to the U.S. presidency—by filling the leadership pipeline with a diverse group of women.

The WISH List
333 North Fairfax Street, Suite 302
Alexandria, VA 22314
Phone: (703) 778-5550
Fax: (703) 778-5554
WISH@thewishlist.org

WISH stands for Women in the Senate and House. It raises money to identify, train, and support pro-choice Republican women to public office at all levels.

The Women's Campaign Forum
734 15th Street, NW, Suite 500
Washington, DC 20005
Phone: (202) 393-8164
Fax: (202) 393-0649
www.wcfonline.org

The Forum supports women leaders in politics as volunteers, donors, campaign professionals, and most importantly, candidates. It is pro-choice, nonprofit, and nonpartisan and helps recruit and train women candidates.

Political Parties

Democratic National Committee
www.democrats.org

Republican National Committee
www.rnc.org

National Republican Senatorial Committee
www.nrsc.org

Democratic Senatorial Campaign Committee
www.dscc.org

Democratic Congressional Campaign Committee
www.dccc.org

National Republican Congressional Committee
www.nrcc.org

Notes

All the quotations, unless otherwise noted, were interviews conducted by me and my assistants between May and October 2007.

Introduction

1. First National Women's Conference, Houston, Texas, November 18–21, 1977.
2. Jessica Riegel, The White House Project, "Inside Go Run New York," blog. thewhitehouseproject.org/2007/08/07inside-go-run-new-york. August 7, 2007.

Chapter 1

1. Maureen Dowd, "Obama's Big Screen Test," *The New York Times*, February 21, 2007.
2. Lyndall Gordon, *Vindication, A Life of Mary Wollstonecraft*, p. 125. New York: HarperCollins Publishers, 2005.
3. Alice S. Rossi, *The Feminist Papers*, p. 29. Boston: Northeastern University Press, 1988.
4. Ibid, p. 32.
5. Ibid, p. 37.
6. Gordon, p. 389.
7. Alice S. Rossi, *The Feminist Papers*, p. 58. Boston: Northeastern University Press, 1988.

Chapter 2

1. Jennifer I. Lawless and Richard L. Fox, *It Takes a Candidate: Why Women Don't Run for Office*, p. 11. New York: Cambridge University Press, 2005.
2. Ibid., p. 2.
3. SurveyUSA poll, www.surveyusa.com, September 2005.
4. Fox, Margalit, "Betty Friedan, Who Ignited Cause in 'Feminine Mystique,' Dies at 85," *The New York Times*, Feb. 5, 2006. (http://www.nytimes.com/2006/02/05/national/05friedan.html)
5. "Excerpts from *The Feminine Mystique*, "The Problem That Has No Name," p. 11. New York: Dell Publishing Company, 1963.
6. Ibid., p. 364.
7. Ellen Carol DuBois, editor, *Elizabeth Cady Stanton, Susan B. Anthony Correspondence, Writings, Speeches*, p.28. Boston: Northeastern, 1992. Elizabeth Cady Stanton, "Address to the First Anniversary of the American Equal Rights Association," May 9, 1867.
8. Author conversation with Mary V. Hughes of Stanton Hughes. San Francisco, California, June 26, 2007.
9. Catherine Whitney. *Nine and Counting: The Women in the Senate*, p. 215. New York: HarperCollins, 2001.
10. Whitney, p, 99.
11. Ibid, p. 101.
12. Whitney, p. 40.

Chapter 3

1. Whitney, p. 55.
2. Jewish Women's Archive. Available at www.jwa.org/exhibits/wov/abzug/subway.html
3. Jewish Women's Archive www.jwa.org/exhibits/wov/abzug/
4. Whitney, p. 44.
5. Ibid., pp. 28–30.
6. Ibid., p. 170.
7. Whitney, p. 118.

Chapter 4

1. Lee Iacocca and Catherine Whitney, *Where Have All the Leaders Gone?* Scribner, New York 2007.
2. Jakobsh, Doris R., *Encyclopedia of Leadership*, Vol. 4, page 76. George R. Goethals, General Editor, Georgia J. Sorenson, General Editor, James MacGregor Burns, Senior Editor. SAGE Publications, Thousand Oaks, London, New Delhi 2004.
3. Ibid., p. A.2004.
4. Leadership Effectiveness and Gender, p 14. Christine R. Gedney, Major, USAF. A Research Report Submitted to the Faculty in Partial Fulfillment of the Graduation Requirements, Air Command and Staff College, Air University, Maxwell Air Force Base, Alabama. April 1999.
5. Tracey T. Manning, "Gender, Managerial Level, Transformational Leadership and Work Satisfaction," *Women in Management Review*, Vol. 17, Number 5 (2002), p. 208.
6. Robert Kabacoff and Helen Peters. "The Way Women and Men Lead—Different, but Equally Effective," *Management Research Group*, 1998.
7. Martha J. M. Kelley, Lt Col, U.S. Air Force, *Gender Differences and Leadership, a Study*, p. 29. Air War College, Air University Maxwell Air Force4 Base, Alabama. 1997.
8. Ibid., p. 29.
9. Jacobsh, p. 78.
10. Kathleen Hall Jamieson. *Beyond the Double Bind*. New York: Oxford University Press, 1995.
11. Alice H. Eagly and Linda L. Carli. "Women and the Labyrinth of Leadership," *Harvard Business Review*, September 2007, p. 66.
12. Excerpts from "Conversations with Alice Paul: Woman Suffrage and the Equal Rights Amendment, conducted by Amelia R. Fry." The Regents of the University of California, 1976.
13. Ibid.
14. Encyclopedia of Leadership. p. 1664 Karen O'Connor and Alixandra B. Yanus.
15. Eagly and Carli, p. 429.
16. *The New York Times*, Friday, November 17, 1978, op ed page.
17. Daniel Goleman. *Emotional Intelligence*, Appendix B 253, 254. New York: Bantam Books, 2006.
18. Encyclopedia of Leadership. p. 1656. Candida G. Brush
19. Judith Rosener, " Ways Women Lead". p. 68 *Harvard Business Review*, Nov.-Dec, 1990.
20. Excerpts from a speech at the Miami Leadership Round Table, Miami Dade University. Sept. 10, 2007.
21. Carly Fiorina. *Tough Choices*, p. 39. New York: The Penguin Company, 2006.

22. *Report Prepared for the Canadian Forces Leadership Institute, Leadership Development Programs in the Canadian Armed Forces,* reference number: DND 2002/0628, pp. 8, 11, 17. March 31, 2003.

23. Ibid., p. 21.

24. Ibid., p. 28.

25. *Harvard University Gazette* online, May 3, 2007. Access article at: www.news.harvard.edu/gazette/2007/05,03/99-ivypresidents.html

26. Jesse Harlan Alderman, Associated Press Writer, May 3, 2007. *The Boston Globe*

27. The law states: "No person in the United States shall, on the basis of sex, be excluded from participation in, be denied the benefits of, or be subjected to discrimination under any educational program or activity receiving Federal financial assistance."

28. The requirements are defined as: (1) participation opportunities; (2) athletic financial assistance, and (3) equal treatment/benefits. The legislation was passed by the U.S. Congress, June 23, 1972.

29. *2005 Annual Report.* Available at Womenssportsfoundation.org.

30. Mona Harrington and Helen Hsi. *A Report of MIT Workplace Center Surveys on Comparative Career Decisions and Attrition Rates of Women and Men in Massachusetts Law Firms,* Massachusetts Institute of Technology, Spring 2007.

31. Ibid, pp. 4, 5.

32. *The Christian Science Monitor,* June 30, 2003.

33. MacNeil/Lehrer Productions, *OnLine NewsHour,* "Pivotal Justice," July 1, 2005.

34. http://www.yubanet.com/cgi-bin/artman/exec/view.cgi/22/55069.

35. Jennifer Freyd, Department of Psychology, University of Oregon. "References on Chilly Climate for Women Faculty in Academe." Available at http://dynamic.uoregon.edu//chillyclimate.html. May 13, 2003.

36. Ibid.

37. Sumru Erkut. "Leadership: What's Motherhood Got to Do with It?" Wellesley, MA: Wellesley Centers for Women, 2006, p. 3.

38. Ibid., p. 7.

Chapter 5

1. After the United States declared war on Japan during World War II, 110,000 Japanese Americans were taken from their homes and sent to internment camps for "reasons of national security."

2. "Women, State Legislators: Past, Present and Future." New Brunswick, N.J.: Center for American Women and Politics, Eagleton Institute of Politics, Rutgers University, 2001.

3. Ibid., p. 5.

4. Deborah L. Rhode. *The Difference "Difference" Makes.* Stanford, CA: Stanford University Press, 2003, p. 22.

Chapter 6

1. "Mom's in the House, With Kids at Home," July 19, 2007. Available at WashingtonPost.com.

2. "Climbing," *Dartmouth Alumni Magazine,* November/December 2007, p. 49.

3. "Member Mom." *National Journal,* April 2007.

4. Op cit., *Washington Post.*

5. Governor Jennifer Granholm, teleconference at governor's training session, Washington, DC, June 2007.

Chapter 7

1. Catherine H. Roehig, Renee Dreyfus, and Cathleen A. Keller. "Introduction," in *Hatshepsut, from Queen to Pharaoh,* p. 9. New York: Metropolitan Museum of Art, and New Haven and London, Yale University Press, 2006.

2. Ibid., p. 4.

3. "About COM: Women's History." Available at http://womenshistory.about.com/od/quotes/a/m_thatcher.htm?p=1. July 2, 2007.

4. "NewYork Times.com, On This Day." Available at www.nytimes.com/learning/general/onthisday/20071119.html.

5. BBC News. Available at http:newsvote.bbc.co.uk/mpapps/pagetools/print.news.bbc.co.uk/2/hi/south_Asia/3960877.

6. Metropolitan State College of Denver website. Available at www.mscd.edu/~golda/Norm%20Stuff/CENTER%20FAVORITES.html.

7. "About COM: Women's History." Available at http://womenshistory.about.com/od/quotes/a/golda_meir.htm.

8. Roger Cohen, "Her Jewish State." *The New York Times Magazine* July 8, 2007, p. 4.

9. "About COM: Women's History." Available at www.womenshistory.about.com/od/quotes/a/corazon_aquino.htm

10. Available at www.msnbc.com/id/10865705.

11. Available at www.com/mld/philly/news/13649013.

12. Available at www.newzimbabwe.com/pages/opinion107-13670.13670.html.

13. "For Liberia's 'Iron Lady,' Toughness Part of the Territory," *Washington Post,* Dec. 16, 2005.

14. The Aspen Ideas Festival, Dialogue, Summer 2007.

15. *Time* magazine website. Available at www.time.com/time/magazine/article/0,9171,1132777,00.html.

16. Jon Lee Anderson, "Letter from Liberia," *The New Yorker,* March 27, 2006, p. 63.

17. Ibid., p. 65.

18. Monte Reel. "Female, Agnostic and the Next Presidente?" *Washington Post,* Dec. 10, 2005.

19. AFX News Limited, AFX International Focus, March 9, 2007.

20. Available at www.opendemocracy.net/node/3183/print

21. Radio Coopertiva. Available at www.cooperativa.cl/p4noticias/site/artic/20041224/pags/20041224122418htm.

22. *Yes!* Summer 2007. Available at www.yesmagazine.org/article.asp?id=1734.

23. Mark R. Thompson and Lyudmila Lennartz. "The Making of Chancellor Merkel." 'German Politics,' Vol. 15, No.1, March 2006, pp. 105, 110.

24. Susanne Gaschke. "Was Merkel so anders macht." *Die Zeit.* August 25, 2005.

25. Myra Marx Ferree. "Angela Merkel: What Does It Mean to Run as a Woman?" *German Politics and Society, 24* (Spring 2006): pp. 97–110.

26. Ibid., p. X.

27. Thompson and Lennartz, p. 101.

28. Ibid., p. X.

29. Ibid., p. 105.

30. Ibid.,p. 106.

31. Ibid., p. 99.

32. Gro Harlem Brundtland. *Madame Prime Minister, Living a Life in Power and Politics,* p. 173. New York: Farrar, Straus and Giroux, 2002.

33. Brandeis University, "Women Leaders and Transformation in Developing Countries." Available at www.unet.brandeis.edu/~dwilliam/profiles/brundtland.htm.

34. Elaine Sciolino "Before French Vote, Candidate Asks Women to Pick Her," *The New York Times,* April 19, 2007.

35. "A Conservative to Face a Socialist in French Presidential Runoff Election" *The New York Times,* April 23, 2007, p. A10.

36. Maureen Dowd, "Ségomania," *The New York Times,* dateline Lille, France; May 7, 2007.

37. *L'Express,* May 25, 2007

38. *L'Express,* June 8, 2007

39. Thomas E. Skidmore and Peter H. Smith. *Modern Latin America,* 5th edition, p. 343. New York and Oxford: Oxford University Press, 2001.

40. Ibid, p. 345.

41. Additional information provided by Caroline Beer, Assistant Professor of Political Science, University of Vermont.

42. Alexei Barrionneuvo, "News of the Week in Review: The Political Tango, Women in the Lead." *The New York Times,* November 4, 2007, p. 4.

43. Paper written by Antoinette Habinshuti, a Rwandan student at the University of Vermont.

Chapter 8

1. Carolyn G. Heilbrun. *The Education of a Woman—The Life of Gloria Steinem,* p. xxii. New York: The Dial Press, 1995.

2. Ibid., p.xxii.

3. Ibid., p. 355.

4. Gloria Steinem, *Outrageous Acts and Everyday Rebellions,* p. 108. New York: Henry Holt and Company, 1995.

5. Ibid., p. 122.

6. Available at www.brainyquote.com.

7. Gloria Steinem, Commencement address at Smith College, June 19, 2007.

8. The others were Governor Jane D. Hull, Treasurer Carol Springer, and Superintendent of Public Instruction Lisa Graham Keegan. All were Republicans, except Napolitano.

9. Eleanor Clift and Tom Brazaitis. *Madam President: Women Blazing the Leadership Trail,* p. 79. New York and London: Routledge, 2004.

Chapter 9

1. Ruth B. Mandel. *She's the Candidate!*, p. 1. New Brunswick, NJ: Center for American Women and Politics, Eagleton Institute of Politics, Rutgers University, 2007.

2. Ibid, p. 2.

3. Moseley Braun had not endorsed either Clinton or Obama at the date of this conversation, August 7, 2007.

4. David McCullough. *John Adams*, p. 57. New York: Simon & Schuster, 2001.

5. Ibid., p. 104.

6. Alice S. Rossi. *The Feminist Papers*, p. 11. Boston: Northeastern University Press, 1988.

7. Mandel, p. 6.

8. CBS News/*New York Times* Poll, July 9–17, 2007.

9. *The Wall Street Journal*, Dec. 8, 2007, p. 1.

10. Ibid., p. 8.

11. *Mother Jones* website Available at www.motherjones.com/news/feature/2007/01/harpy_hero_heretic_hillary-3.html.

12. Catalyst.org website. Available at www.catalystwomen.org/pressroom/pressdoublebind.shtml. July 17, 2007.

13. Interview aired on Dec. 10, 2007.

14. Interview aired on Dec. 7, 2007.

15. "Pretty Formidable in Pink" Ruth Marcus, *The Washington Post*, July 25, 2007, p. A15.

16. MSNBC, YouTube debate, July 23, 2007.

17. Anna Quindlen, "The Brand New And Same Old" *Newsweek*, May 28, 2007. p. 74

18. *The Burlington Free Press*, August 13, 2007, p. 5A.

Chapter 10

1. Alice S. Rossi. *The Feminist Papers*, p. 382. Boston: Northeastern University Press, 1988.

2. Ibid., p. 379.

3. Ibid., pp. 61–62.

4. Ibid., p. 380.

5. Ellen Carol DuBois. *The Elizabeth Cady Stanton-Susan B. Anthony Story Reader, Correspondence, Writings, Speeches*, p. 54. Boston: Northeastern University Press, 1992.

6. Rossi, p. 416.

7. DuBois, p. 28.

8. Ibid, pp. 152-154.

9. Lynne A. Bond, Sheila Kirton-Robbins, and Lynne Babchuck. "Effects of Women's Community Leadership on Leaders' Own Development and Well-Being," p. 18. Uncorrected proof. Draft for publication.

10. The White House Project, press release, "Inside Go Run New York," August 7, 2007.

11. Arianna Huffington. "My Journey to the Top," *Newsweek*, November 15, 2007, p. 49.

12. Verlyn Klinkenborg, "Politeness and Authority at a Hilltop College in Minnesota" *The New York Times*, October 15, 2007.

13. The methodology used may not be comparable to my term as governor.

Chapter 11

1. Simone de Beauvoir, *The Second Sex*, pp. 675–676. From Simone de Beauvoir, *The Second Sex*. Translated by H. M. Parshley. New York, Alfred A. Knopf, 1953.

2. Tobi Walker. "Service as a Pathway to Political Participation: What Research Tells," *The Pew Charitable Trusts, Applied Developmental Science*, Vol. 6, No. 4 (2002), p. 183.

3. Ibid., p. 188.

4. Donna Brazile. *Cooking with Grease*, p. 79. New York: Simon & Schuster, 2004.

5. Jennifer Baumgardner and Amy Richards. *ManifestA: Young Women, Feminism, and the Future*. New York: Farrar, Straus and Giroux, 2000. xxvii.

6. Interview.

7. Rory Dicker and Alison Piepmeier, eds. *Catching a Wave, Reclaiming Feminism for the 21st Century*. Boston: Northeastern University Press, 2003. p. 8.

8. Ibid., p. 169.

9. Barbara Burrell. "Political Parties and Women's Organizations," in Susan Carroll and Richard L. Fox, eds., *Gender and Elections*, p.152. New York: Cambridge University Press, 2006.

10. Ibid., p. 146.

11. Ibid., p. 146.

12. In clean election states, candidates are not allowed to accept outside donations or use their own money. Maine has had such a law since 2000; Connecticut passed a clean elections law in 2005, and the cities of Portland, Oregon, and Albuquerque, New Mexico also have such laws. California defeated a clean elections initiative in 2006 by a wide margin.

13. A. Ellin. February 29, 2004, p. BU7.

14. "The Feminine Critique," *The New York Times*, November 1, 2007.

15. Press release, Center for American Women and Politics, November 7, 2007.

16. Anne Firor Scott. *The Southern Lady*, p. 170. Chicago, IL: The University of Chicago Press, 1970.

17. Ibid., p. 225.

Index

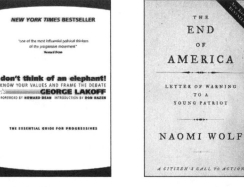

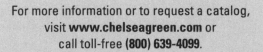